Conducting Drug Abuse Research with Minority Populations: Advances and Issues

Conducting Drug Abuse Research with Minority Populations: Advances and Issues has been co-published simultaneously as *Drugs & Society*, Volume 14, Numbers 1/2 1999.

Conducting Drug Abuse Research with Minority Populations: Advances and Issues

Mario R. De La Rosa, PhD
Bernard Segal, PhD
Richard Lopez, PhD
Editors

Conducting Drug Abuse Research with Minority Populations: Advances and Issues has been co-published simultaneously as *Drugs & Society*, Volume 14, Numbers 1/2 1999.

Routledge
Taylor & Francis Group
NEW YORK AND LONDON

First published 1999 by
The Haworth Press, Inc.

Published 2014 by Routledge
711 Third Avenue, New York, NY 10017, USA
27 Church Road, Hove, East Sussex BN3 2FA

First issued in paperback 2015

Routledge is an imprint of the Taylor and Francis Group, an informa business

Conducting Drug Abuse Research with Minority Populations: Advances and Issues has been co-published simultaneously as *Drugs & Society*™, Volume 14, Numbers 1/2 1999.

The development, preparation, and publication of this work has been undertaken with great care. However, the publisher, employees, editors, and agents of The Haworth Press and all imprints of The Haworth Press, Inc., including The Haworth Medical Press® and Pharmaceutical Products Press®, are not responsible for any errors contained herein or for consequences that may ensue from use of materials or information contained in this work. Opinions expressed by the author(s) are not necessarily those of The Haworth Press, Inc.

Cover design by Thomas J. Mayshock Jr.

Library of Congress Cataloging-in-Publication Data

Conducting drug abuse research with minority populations : advances and issues / Mario R. De La Rosa, Bernard Segal, Richard Lopez, editors.
    p. cm.
    [This work] has been co-published simultaneously as Drugs & society, volume 14, numbers 1-2 1999.
    Includes bibliographical references and index.
    ISBN 0-7890-0530-1 (alk. paper)
    1. Minorities–United States–Drug use–Research. 2. Drug abuse–Research–United States. I. De La Rosa, Mario R. II. Segal, Bernard, 1936- . III. Lopez, Richard. IV. Drugs & society (New York, N.Y.)
HV5824.E85C66 1998
362.29'12'08900973–DC21
                                             98–36242
                                               CIP

ISBN 13: 978-1-138-00236-4 (pbk)
ISBN 13: 978-0-7890-0530-4 (hbk)

Conducting Drug Abuse Research with Minority Populations: Advances and Issues

CONTENTS

ABOUT THE EDITORS

Mario R. De La Rosa, PhD, is Visiting Associate Research Professor at Boston University School of Social Work and Health Science Administrator with the National Institute on Drug Abuse (NIDA). Throughout his research career, Dr. De La Rosa has focused his work toward understanding the psychosocial factors responsible for the drug behaviors of minority populations. While at NIDA, he has developed and managed an internationally and nationally acclaimed research program on the epidemiology of drug use in minority populations and the drug use/crime connection. He has been actively involved in encouraging minority researchers to submit grants to NIDA, and he has served on national panels and research review committees, authoring numerous publications on the drug use behavior of minorities.

Bernard Segal, PhD, is Director of the Center for Alcohol and Addiction Studies and Professor of Health Sciences at the University of Alaska Anchorage. Before coming to Anchorage, Dr. Segal taught at the University of Rhode Island and Murray State University in Kentucky, where he held the Directorships of both the clinical training and psychological centers, and where he also worked as a Police Psychologist with the Murray Police Department. He has maintained this interest and serves as a Police Psychologist with the Anchorage Police Department. His research interests encompass the etiology, epidemiology, and biobehavioral aspects of drug-taking behavior, with a special emphasis on cross-cultural issues, particularly as they pertain to Alaskan issues. A recipient of both NIH and state grants, he has authored several books, numerous publications and presentations, and collaborated with researchers in Israel, Japan, and Russia.

Richard Lopez, PhD, JD, is Director of the Substance Abuse Program, Chief Psychologist, and Associate General Counsel at D.C. General Hospital in Washington, D.C. Previously, he was Deputy Chief of the Center for Minority Group Mental Health Programs at the National Institute of Mental Health and was responsible for the Minority Research and Development Centers and Fellowship Programs. Dr. Lopez has served on national panels and research review committees and has authored 16 publications. In addition, he has conducted research on drug abuse and drug treatment, minority group mental health, mental testing as an obstacle to access to higher education, and theories of socialization and acculturation of minority groups.

Foreword

PURPOSE

The purpose of this book is to provide a forum for drug abuse researchers to describe and discuss their experiences and concerns in their conduct of research on the drug-taking[1] behavior of minority populations.[2] The information and ideas presented in this collection emanate from the many years of experiences that the authors have in conducting drug abuse research with minorities. The information and ideas presented have also been influenced by the authors' personal experiences of growing up and living in a minority community or their personal experiences while working with those livign in those living in minority communities. Each of the authors discuss specific theoretical or methodological issues and concerns which they consider of significance in their research with minority populations. Also, each of the authors provide in their papers recommendations and strategies concerning how to be more effective and efficient when conducting research with minority populations.

Imbedded within all the authors' discussions is the central issue of understanding the impact of cultural values, attitudes, and norms in the drug-taking behavior of minority persons and in the conduct of drug abuse research with minority populations. A second overarching issue which the authors consider is the importance of community involvement or participation in drug abuse research studies that focus on minority populations. The editors of this collection anticipate that the information and ideas presented by the authors will be used by new and experienced drug abuse

---

Opinions expressed in this paper are those of the authors and do not necessarily reflect the opinions or official policy of the National Institute on Drug Abuse (NIDA) or any part of the U.S. Department of Health and Human Services.

[Haworth co-indexing entry note]: "Foreword." De La Rosa, Mario R., Bernard Segal, and Richard Lopez. Co-published simultaneously in *Drugs & Society* (The Haworth Press, Inc.) Vol. 14, No. 1/2, 1999, pp. xv-xxiii; and: *Conducting Drug Abuse Research with Minority Populations: Advances and Issues* (ed: Mario R. De La Rosa, Bernard Segal, and Richard Lopez) The Haworth Press, Inc., 1999, pp. xvii-xxv. Single or multiple copies of this article are available for a fee from The Haworth Document Delivery Service [1-800-342-9678, 9:00 a.m. - 5:00 p.m. (EST). E-mail address: getinfo@haworthpressinc. com].

researchers to enhance their abilities to conduct meaningful drug abuse research with minority populations. To that end, this publication seeks to improve and expand our current state of knowledge regarding drug abuse research with minority populations.

BACKGROUND AND JUSTIFICATION

During the past decade, research on the etiology[3] of drug abuse among minority populations has yielded a wealth of information on some of the underlying factors responsible for the drug abuse behavior of minority persons. This research has determined that Hispanic[4] and African-American youth[5] who use drugs are more likely to come from impaired families where the use of drugs is more common than Hispanic and African-American youth who do not use drugs (De La Rosa & White, in press; Brook, 1996; Blackmore-Gomez, 1996). Data from this research also have indicated that Hispanic and African-American youth who use drugs have lower self-esteem than Hispanic and African-American youth who do not use drugs (Warheit et al., 1995).

The results from these studies also have suggested that Hispanic and African-American youth who use drugs are more likely to have peers who use drugs than Hispanic and African-American youth who do not use drugs (Rodriguez, 1995; Thornberry, 1996; Valdez, 1996a). In addition, research has shown that Hispanic and African-American youth who do not attend religious services are more likely to use drugs than Hispanic and African-American youth who attend religious services (Chard-Wierschew, 1996; Wallace, 1996). Further, research on the drug taking behaviors of Hispanic youth has revealed that Hispanic youth who have stronger linkages with their cultural heritage are less likely to use drugs than Hispanic youth with weak linkages to their culture heritage[6] (Gil & Vega, in press; Vega, 1996a, 1996b).

Despite these research advances, significant gaps remain in understanding the etiology of drug use among minority populations. One major gap is the lack of theory-driven research on the impact that societal and community level[7] variables have on the drug-taking behavior of minority persons. A second major deficiency is the lack of studies that investigate resiliency[8] factors in preventing or reducing the use of drugs among minority populations. These research limitations are, to a large extent, due to the theoretical orientations of past etiological drug abuse research with minority and non-minority populations. This prior research resulted from theoretical models of risk-taking behaviors that focus on the investigation of the impact of individual level social psychological variables on the drug using behavior of minority as well as non-minority persons (see Jessors's problem behavior theory, 1997; Aker's learning theory, 1977; Kaplan's self derogation model, 1975; Kandel's socialization approach, 1975; Brook's family interactional approach, 1990; Hawkins and his colleagues' social development model, 1992). Yet, the impact that resiliency factors and societal and community level factors have on the drug using behaviors of minority populations have until recently remained unexplored (De La Rosa, Recio-Adrados, Kennedy, & Milburn, 1993). A third major problem is the lack of theory driven research on the etiology of drug use among Asian/Pacific Islanders,[9] American Indian,[10] and Alaskan Native[11] populations (De La Rosa et al., 1993). These research limitations are mainly due to the fact that until recently most drug abuse research on minority populations has focused on studying the etiology of drug abuse among Hispanic and African-American populations.

Similarly, while there has been progress to improve data collection techniques[12] for research in the drug abuse field with the general population, serious deficiencies in research methodology, nevertheless, continue to plague studies of minority populations (De La Rosa et al., 1993). No clear guidelines exist to advise drug abuse researchers on the development of effective strategies to access, recruit, and retain minority populations in research studies. Moreover, little information exists to guide the efforts of drug abuse researchers to involve members of the community in research studies as a technique to improve their data collection activities with minority populations.

This lack of guidance in the development and implementation of drug abuse research with minority populations comes at critical time in the evolution of this area of research. Efforts by the National Institute on Drug Abuse (NIDA) during the past decade to increase the number of funded studies that focus on the drug-taking behaviors of minority populations, have resulted in a resurgence of interest in this topic. These efforts have led to the funding of drug abuse research studies that consider such issues as: (1) the impact of the crack use/trade on the well-being of minority communities; (2) the relationship between intravenous drug use and HIV infection among African-American and Hispanic drug users; and (3) what role familial factors, cultural values and attitudes, peer influences, and affiliation to religious institutions have on the drug-taking behavior of Hispanic, African-American, Asian/Pacific Islander, and America Indian youth (National Institute on Drug Abuse, 1996a).

The need to develop guidelines to conduct drug abuse research with minority populations also comes at time when recognition by the scientific community of the need to expand minority participation is increasing within all behavioral and biomedical research. The National Institutes of Health (NIH) stressed the scientific community's concern in this area when in 1994 it issued strict guidelines that require, absent a clear scientific rationale for their exclusion, that all research it funds include women and persons of ethnic/racial minority populations (*Federal Register,* March 28, 1994).

Further, the need to develop guidelines to conduct drug abuse research with minority populations comes at a time when drug abuse researchers increasingly report difficulty in gaining the trust and participation of minority persons and communities in their studies (National Institute on Drug Abuse, 1996b).

This distrust toward drug abuse researchers may be due to the recognition by leaders in minority communities that participation by such communities in drug abuse studies has resulted in little or no benefit to their communities (National Institute on Drug Abuse, 1996b). These leaders see that many drug abuse researchers come to their communities and, once they have collected their data, disappear. According to leaders in these communities, researchers often do not provide benefits to the community they are studying (i.e., funds, jobs, referrals to drug treatment or social services) in exchange for the community participation in their research.

Moreover, this distrust by minority persons toward drug abuse researchers may be due to the long-term negative experiences that minority populations have had with the scientific community in general. "Fueled by past experiences with the scientific community minority persons are in many instances reluctant to allow access to drug abuse researchers into their communities" (Debro & Conley, 1993, p. 343). The increased reluctance of minority persons to participate in drug abuse research studies may also lie in their fears that any information they provide to drug abuse researchers could be used against them. These fears may be stronger among minority persons who have the most to lose and the least to gain by providing information on their illicit drug use behaviors to researchers, persons such as illegal immigrants, welfare recipients, and drug dealers/users. For example, Hispanic or Asian/Pacific Islander illegal immigrants may be reluctant to participate in drug abuse studies for fear that the information they provide to researchers will be used to deport them from the country. Moreover, drug dealers and users may be reluctant to provide information on their drug using and dealing to researchers for fear that law enforcement officials may use this information to incarcerate them.

This renewed and expanded interest to investigate the etiology of drug use among minority populations, and the need to develop guidelines for the conduct of drug abuse research with these populations, led to a meeting sponsored by NIDA. The purpose of this meeting was to discuss theoretical and methodological issues and concerns that affect etiologic drug abuse research in minority populations. The meeting was held in Washington, D.C. on September 26-27, 1996. Six panels composed of 20 researchers presented information that emanated from their research on minority populations, and discussed the lessons they learned from their research endeavors. The completed and edited manuscripts from this meeting form the basis for this book.

OUTLINE

This collection is divided into two parts. Part I consists of two topical sections. The first section of Part I focuses on theoretical advances and issues. Included in this section are papers by Brunswick, Wallace, Su, and Vega and Gil. The second section of Part I focuses on community involvement advances and issues. Included in this section are papers by Baldwin, Delgado, and Sterk. Part II also consists of two topical sections and a final component that sets forth conclusions and recommendations. The first section of Part II focuses on access, recruitment, and retention advances and issues. Included in this section are papers by Dunlap and Johnson; Nemoto, Huang, and Aoki; Beauvais; Krohn and Thornbery; and Valdez and Kaplan. The second section of Part II considers training advances and issues. Included in this section are papers by Alegría and Vera, and Grills and Rowe. In the conclusions and recommendation section, De La Rosa, White, Segal, and Lopez offer their comments on the subject matter and advise for future epidemiologic drug abuse research with minority populations. Each section of this publication commences with a brief introduction to the salient issues which the authors address and an overview to the articles that constitute the section.

CONCLUSION

Developing a more scientific foundation for the conduct of drug abuse research with minority populations is important to the well-being of our society. Drug abuse continues to be a serious problem that affects our society; it is particularly evident in many inner city minority communities. Moreover, data from several National Drug Abuse Surveys suggest that drug abuse is becoming an even more serious problem for minority youth than it is for non-minority youth (Johnston et al., 1995; Johnston et al., in press). Further, data from a number of local community-based studies also provide ample evidence of the devastating consequences of drug use/dealing on the economic and social well-being of minority communities. The contents of this book, however, do not reflect the wealth of drug abuse prevention and intervention efforts in minority populations across the country. Many of the efforts of local communities go unnoticed, and information about their work goes unpublished.

With minority populations playing an increasingly active role in the social, economic, political, and cultural life of the United States, efforts to better understand the drug using behavior of minority populations present a clear and urgent need. This book is a step toward that goal. The scientific papers included in this collection attempt to lay the foundation for more reliable and comprehensive research on the drug using behavior of minority populations.

Mario R. De La Rosa, PhD
Bernard Segal, PhD
Richard Lopez, PhD, JD

NOTES

1. The term "drug taking" refers to the lifetime, past month, and weekly use of alcohol and other illicit drugs, such as marijuana, cocaine, heroin, and PCP.

2. The term "minority populations" refers to individuals of African-American, American Indian/Alaskan Natives, Asian/Pacific Islander, and Hispanic ancestry.

3. The term "etiology" refers to underlying or causal factors responsible for the drug using behaviors of minority populations (e.g., self-esteem, parental drug use, peer drug use, family support, school support, family economic conditions, etc.).

4. The term "Hispanic" refers to individuals of Cuban-American, Mexican-American, Puerto Rican, and South and Central-American ancestry, regardless of race, who live in the mainland United States and the island of Puerto Rico.

5. The term "youth" refers to individuals aged 13 to 21.

6. The phrase "cultural heritage" refers to the mores and beliefs that help to determine behavior or thinking toward specific issues or problems, such as drug abuse. It does not include the issue of acculturation or assimilation into a culture.

7. The phrase "societal and community level variables" refers to such factors as poverty; racism; employment opportunities; lack of good schools, housing, and clean streets; availability of drug networks in neighborhoods; lack of proper law enforcement efforts to deal with drug dealing/using; lack of community recreational facilities and neighborhood youth sport activities; lack of residents' involvement in the political, social, and economic activities of their communities; etc.

8. The term "resiliency" refers to factors that protect an individual from the use of drugs (e.g., strong and warm parent-child relationships, no drug use in the family, peers who do not use drugs, effective school and community drug prevention programs, high self-esteem, high attendance in religious services, etc.).

9. The term "Asian/Pacific Islander" refers to individuals of Chinese, Japanese, Filipino, Indian, Vietnamese, Korean, Cambodian, Thai, Malaysian, Burmese, and Polynesian ancestry.

10. The term "American Indian" refers to individuals belonging to one of the more than 200 Indian tribes in the United States (e.g., Seminole, Sioux, Cherokee, Blackfoot, Navajo, Hopi, etc.).

11. The term "Alaskan Native" refers to the indigenous peoples of Alaska.

12. The term "data collection techniques" refers to the qualitative and quantitative methods and procedures utilized by researchers to access, recruit, retain, interview, and follow up of subjects in their studies.

REFERENCES

Akers, R. L. (1977). *Deviant behavior: Social learning approach*. Belmont, CA: Wadsworth Press.

Blackmore-Gomez, J. R. (1996). *Family function/drug use of Mexican American adolescents* (National Institute on Drug Abuse Research Grant Number DA05553). Unpublished report submitted to the National Institute on Drug Abuse, Rockville, MD.

Brook, J. S. (1996). *Drug use and problem behavior in minority youth* (National Institute on Drug Abuse Grant number DA0502). Unpublished report submitted to the National Institute on Drug Abuse, Rockville, MD.

Brook, J. S., Brook, D. W., Gordon, A. S., Whiteman, N., & Cohen, P. (1990). The Psychosocial etiology of adolescent drug use: A family interactional approach. *Genetic, Social, and General Psychology Monograph, 116*(2).

Chard-Wierschem, D. (1996). *In pursuit of the "true" relationship: A longitudinal study of the effects of religiosity on delinquency and substance use*. Unpublished doctoral dissertation, School of Criminal Justice, State University of New York at Albany.

Chavez E. L. (1996). *Mexican American dropouts and drug use* (National Institute on Drug Abuse Grant Number DA04777). Unpublished report submitted to the National Institute on Drug Abuse, Rockville, MD.

Debro, J., & Conley, D. J. (1993). School and Communities Politics: Issues, Concerns, and Implications when conducting Research in African-American Communities. In M. R. De La Rosa and J. Recio-Adrados (Eds.), *Drug abuse among minority youth: Advances in research and methodology* (NIDA Monograph 130, NIH Publication No. 93-3479, pp. 321-340). Washington, DC: Government Printing Office.

De La Rosa, M. R., Recio-Adrados, J., Kennedy, N., & Milburn, N. (1993). Current gaps and new directions for studying drug use and abuse behavior in minority youth. In M. R. De La Rosa and J. Recio-Adrados (Eds.), *Drug abuse* among minority youth: Advances in research and methodology* (NIDA Monograph 130, NIH Publication No. 93-3479, pp. 321-340). Washington, DC: Government Printing Office.

De La Rosa, M. R., & White, M. (In press). The role of social support systems in the drug use behavior of Hispanics revisited. *Journal of Health and Social Policy.*

Gil, A., & Vega, W. (in press). Two different worlds: Acculturation stress and adaptation among Cuban and Nicaraguan families. *Journal of Personal and Social Relationships.*

Hawkins, J. D., Catalano, R. F., Morrison, D. M., O'Donell, R. D., & Abbott, L. E. (1992). The Seattle social development project: Effects of the first four years on protective factors and problem behaviors. In J. McCord and R. Trembleay (Eds.), *The prevention of antisocial behavior in children.* New York: Guilford Press.

Jessor, R., & Jessor, S. L. (1977). *Problem behavior and psychological development: A longitudinal study of youth.* New York: Academic Press.

Johnston, L. D., O'Malley, P. M., & Bachman, J. G. (1995). *National survey results on drug use from the monitoring the future study, 1975-1993* (NIH Publication. No. 94-3809, Vol. I). Rockville, MD: National Institute on Drug Abuse.

Johnston, L. D., O'Malley, P. M., & Bachman, J. G. (in press). *National survey results on drug use from the monitoring the future study, 1975-1995*(NIH Publication. No. 96-4139, Vol. I). Rockville, MD: National Institute on Drug Abuse.

Kandel, D. (1975). Stages in adolescent involvement in drug use. *Science, 181,* 1067-70.

Kaplan, H. B. (1975). *Self attitudes and deviant behavior.* Pacific Palisides, CA: Goodyear Press.

National Institute on Drug Abuse (1996a). Division of Epidemiology and Prevention Research. Unpublished Report.

National Institute on Drug Abuse (September, 26-27, 1996b). *Proceedings from the Meeting on Drug Abuse Research Among Minority Populations: Methodological Issues and Concerns.* Unpublished manuscript, National Institute on Drug Abuse, Rockville, MD.

Page, B. J. (1996). *Comparative study of needle use in Miami and Valencia* (National Institute on Drug Abuse Grant number DA 08802). Unpublished report submitted to the National Institute on Drug Abuse, Rockville, MD.

Rodriguez, O. (1995). Causal models of substance abuse among Puerto Rican adolescents: Implications for prevention. In G. Botvin, S. Schinke, & M. Orlandi (Eds.), *Drug abuse prevention with multiethnic youth* (pp. 130-146). London: Sage Publications.

Substance Abuse and Mental Health Services Administration (1994). *National household survey on drug abuse: Population estimates: October, 1994* (DHHS publication No. 94-3017). Washington, DC: U.S. Government Printing Office.

Thornberry, T. (1996). *Social network approach to drug use* (National Institute on

Drug Abuse grant number DA 05512). Unpublished report submitted to the National Institute on Drug Abuse, Rockville, MD.

U.S. Bureau of the Census (1992). *Persons of Spanish origin by states: 1990* (PC8-051-7). Washington, DC: U.S. Department of Commerce.

U.S. Government Printing Office (March 28, 1994). *Federal register* (Volume 59, pp. 14508-14513). Washington, DC: U.S. Government Printing Office.

Valdez, A. (1996a). *Substance use among Mexican American school-age youth* (National Institute on Drug Abuse grant number DA 07234). Unpublished report submitted to the National Institute on Drug Abuse, Rockville, MD.

Vega, W. (August, 1995). *Acculturation stress and Latino adolescent drug use.* Paper presented at the National Institute of Mental Health meeting on Stress, Psychological Disorders, and Prevention Strategies, Bethesda, MD.

Vega, W. (1996). *Patterns of drug use: Hispanic and non-Hispanic male teens* (National Institute on Drug Abuse grant number DA0512). Unpublished report submitted to the National Institute on Drug Abuse, Rockville, MD.

Wallace, J. (1996). *Race, religion, and drugs* (National Institute on Drug Abuse grant number DA09106). Unpublished report submitted to the National Institute on Drug Abuse, Rockville, MD.

Warheit, G., Biafora, F., Zimmerman, R., Gil, A., Vega, W., & Apospori, G. (1995). Self-rejection/derogation, peer factors, and alcohol, drug, and cigarette use among a sample of Hispanic, African American, and White non-Hispanic adolescents. *The International Journal of the Addictions, 30,* 97-116.

PART I

THEORETICAL ADVANCES
AND ISSUES

This section focuses on the presentation of theoretical models most appropriate to understanding drug behaviors of minority populations. These theoretical models share a number of common themes. The authors suggest that such a model should investigate: (1) the interactive effects of societal, community, and individual level psychosocial variables on the drug-taking behaviors of minority persons; (2) how the drug using and dealing activities of their residents impact the social and economic well-being of minority communities; (3) the relationship between drug use among Hispanic and Asian/Pacific Islanders and stress associated with their experiences of assimilation into American society; (4) the role of gender in the drug-taking behaviors of minority persons; and (5) the role of protective factors, as well as risk factors, in the drug-taking behaviors of minority populations. Included in this section are papers by Brunswick, Wallace, Su, and Vega and Gil.

Brunswick's paper posits the development of an integrative ecological system model that will serve as a theoretical framework for exploring drug abuse behavior among African-American individuals. Wallace's paper addresses the issue of economic disempowerment as an important variable which is directly related to the differential patterns of drug use found among middle class and lower income African-American youth. Su's paper discusses the need to develop a culturally relevant and multidimensional theoretical approach that can appreciate the drug using behavior of the various Asian/Pacific Islanders' population groups. Vega and Gil's paper proposes the development of an integrative model that assumes that the process of acculturation to American society plays a significant role in the drug-taking behavior of Hispanic youth.

3

Structural Strain:
An Ecological Paradigm for Studying African American Drug Use

Ann F. Brunswick, PhD

SUMMARY. Social structural factors (gender, age, income/wealth and geographic variations) are often ignored as descriptive or explanatory variables in drug studies. They are critical for differentiating drug use patterns, whether within an ethno-racial group or between ethno-racial groups. Within the African American community, specifically, drug involvement differences are best explained by heterogeneity in degrees of success in and attachment to mainstream social institutions (family, church, schools, workplace).

These considerations predominate in structural strain theory, offered here for explaining African American drug use patterns. An ecological model operationalizes the theory and posits three different interlinking levels of social influence on individual drug use behavior: social structural, institutional, and interpersonal networks (macrosystem, exo-

Ann F. Brunswick is Senior Research Scientist in Public Health/Sociomedical Sciences, Columbia University.

Research reported in this paper has been supported by the National Institute on Drug Abuse through research grants 5R18DAO3287 and 5RO1DAO5142, Ann F. Brunswick, PhD, Principal Investigator. Theory and empirical findings discussed in this paper were derived from the Longitudinal African American Cohort study, which Dr. Brunswick has been directing for 30 years. Points of view and opinions expressed herein are those of the author, not of the NIDA.

This is a revision of a paper presented at the Conference on Drug Abuse Research with Minority Populations: Methodological and Theoretical Issues and Concerns, Washington, DC, September 26-27, 1996.

[Haworth co-indexing entry note]: "Structural Strain: An Ecological Paradigm for Studying African American Drug Use." Brunswick, Ann F. Co-published simultaneously in *Drugs & Society* (The Haworth Press, Inc.) Vol. 14, No. 1/2, 1999, pp. 5-19; and: *Conducting Drug Abuse Research with Minority Populations: Advances and Issues* (ed: Mario R. De La Rosa, Bernard Segal, and Richard Lopez) The Haworth Press, Inc., 1999, pp. 5-19. Single or multiple copies of this article are available for a fee from The Haworth Document Delivery Service [1-800-342-9678, 9:00 a.m. - 5:00 p.m. (EST). E-mail address: getinfo@haworthpressinc.com].

5

system, and microsystem, respectively). Findings then are presented from a 25-year study conducted with one community representative African American cohort that supports the importance of the structural strain premise in explaining African American drug use patterns. An example of study measures arrayed according to the ecological paradigm is provided. Finally, its utility is demonstrated in enumerating sources of error that have led to incomplete and sometimes contradictory findings regarding African American drug use. *[Article copies available for a fee from The Haworth Document Delivery Service: 1-800-342-9678. E-mail address: getinfo@haworthpressinc.com]*

INTRODUCTION

Research designs too seldom have acknowledged the axiom that drug use is a complex behavior with multiple determinants. Determinants or influences on initiating, continuing, discontinuing, and, finally, terminating drug use derive from every level of social and individual organization. Levels of individual organization range from cellular to synaptic and neurotransmittal to, importantly, cognitive functions expressed in beliefs, goals, and expectations. Progressively more complex levels of social organization enter into the choice, duration, etc., of drug use. These include not only social networks of family, peer, school, work but also of community affiliations and of interactions with social institutions (school, health care, legal, criminal justice system, and so on). Less visible and, perhaps most powerful in the case of African Americans, are broader levels of social organization that reflect the allocation of social resources and time linked values and norms. These vary with ethno-racial, economic, gender, age, and geographic factors that stratify U.S. society.

The relative strength and interlinkage of individual and social influences varies with life stage progression which is experienced differently both by minority and majority groups and the men and women within them. Thus, adolescence, varyingly defined as to specific ages that it subsumes, has been identified uniformly in the U.S. as the critical life stage for onset of illicit drug use, with abatement of its use linked to subsequent assumption of adult roles and responsibilities. The age parameters for abatement of use also vary systematically with social stratification factors. Unless the complex, multi-causal nature of drug use behavior receives due credence and unless the resultant variations in patterns and determinants of that behavior receive due recognition, appropriate research programs and policy cannot be formulated. These are the issues that the following theoretical and methodological discussion addresses.

Historically, intra-individual factors in drug use have been, for the most part, the focus of theories of drug use. Psychology/psychiatry's classification of drug use as "disorder" and sociology/criminal justice's classification of drug use as deviant behavior are examples of this pattern. Within the past two decades, perspectives on drug use have broadened with social learning theory (Rotter, Chance, & Phares, 1972). Problem behavior theory (Jessor & Jessor, 1977) and social control theory (Thompson, Smith-DiJulio, & Matthews, 1982) have gained a toe-hold in explanatory models. (See Brunswick, Messeri, & Titus, 1992 for a more detailed review of these and other theories of drug use.) While these encompass a broader view of drug use compared to earlier psychopathy/sociopathy models of drug use, they have not been explicated or tested specifically for their efficacy in explaining African American drug use patterns.

Finally, drug use patterns sometimes are linked to and explained by variations in stress (see Su in this book). Stress like drug use, however, implicates social structural determinants (e.g., age, gender, geography, socioeconomic status [SES]) which have been minimalized in studies of stress (Turner, Wheaton, & Lloyd, 1995). This is a shortcoming of considerable magnitude when what is at issue is the behavior of a minority group, identified so strongly by their attributed and attained position in the social structures.

Socio-economic phenomena loom large in understanding African American drug use behavior, based on: (1) the out-migration of middle-class and/or other stable working African Americans from inner city communities (Wacquant & Wilson, 1989; Wilson, 1987) that has led to an absence of appropriate African American male role models in inner-city communities, and (2) the decline in blue collar and unskilled jobs traditionally filled by African Americans (Glazer & Moynihan, 1967; Kasarda, 1989; Wilson, 1987). These have resulted both in inner city African American male youths' high actual rates of joblessness and in lowered expectations for future employment (Brunswick, 1980; Brunswick & Rier, 1995; Brunswick, Lewis, & Messeri, 1992; Brunswick, Messeri, & Aidala 1991; Brunswick, Messeri et al., 1992; Massey & Eggers, 1990; Swinton, 1989; Wilson, 1978). Further, African American youth's employment and affiliation needs add to the functions drugs serve. This means that among young inner city African Americans drugs have posed an attractive alternative pathway for occupational and affiliation needs. Just as the concentration of the unemployed and impoverished in the inner cities have tended to produce a polarized African American community, patterns of drug use have been skewed following this schism.

In sum, a theory and model of African American drug use needs to adjust to the heterogeneity of a society in schism, the alternative economic functions served by drugs, and both the perceived and actual exclusion of segments of inner-city African Americans from the opportunity structure. As Brunswick and Rier (1995) previously noted:

Understanding the status of drug use in Black America today requires a perspective on the heterogeneous composition of the African American youth population, a group deeply and increasingly polarized-economically and, subsequently, socially–into segments of haves and have-nots. Managing drug use behavior similarly requires a changed perspective, in which it is seen as one symptom of a broader, underlying isolation from mainstream opportunities and rewards to which we have applied the term "structural strain." (p. 240)

STRUCTURAL STRAIN: AN ECOLOGICAL PARADIGM FOR AFRICAN AMERICAN DRUG USE

A paradigm or model is required that can capture both the diversity of influences on drug use within the African American group and the intergroup differences between them and other minorities and varying subgroups of the white majority. Given the distinct racial history that African Americans share, their minority status, and the socioeconomic disadvantage experienced by a sizeable portion of the group, the paradigm needs to emphasize social structural and situational factors. These are the focus of structural strain theory (Brunswick & Rier, 1995; Brunswick, Messeri et al., 1992). The theory essentially expands on Merton's theory of social strain (Farnsworth & Leiber, 1989; Merton, 1957) which referred to the tension between socially accepted goals and inability to achieve them through socially accepted channels. The theory predicts that this strain will prompt excluded individuals to seek success through alternative (non-normative or socially disapproved) means. In applying the theory to African American drug use, it has been re-labeled "structural strain" to emphasize the role of social structural determinants in the socially and economically disarticulated segment of the group who are the ones most frequently and most heavily involved with drugs. Figure 1 expresses this relationship.

Moving beyond articulating a theoretical model, a framework is needed to operationalize it and guide research into African American drug use behavior. Toward this end, influences on drug use behavior have been arrayed according to an ecological paradigm first suggested by Bronfenbrenner's (1979) theory of "nested contexts" of behavioral influences. Figure 2 depicts this paradigm.

The ecological model is an apt graphic paradigm for structural strain theory because: (1) It emphasizes contextual, situational factors within which the individual develops and exercises his/her behavioral repertoire; (2) it explicates four levels of influence that are increasingly complex as one moves from the most proximal, intra-individual factors to the most distal indirect social structural ones. The model also emphasizes the interlinkages

FIGURE 1. Structural Strain Model

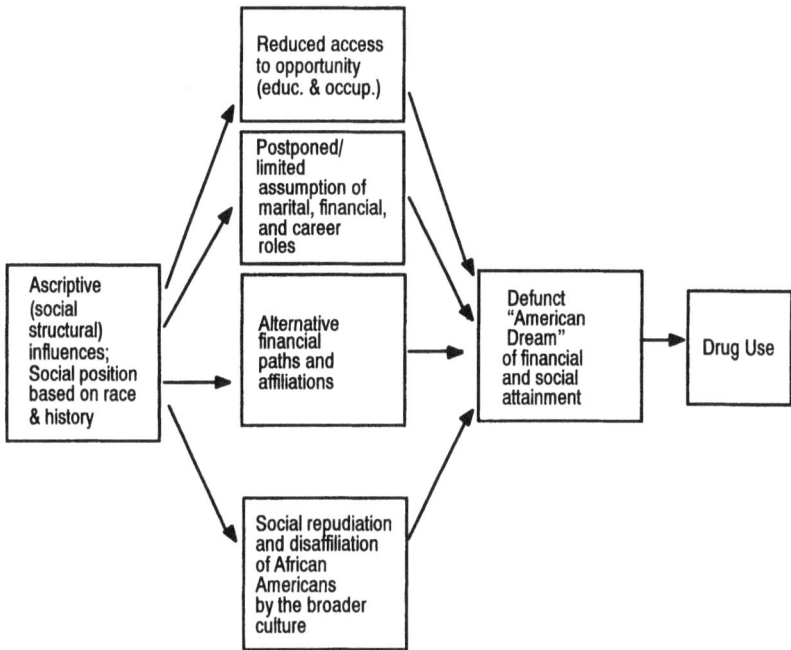

between levels, capturing the interplay between interpersonal, legal, political, economic, and social value influences and the individual's behavior.

In brief, from most distal to proximal to the individual, the model postulates that drug use behaviors develop and are maintained within the context of (1) the individual's socially ascribed position and opportunities conditioned on his/her ethno-racial-gender identity (macrosystem); (2) legal and institutional arrangements that either enable or erect barriers to drug use (exosystem); (3) interpersonal interactions and networks within the community (schools, work, church, courts, and so on), as well as primary networks of family and peers (microsystem); and (4) intra-individual perceptions, aspirations (values, beliefs) and attitudes regarding self and society (ontogenic system). (See Brunswick, 1994 for detailed explication of these four domains.)

Historically, much drug and psychosocial research has been focused on

FIGURE 2. Ecological "Nested Contexts" Paradigm of Influences on Drug Involvement

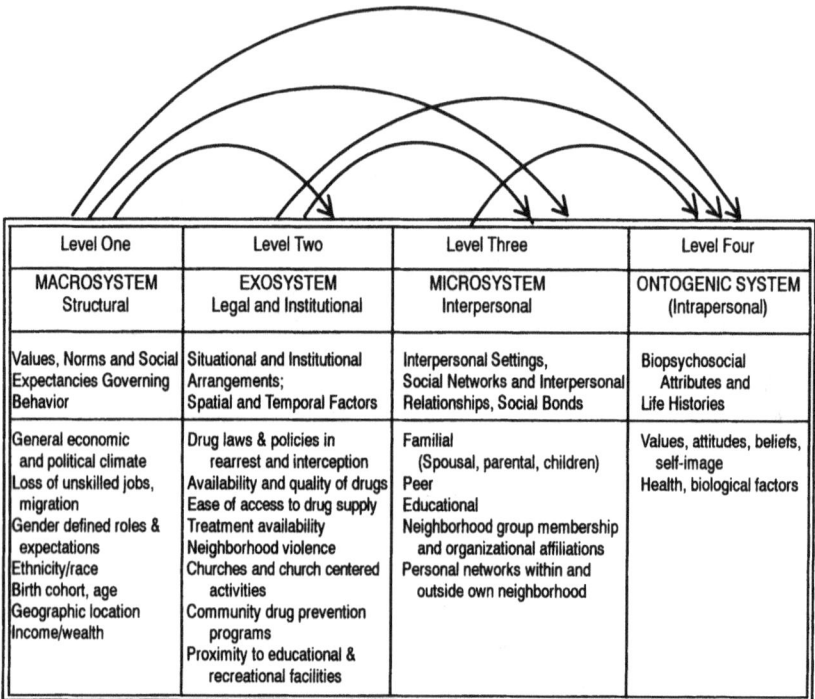

Level One	Level Two	Level Three	Level Four
MACROSYSTEM Structural	EXOSYSTEM Legal and Institutional	MICROSYSTEM Interpersonal	ONTOGENIC SYSTEM (Intrapersonal)
Values, Norms and Social Expectancies Governing Behavior	Situational and Institutional Arrangements; Spatial and Temporal Factors	Interpersonal Settings, Social Networks and Interpersonal Relationships, Social Bonds	Biopsychosocial Attributes and Life Histories
General economic and political climate Loss of unskilled jobs, migration Gender defined roles & expectations Ethnicity/race Birth cohort, age Geographic location Income/wealth	Drug laws & policies in rearrest and interception Availability and quality of drugs Ease of access to drug supply Treatment availability Neighborhood violence Churches and church centered activities Community drug prevention programs Proximity to educational & recreational facilities	Familial (Spousal, parental, children) Peer Educational Neighborhood group membership and organizational affiliations Personal networks within and outside own neighborhood	Values, attitudes, beliefs, self-image Health, biological factors

Source: Adapted from Brunswick 1985 and 1994

the fourth level in Figure 2, that of ontogenic factors. The ecological paradigm was formulated to redress this inappropriate emphasis and exclusivity when studying minority groups whose very label denotes a structural, not a personal, attribute (Brunswick, Messeri, & Titus, 1992; Brunswick & Rier, 1995). Not only does concentration on intra-individual factors ignore the social settings, that is, the contexts that importantly influence individual's behavior, it imbues those lives with a regularity and coherence that ofttimes are not present. This writer's Longitudinal African American Cohort Study provides a simple example of this fallacy of constant lives. When cross-classifying men's reported income by drug involvement, better than a third of men heroin users did not report income. The actual interviews revealed that this was not a result of unwillingness to respond, as might appear at first. Instead, the question, "How much money do you make? You can tell me by the week, or the month, or the year," was unanswerable by those whose earnings were irregular and might be described best as, "catch as catch can."

The ecological paradigm's implications for research design and procedures are discussed more systematically below, after reviewing some empirical instances that support the model and its underlying theory. These come from three different studies of the same African American cohort cited above.

THEORY GUIDED RESEARCH
AND RESEARCH GUIDED THEORY

The impetus for articulating structural strain theory and the ecological paradigm that translates it came from the investigator's experience with the Longitudinal African American Cohort Study. The Longitudinal African American Cohort Study is a life course study of drug use and health trajectories that began in 1968 as the first area representative sample survey of health status and needs for health care among African American adolescents (Brunswick, 1984; Brunswick & Josephson, 1972). The research now includes five waves of data collection that span 25 years. The study cohort initially was drawn from every 2 in 25 households in the Central Harlem (New York City) Health District where one or more adolescents aged 12 to 17, inclusive, resided. Initially numbering 668 in adolescence, with death and moving away from the New York City area as the major sources of attrition, at the fifth round of data collection 25 years later (1993), the participating study cohort numbered 347. This constituted 75% of those who were interviewable from the initial study wave. Because interviewing in each subsequent round has been limited to those then residing within 60 miles of the city limits, findings are deemed generalizable to African Americans in the metropolitan New York City area who were born in the 1950s (Brunswick, 1991).

The utility of the ecological model in interpreting African American drug use patterns became apparent in a birth cohort analysis of prevalence and timing of onset in adolescence use of four major drugs (marijuana, cocaine, heroin, and psychedelics). Prevalence of particular drugs varied by birth cohort but age at initiation did not. Onset of drug use was a maturational phenomenon (a linkage of level four with contributions from levels one through three, Figure 2), while identification of particular drugs of choice was subject to period factors tied to changing substance availability and group norms of acceptability (ecological model level two). (See Brunswick & Boyle, 1979, for further details of this analysis.)

Another example of situational (level two) influences was observed when analyzing the chronological concurrence of the decline in heroin use in the 1970s with fluctuations in heroin price and purity. The latter are commonly used indicators of government efforts to control drug supply. Fluctuations in drug use prevalence and price/purity were poorly correlated. Data from personal interviews showed that direct observation of effects on drug users and changing perceptions of educational and job opportunity in the late 1960s and early 1970s differentially affected successive birth cohorts as they entered the adolescent period at risk for heroin initiation (which, in this sample, began at age 13). This reduced the attractiveness of initiating and, to some extent, of continuing heroin use. These perceptions and broader social changes best explained the dramatic drop in rates of heroin use from that in the oldest (28%) to the youngest birth cohorts (3%) in this study cohort (Boyle & Brunswick, 1980; Messeri & Brunswick, 1987).

A direct test of structural strain theory was performed in another study which was formulated to disentangle the opposing functions attributed to substance use–one as causal of stress and the other as buffer or coping mechanism (mediator) for that stress, that is, distress effects. Gender specific longitudinal models controlled for baseline levels of distress. The first series of models posited acute life events as predictors of distress; the second series tested enduring unemployment (hypothesized from structural strain theory) as the predictor chronic stressor. Results showed, first, that acute negative life events were not stressors, that is, did not increase levels of distress in the African American sample. But the chronic stressor of unemployment did have significant impact on distress. When the role of drugs was tested for its causal *vs.* mediating or buffering role in this relationship, different processes were observed for men and women. For men, moderate to heavy (weekly to daily) drug use exacerbated the distressful effects of chronic unemployment; drug use was not stressful in the absence of unemployment (i.e., if employed). For women, the stress of chronic unemployment was ameliorated modestly by light (less than weekly) use of an illicit drug. Heavier use (weekly or greater use of any drug) was stressful for women independent of and in addition to unemployment. This was evidence of the stricter anti-drug use norms that apply for African American women than men, another level one effect encompassed by structural strain theory.

THE ECOLOGICAL MODEL AS A METHODOLOGICAL GUIDE FOR STUDY INSTRUMENTATION AND PROCEDURES

The ecological model is useful as a framework for reminding the researcher of the multiple domains of influence on substance use that vary according to particular minority group status (*vis à vis* the dominant culture) and according to the individual's status within the minority group.

An example of this heuristic or research guiding function is shown in Table 1, where predictor variables that have been measured in the writer's Longitudinal African American Cohort study are arranged according to their level in the ecological model.

Because theory cannot be separated from methods nor methods from theory, the ecological structural strain perspective has implications for each stage of study design and execution, from cohort selection (community cross-section or drug user sample, multi-ethnic or race specific) and sampling procedure (probability or purposive), to data collection rules and protocol, to the requirement of pretesting at successive stages of instrument and protocol development, to designing instruments that minimize response bias and social desirability effects and that incorporate cognitively appropriate question wording, sequencing and response categories.

Elsewhere, the writer has classified sources of measurement bias that confound valid measurement of African American drug use (Brunswick, in press). These arise when distinct ethno-race-gender related structural, situational and interpersonal qualities are ignored. Three broad categories of bias were identified: logical fallacies, sampling, and non-sampling error.

Logical Fallacies

Three fallacies have ramifications in both sampling and non-sampling bias:

Geographic generalization fallacy: Drug use and minority populations both are unevenly distributed throughout the U.S., a skew and heterogeneity that are insufficiently redressed in most sample designs, data analytic methods and reporting, e.g., applying uncorrected means and mean based deviation statistics.

Intra-group homogeneity fallacy: Differences in within group variance or heterogeneity, e.g., different correlations between class and substance use in African American and white populations, too often are neglected in cross-group analyses. Increased multivariate analysis will but partially redress this oversight. Specifically, the distribution of drug involvement is more skewed in the African American population; high levels of use are concentrated among a minority of the population, such as reflected in the 13% of 25 to 29 year old and 14% of 30 to 34 year old black males that census officials acknowledge they undercount (NRC, 1995).

This skewed distribution is a particular threat to the validity of school surveys, where Black youths captured in school–regardless of their real dollar SES–will be more middle class in value orientation and behavior norms than their white equivalents. Research has shown also that African American students are not only more likely to be absent from school but to

TABLE 1. Conceptual Variable List: Longitudinal Harlem Cohort Study

A. DRUG USE AND DRUG TREATMENT (OUTCOME/DEPENDENT) VARIABLES:

1. Drug Use Patterns: Cigarettes, alcohol, marijuana, cocaine, heroin, methadone, other opiates, PCP, other psychedelics, amphetamines, barbiturates, glue/other inhalants
   Ever use
   Frequency of use
   Recency of use
   Onset of use
   Duration of use
   Amount used (tobacco, alcohol, marijuana)
   Attitude toward own tobacco, alcohol use
   Mode of administration
   Continuous/interrupted use
   Trouble as a result of use
   Drug combinations (simultaneous use)
   Polydrug use

2. Drug Treatment Experience
   Perceptions of treatment
   Exposure
   Sources of influence on entry
   Treatment environment
   Motivations for entering
   Treatment modality
   Preferences
   Treatment effects
   Treatment barriers

3. Perceptions of and Attitudes Toward Drug Use
   Salience of drug problems
   Tolerance of drug use
   Health consequences attributed to drugs

B. PREDICTOR VARIABLES (ARRANGED BY ECOLOGICAL MODEL)

1. Social Structure (level 1)
   Current life role/activity
   Household composition
   Economic status (source, level and adequacy of income)
   Mobility
   Age/cohort
   Gender

2. Spacial and temporal
   Census tract and address of residence
   Wave (timing) of interview

3. Social Contexts (level 3 linked to level 1)
   Living arrangements
   Support networks
   Network size and diversity
   Kin networks
   Friend networks
   Drug and alcohol use in friend networks
   Alternative network norms & exposure
   Network strain
   Stability of networks
   Community participation
   Life stress events

4. Ontogenic System: Personal resources (self attitudes and outlooks on life) and coping strategies
   Mood/depression
   Anxiety/worry/fears
   Hostility/anger
   Self esteem
   Sense of personal efficacy/control/mastery
   Alienation/hopelessness
   Time orientation
   Perceptions of parents
   Values orientation
   Coping strategies adaptive/not
   Perceived strains: general, economic, health, education, parenting, conjugal, and job

return incomplete drug reports if present (Bachman, O'Malley, & Johnson, 1984; Josephson & Rosen, 1978).

Fallacy of homogeneity in cognitive processing and response styles: Little research on ethno-race variability in cognitive styles has been reported, whether in regard to processing questions, memory storage, recall cues or response styles. Unforeseen bias from this source is associated with ethno-race varying values, norms, and experiences (frames of reference) which ethnographic research plus rigorous instrument pretesting can avert.

Sampling Bias

Non-inclusivity: Household and school surveys, as is commonly acknowledged, underrepresent the most socially distressed, or in W. J. Wilson's (1987) term, socially disarticulated, segments of the black population. Drug use is concentrated more heavily among "floaters" (those who move from one acquaintance to another), others with transient housing, prison populations, and people lacking any official residence and/or who are not acknowledged as part of the screened dwelling unit. The National Household Survey on Drug Abuse (NHSDA) now samples shelters and certain group residences as a step toward reducing non-inclusivity bias.

Selection bias: This refers to biased or race-differentiated survey participation rates based on unavailability or unwillingness of selected respondents to be interviewed. It differs from non-inclusivity (above) which is a function of sample design. Appropriate interviewer selection and training, as well as respondent appropriate instrumentation and incentives can limit bias from this source.

Sample weighting fallacy: For obvious reasons, weighting up the obtained sample responses to census proportions will not correct for non-inclusivity, selection, and other sampling, as well as response bias, which is discussed later.

Field rule or protocol bias: Constraints on call-backs and time in the field contribute to biased, i.e., differential, drug use reports. Howard (1997), using data from the Longitudinal African American Cohort Study, compared substance use reports of African American men and women under conditions of relatively unlimited time in field to those obtained from age, race, and gender matched individuals interviewed within 180 days of first assignment. She found significantly higher heavy alcohol consumption for men and significantly more heavy alcohol and heroin use reports for women under the relaxed time limit condition.

Non-Sampling Sources of Measurement Bias

Interviewer characteristics: Concordance of interviewer's race, gender, and class with respondent's characteristics influences quality of response on sensitive issues. The broader question of what constitutes a sensitive issue on which interviewer characteristics have a stronger effect is itself subject to varying ethno-racial, gender, and age or period norms.

Modality bias: Evidence is accumulating regarding modality bias, i.e., variability linked to the modality or setting in which drug reports are collected. Importantly, the few investigators who have examined race differences in modality effects have found them. Aquilino and LoSciuto (1990) found greater divergence between what black respondents reported on personal *versus* phone interviews than appeared for whites; similarly, Fendrick and Vaughn (1994) found blacks had twice the odds of telephone underreport compared to telephone versus personal interview differences in other groups. Importantly, and contradicting the effect for whites, Aquilino (1992) found that black respondents reported more drug use on personal interviews than on self-administered questionnaires (SAQs).

Instrumentation bias: Question wording, meaning, ease of comprehension, and appropriateness or proximity to everyday experience have obvious ethno-race variability. Twenty-five years of interviews with an African American sample has taught this investigator to avoid questions that require numeric replies and quantitative estimates; to avoid the term "problem" when inquiring into experiences with respect to health, drug use, and so on.

Instrumentation bias can be reduced by paying particular attention to ethno-race (gender, age, and region) differences in pretesting and then modifying instruments in light of these differences. Some investigators who have reported greater inconsistency in African American reports of drug use (Fendrich & Vaughn, 1994; Mensch & Kandel, 1988), for example, may well have uncovered instances of instrumentation bias and neglect of cognitive style differences.

CONCLUSION

Drug use behavior and its reporting are complex context-driven phenomena regulated by varying gender, ethno-racial, age, occupational, and income/wealth as well as temporal and regionally defined expectations and norms of social acceptance.

In theory and in practice, research with minority populations needs to be attentive to and capture these varying social contexts. The one theory-one methodology approach ill serves elucidating minority group illicit drug use and the intra- as well as inter-group differences that prevail in regard to both its parameters and causative influences. Structural strain theory has been articulated here, based on the writer's 25 year African

American Cohort Study, that encapsulates the dominant influences on African American patterns of drug use, with special attention to the minority of African Americans who are heavily drug involved. Concordant with the theory, an ecological paradigm was outlined that identifies successive "layers" of societal influence. It can serve as a heuristic tool in developing appropriately comprehensive study designs and procedures for obtaining valid measures of drug use among African Americans and other minority groups. Examples from the writer's own research were provided in support of the utility of the theory and the ecological model. Some errors in study design, data collection, and analysis procedures that threaten internal and external validity then were summarized. Investigators are encouraged to recognize and report the limitations of their studies' validity and generalizability, two hallmarks of the scientific endeavor. Improved understanding of the commonalities and distinctions among minority groups and between them and the dominant white population's drug use patterns, determinants, and consequences hopefully, will follow from attention to these issues. Only in this way will research address adequately the complex and changing phenomena of drug use behavior.

REFERENCES

Aquilino, W. S. (1992). Telephone versus face-to-face interviewing for household drug use surveys. *International Journal of the Addictions, 27*, 71-91.

Aquilino, W. S., & LoSciuto, L. A. (1990). Effects of interview mode on self-reported drug use. *Public Opinion Quarterly, 54*, 362-395.

Bachman, J. G., O'Malley, P. M., & Johnson, L. D. (1984). Drug use among young adults: The impacts of role status and social environment. *Journal of Personality & Social Psychology, 47*, 629-645.

Boyle, J. & Brunswick, A. F. (1980). What happened in Harlem? Analysis of a decline in heroin use among a generation unit of urban Black youth. *Journal of Drug Issues, 10*(1), 109-130.

Bronfenbrenner, U. (1979). *The ecology of human development.* Cambridge, MA: Harvard University Press.

Brunswick, A. F. (1980). Social meanings and developmental needs: Perspectives on Black youth's drug use. *Youth and Society, 11*(4), 449-473.

Brunswick, A. F. (1984). Health consequences of drug use: A longitudinal study of urban Black youth. In S. A. Mednick, M. Harway, & K. M. Finello (Eds.), *Handbook of Longitudinal Research in the U.S., 2* (pp. 290-314). New York, NY: Praeger Press.

Brunswick, A. F. (1991). Health & substance use behavior. *Journal of Addictive Diseases, 11*, 119-137.

Brunswick, A. F. (1994). Bringing the context in from the cold: Substantive, technical and statistical issues for AIDS research in the second decade. In R. J. Battjes, Z. Sloboda, & W. C. Grace (Eds.), *The context of HIV risk among drug users and their sexual partners* (NIDA Research Monograph 143, pp. 187-201). Rockville, MD: The National Institute on Drug Abuse.

Brunswick, A. F. (in press). *Racial differences in surveys of drug prevalence: More than measurement error?* In A.S.A./A.A.P.O.R. Joint 1997 Proceedings of the 52nd Annual Conference, American Association for Public Opinion Research, Norfolk, VA.

Brunswick, A. F., & Boyle, J. (1979). Patterns of drug involvement: Developmental and secular influences on age at initiation. *Youth and Society, 11*(2), 139-162.

Brunswick, A. F., & Josephson, E. (1972). Adolescent health in Harlem. *American Journal of Public Health, 62*(Suppl 10), 1-62.

Brunswick, A. F., & Rier, D. A. (1995). Structural strain: Drug use among African American youth. In R. L. Taylor (Ed.), *African American youth: Their social and economic status in the United States* (pp. 225-246). Westport, CT: Praeger.

Brunswick, A. F., Lewis, C. S., & Messeri, P. A. (1992). Drug use and stress: Testing a coping model in an urban African American sample. *Journal of Community Psychology, 20*, 148-162.

Brunswick, A. F., Messeri, P., & Aidala, A. (1991). Changing drug use patterns and treatment behavior: A longitudinal study of urban Black youth. In R. R. Watson (Ed.), *Drug and Alcohol Abuse Prevention* (pp. 263-311). Clifton, NJ: Humana Press.

Brunswick, A. F., Messeri, P. A., & Titus, S. P. (1992). Predictive factors in adult substance abuse: A prospective study of African American adolescents. In M. D. Glantz & R. W. Pickens (Eds.), *Vulnerability to drug abuse* (pp. 419-472). Washington, DC: APA Press.

Farnsworth, M., & Leiber, M. J. (1989) Strain theory revisited: Economic goals, educational means, and delinquency. *American Sociological Review, 54*, 263-274.

Fendrick, M., & Vaughn, C. (1994). Diminished lifetime substance use over time. *Public Opinion Quarterly, 54*, 96-123.

Glazer, N., & Moynihan, D. P. (1967). *Beyond the melting pot.* Cambridge, MA: Massachusetts Institute of Technology.

Howard, J. M. (1997). *Reaching African Americans in inner-city communities: The impact of irregular living situations.* Unpublished doctoral thesis, Columbia University, New York, NY.

Jessor, R., & Jessor, S. L. (1997). *Problem behavior and psychosocial development: A longitudinal study of youth.* San Diego, CA: Academic Press.

Josephson, E., & Rosen, M. A. (1978). Panel loss in a high school drug study. In D. Kandel (Ed.), *Longitudinal research in drug use: Empirical findings & methodological issues* (pp. 115-33). Washington, DC: Hemisphere Press-John Wiley.

Kasarda, J. D. (1989). Urban industrial transition and the underclass. *Annals of the American Academy of Political and Social Sciences, 501*, 26-47.

Massey, D. S., & Eggers, M. I. (1990). The ecology of inequality: Minorities and the concentration of poverty, 1970-80. *American Journal of Sociology, 95*, 1153-1188.

Mensch, B. S., & Kandel, D. B. (1988) Underreporting of substance use in a national longitudinal youth cohort. *Public Opinion Quarterly, 52*, 100-124.

Merton, R. K. (1957). Social theory and social structures. New York: The Free Press.

Messeri, P., & Brunswick, A. F. (1987). Heroin availability and aggregate levels of use: Secular trends in an urban Black cohort. *American Journal of Drug & Alcohol Abuse, 13*(1&2),105-129.

National Research Council (NRC 1995). Panel on census requirements in the year 2000 and beyond. In B. Edmonston & C. L. Schultze (Eds.), *Modernizing the U.S. census* (pp. 30-43). Washington, DC: National Academy Press.

Rotter, J. B., Chance, J. E., & Phares, E. J. (1972). *Applications of a social learning theory of personality*. New York: Holt, Reinhart, and Winston.

Su, S. S. (1999). Stress and coping as a conceptual framework for studying alcohol and drug use among Asian American adolescents. In M. R. De La Rosa, B. Segal & R. Lopez (Eds.), *Conducting Drug Abuse Research with Minority Populatons: Advances and Issues* (pp. 37-56). New York, The Haworth Press, Inc.

Swinton, D. H. (1989). Economic status of Black America. In J. Dewart (Ed.), *The State of Black America 1988* (pp. 9-39). New York: National Urban League.

Thompson, E. A., Smith-DiJulio, K., & Matthews, T. (1982). Social control theory: Evaluating a model for the study of adolescent alcohol and drug use. *Youth & Society, 13*, 303- 326.

Turner, R. J., Wheaton, B., & Lloyd, D. A. (1995). The epidemiology of social stress. *American Sociological Review, 60*, 104-125.

Wacquant, L. J. D., & Wilson, W. J. (1989). The cost of racial and class exclusion in the inner city. *Annals of the American Academy of Political & Social Sciences, 501*, 8-25.

Wilson, W. J. (1987). *The truly disadvantaged*. Chicago: University of Chicago Press.

Explaining Race Differences in Adolescent and Young Adult Drug Use: The Role of Racialized Social Systems

John M. Wallace, Jr., PhD

SUMMARY. Despite a growing literature on race differences in drug use, few studies have offered theoretical explanations for their existence. In light of this limitation, this paper describes a conceptual framework for understanding race differences in adolescent and young adult drug use. The central argument of the paper is that in order for researchers to understand race differences in drug use outcomes, developmental processes, and mean level differences on antecedent influences on drug use, they must understand the ways in which social systems influence individual, interpersonal, and community level risk and protective mechanisms that are linked to race and that, in turn, are responsible for racial variation in drug use. *[Article copies available for a fee from The Haworth Document Delivery Service: 1-800-342-9678. E-mail address: getinfo@haworthpressinc.com]*

INTRODUCTION

Among adolescents, Black youth are no more likely, and in many instances have been found to be less likely, than White youth to be past,

John M. Wallace, Jr. is Assistant Professor, University of Michigan, School of Social Work, and is affiliated with the Institute for Social Research.

This work was supported by a research grant from the National Institute on Drug Abuse (NIDA) R29DA09106. The opinions expressed in this paper are those of the author, not of the NIDA.

[Haworth co-indexing entry note]: "Explaining Race Differences in Adolescent and Young Adult Drug Use: The Role of Racialized Social Systems." Wallace, Jr., John M. Co-published simultaneously in *Drugs & Society* (The Haworth Press, Inc.) Vol. 14, No. 1/2, 1999, pp. 21-36; and: *Conducting Drug Abuse Research with Minority Populations: Advances and Issues* (ed: Mario R. De La Rosa, Bernard Segal, and Richard Lopez) The Haworth Press, Inc., 1999, pp. 21-36. Single or multiple copies of this article are available for a fee from The Haworth Document Delivery Service [1-800-342-9678, 9:00 a.m. - 5:00 p.m. (EST). E-mail address: getinfo@haworthpressinc.com].

present, or heavy users of licit or illicit drugs (Prendergast, Austin, Maton, & Baker, 1989; Welte & Barnes, 1987; Wallace & Bachman, 1991; Maddahian, Newcomb, & Bentler, 1986; Bachman et al., 1991; Newcomb, Maddahian, & Bentler 1987; Wallace, Bachman, O'Malley, & Johnston, 1995). As Black and White young people make the transition into young adulthood, however, there is evidence that drug use declines significantly among White young adults while it continues to increase among Black young adults (National Institute on Drug Abuse, 1995). Interestingly, irrespective of age, Black adolescents and adults who use drugs have been found to experience greater levels of drug-related problems than their White counterparts (Herd, 1994; Barnes & Welte, 1986).

Cheung (1990-91) observed that despite a significant increase in the amount of research on race differences in drug use and drug-related outcomes, "few studies have offered theoretical explanations for ethnic or racial variations in drug use" (p. 588). In an effort to address this gap in the drug literature, this paper synthesizes concepts and perspectives from a variety of social science disciplines to create an ecological developmental framework within which to examine and understand race differences in drug use. The paper is divided into three sections: the first section describes the framework's theoretical underpinnings; the second section selectively reviews the extant research to elucidate the social ecology of race differences in adolescent and young adult drug use; the third and final section discusses the limitations of the model and provides directions and suggestions for future research.

A CONCEPTUAL FRAMEWORK
FOR UNDERSTANDING RACE DIFFERENCES
IN ADOLESCENT AND YOUNG ADULT DRUG USE

Theoretical Underpinnings

The conceptual framework described here is rooted in what House (1981) has called sociological social psychology, or alternatively, social structure and personality. House (1981) observed that social structure and personality is fundamentally concerned with the relationship between social structure and individual psychology and behavior. He also noted that while psychological explanations for group differences in behavior often view group (e.g., race) differences in behavior "as rooted in the different beliefs and values shared within each group, which in turn are generally seen to arise from the different ways in which these groups have been socialized in early life" (p. 542), structural explanations for group differences highlight the structural constraints and realities that influence beliefs and values as well as behavior. The key concepts within the social structure and personality paradigm are *social system, culture,* and *social structure.*

A social system is defined as "a set of persons and social positions and roles that possess both a culture and a social structure" (p. 542). A social structure is "a persisting and bounded pattern of social relationships (or pattern of behavioral interaction) among the units (that is, persons or positions) in a social system" (p. 542). Culture is defined as "a set of cognitive and evaluative beliefs–beliefs about what is or what ought to be–that are shared by the members of a social system and transmitted to new members" (p. 542).

The conceptual framework presented here argues that race differences in drug use (and other outcomes) result from the fact that American society is a particular kind of social system composed of particular kinds of social structures and a particular culture. Specifically, the framework argues that race differences in drug use are, at least in part, the result of America's being a racialized social system.

Racialized Social Systems

Bonilla-Silva (in press) defined a racialized social system to be a society in which "economic, political, social, and ideological (cultural) levels are partially structured by the placement of actors in racial categories or races" (p. 5). These levels are equivalent to the bounded patterns of social relationships and behavioral interaction that House (1981) identified as social structure. Within a racialized social system, persons in the superordinate positions within the hierarchy receive preference in each domain of the social structure. And while the character and mechanisms of the subordination of the subordinate group may change over time, one fact remains: The life chances of the subordinate group are less than those of the superordinate group (Bonilla-Silva, in press).

America's emergence as a racialized social system resulted, at least in part, from Europeans' desire to expand capitalism into the New World (Bonilla-Silva, in press). The need for labor to permit this expansion resulted in (1) the creation of racial categorizations of people into superordinate and subordinate roles (free versus slave) based upon their place of geographic origin and phenotype (skin color, hair texture, and other physical features); (2) the development of shared racialized cultural ideology (i.e., cognitive attitudes and beliefs) about the inferiority of Black people and their proper role as slaves and the superiority of White people and their proper roles as masters and freemen; and (3) the implementation of racialized practices–discrimination–against Black people in the legal, social, economic, political, educational, and other social structures. In a short period of time, the socially created notion of "race" took on an independent existence. Racialized ideologies, that is, stereotypes and prejudice, became enmeshed in the fiber of the culture, and racialized practices became an inherent part of the social structure, thus firmly establishing America as a racialized social system.

Because "race" became real, many of the societal level factors hypothesized to impact race differences in outcomes like drug use, are not drug specific; rather, they are rooted in the history of America as a racialized social system. Historically, the vast majority of Black people came to America as slaves. The slave status of Black Americans by definition created profound (and lasting) race differentials in access to every social resource sought by those who willingly came to America's shores. As slaves, Black people received no wage for their labor, were denied family, education, and property ownership. In fact, the centerpiece of the American legal structure, the Constitution, in defining slaves as only 3/5ths of a person, did not deem Black people completely human, and only recently have they received the full rights of citizenship through the Voting Rights Act of 1965.

There have been significant gains in the social and material well-being of Black people in America since slavery. Pre- and post-emancipation racialized ideologies and practices, nevertheless, have resulted in large race disparities in material and physical well-being. These disparities continue to exist in virtually every category of life, including income, education, health and wealth (see Allen & Farley, 1986; Oliver & Shapiro, 1995; Williams & Collins, 1995).

Because racialized ideologies and practices are inherent in a racialized social system (its social structure and its culture) they reproduce themselves and are passed on, albeit in different form, from generation to generation (see Omi & Winant, 1994). After becoming reproduced as aspects of the cultural and structural components of the social system, racialized ideologies and practices need not be overtly racist in their intent nor do they require the conscious effort of individual actors to produce racial consequences; in fact, as long as the social system remains racialized, race differences in outcomes are the natural and expected consequence (Bonilla-Silva, in press).

THE SOCIAL ECOLOGY OF RACE DIFFERENCES IN DRUG USE WITHIN A RACIALIZED SOCIAL SYSTEM

The theoretical framework for understanding race differences in drug use that developed here argues that America is a racialized social system comprised of a social structure and a culture that historically and contemporarily categorizes, stereotypes, prejudges, and differentially treats people based upon their "race." The racialized nature of America's social structures and culture have systematically created and maintained mean level differences in the social conditions of people categorized as "Black" and "White," both in the past and in the present.

The model hypothesizes that historical and contemporary racialized practices and ideologies inherent in American social structures and culture directly and indirectly influence race differences in drug use and other outcomes through their influence on the communities in which Black and White live, through the structure and process of their interpersonal relationships, and through their impact on individual level psychology and behavior. Despite the hypothesis that the social system significantly impacts each of these levels, however, the framework does not suggest that individuals, their interpersonal networks, or their communities are simply passive victims of the system. The bidirectional arrows between the social system and community, interpersonal, and individual levels of the framework represent the efforts in which individuals, their interpersonal networks, and their communities attempt to resist and attenuate the influence of the system on their lives. This paper treats below some of the specific mechanisms through which the social system, community, interpersonal, and individual components of the framework are hypothesized to produce racial differences in drug use.

Social System Influences. The framework asserts that the fact that American society is a racialized social system is evident in the American ideology and discourse about race and drugs, and in the ways in which drug policy is developed and applied. For example, despite the fact that approximately three-quarters of America's current drug users are White, drug use in America is largely viewed as a Black problem (Burston, Jones, & Roberson-Saunders, 1995). For example, a sample of approximately 400 respondents were asked, "Would you close your eyes for a second, envision a drug user, and describe that person to me?" More than 95% of the respondents reported that they saw a Black person (Burston et al., 1995). Similarly, respondents reported that they saw a Black person when they were asked to envision a drug trafficker.

America's racialized ideologies concerning the race of drug users and traffickers is also reflected in drug-related legal practices. For example, between January 1995 and September 1996, 73 percent of I-95 motorists detained and searched by Maryland state police were Black (20 percent were White) even though Black motorists comprised only 18 percent of the motorists violating traffic laws and despite the fact that statewide, equal proportions of Black (28.4 percent) and White (28.8 percent) motorists were found with drugs. In another example, researchers found that pregnant drug using Black women were reported to authorities at ten times the rate of their White counterparts despite similar levels of drug use and despite laws mandating reporting of all women testing positive for drug use during pregnancy (Chasnoff, Landress, & Barrett, 1990).

Federal mandatory sentencing laws represent yet another example of the racialization of drug-related legal practice. While these laws are not overtly racist in intent, they clearly differentially categorize and treat drug offenders in a fashion that is racially discriminatory in its outcome. Specifically, the law mandates a 10 year minimum sentence for 1,000 grams of marijuana or five hundred grams of powder cocaine versus only 50 grams of crack cocaine. Given the focus of current drug policies that disproportionately emphasize the arrest of low-level street drug dealers who are most likely to be Black, sentencing laws disproportionately impact Black people and communities (Neuspiel, 1996).

Community Influences. The historical and contemporary practices and cultural ideology of the American social system, "premised upon the inferiority of (B)lacks and the need to avoid contact with them led to the overrepresentation of African Americans in deprived socioeconomic environments" (Williams, in press, p. 17). As a result of race-based residential segregation, Black people, irrespective of their social class level, are much more likely than White people to live in poor communities and to experience the negative social conditions that characterize these communities. These condition include crime, poor schools, lack of jobs, and an increased use and availability of licit and illicit drugs (Massey & Denton, 1993; Sampson & Wilson, 1995; Wilson, 1987; Williams & Collins, 1995). For example, research on community level influences on race differences in drug use suggests that higher levels of crack cocaine use among Black versus White adults is completely explainable in terms of community level predictors such as drug availability (Lillie-Blanton, Anthony, & Schuster, 1993).

Research on licit drug availability suggests that alcohol and tobacco are also more readily available in Black communities than in White communities and that the laws and community norms that govern the availability of these products vary depending upon the race of the persons in question. For example, the physical (e.g., density of retail outlets), social (e.g., billboard and magazine ads), and economic availability (e.g., cost relative to other beverages) of alcohol have been found to be disproportionately high in Black communities (Hacker, 1987; Moore, Williams, & Qualls, 1996; Scott, Denniston, & Magruder, 1992; Strickland & Finn, 1984). The "hyperavailability" of alcohol and other drugs in Black communities is particularly important in light of the research that shows that increased sales, consumption, and various alcohol (and other drug) related problems are related significantly to increased availability (Lillie-Blanton et al., 1993; see Macdonald & Whitehead, 1983 and Moskowitz, 1989 for reviews).

Related to the availability of drugs is the community level exposure and opportunities that community residents, including youth, have to acquire and use drugs. Past research indicates that relative to White youth, Black youth are more likely (1) to perceive that marijuana, cocaine, or heroin would be fairly easy or very easy to obtain in their community, (2) to have seen someone selling drugs in their community occasionally or more often, and (3) to report seeing people who are drunk or high in their community occasionally or more often (National Institute on Drug Abuse, 1995). There is also evidence that retailers are significantly more likely to sell licit drugs to minors in Black communities, and to sell them to Black minors, irrespective of community racial composition (Landrine, Klonoff, & Alcaraz, 1997). It should be noted that Black retailers have been found to be less likely than White, Hispanic, Asian, or Middle Eastern retailers to sell cigarettes to minors (Landrine et al., 1997).

Because Black youth experience a higher level of exposure to community level risk factors for drug use than White youth, it might be expected that drug use should be significantly higher among Black youth than among White youth. An alternative hypothesis, however, is that lower levels of drug use among Black youth result, at least in part, *because* of these adverse conditions. Consistent with the explanation for the decline in heroin use among young people in Harlem in the late 1960s (Boyle & Brunswick, 1980), Black youths' drug involvement might be deterred because they are able to directly witness, if not personally experience, the myriad individual, interpersonal, and community level negative consequences associated with the abuse of drugs. High risk communities in which drugs are widely available and negative consequences are readily observable might also influence Black youths' interpersonal relationships in ways that act to reduce their involvement in drugs, a hypothesis that is addressed in greater detail below.

Interpersonal Influence. Past research indicates that community level risk factors influence adolescents' interpersonal relationships with parents and peers, which in turn influence adolescent problem behaviors (Sampson & Laub, 1994). The race differences framework developed here hypothesizes that race differences in adolescent drug use reflect, at least in part, racial differences in Black and White parents' response to the differing societal and environmental contexts in which they raise their children. As noted by Sampson and Laub (1994), "strong family social controls may serve as an important buffer against structural disadvantage in the larger community" (p. 538). Consistent with this conclusion, the model posits that the absence of high levels of drug use among Black youth, despite their relatively high levels of exposure to environmental risk factors is explainable in part because of the protective effect of diligent and effective family management and parenting practices of Black parents. More specifically, because the communities in which many Black families live are objectively more dangerous, and because drug-related problems disproportionately impact these communities, it is hypothesized that, on average, Black parents will provide less opportunity for their children to use alcohol and other drugs than do White parents, and that Black parents, of necessity, will be more diligent than White parents in their use of protective parenting practices.

Race differences in parental behavior are hypothesized to result not only from Black parents' efforts to shelter their children from the disproportionate availability of drugs in their communities but also to protect their children against the racialized ideologies and practices that helped to create and sustain these conditions. Consistent with this hypothesis, it has been noted that Black parents "encounter unique societal proscriptions that create a dilemma for inculcating a positive group identity in their children" (Thornton, Chatters, Taylor, & Allen, 1990, p. 401). Accordingly, Black parents "must act as a buffer between their offspring and society and function both as a filter of societal information and as a primary interpreter of the social structure" (Thornton et al., 1990, p. 401).

Although past research on Black parent's socialization of their children does not indicate the extent to which the racial socialization process addresses the issue of drugs, Black adults who are highly racially conscious, married, and religious have been found to have extremely negative attitudes toward drug use (Gary & Berry, 1985). Presumably, racially conscious Black parents inculcate in their children both their race consciousness and their negative attitudes toward drugs.

Research on race differences in parental behavior further support the hypothesis that race differences in parental behavior and parenting practices are important explanatory factors in the effort to understand race differences in adolescent drug use. For example, relative to White parents, Black parents have been found to drink less frequently, to hold stronger norms against alcohol use, to perceive alcohol use as more harmful, and to involve their children less in family alcohol use (Peterson, Hawkins, Abbot, & Catalano, 1994).

With regard to parenting practices, relative to White parents, Black parents have been found to monitor their children's whereabouts more closely, exert more control over the peers with whom their children spend time, be more authoritarian in making decisions about where their children go, and be more likely to use physical punishment versus withdrawal of love or reasoning as disciplinary strategies (Gillmore et al., 1990; Giordano, Cernkovich, & Demaris, 1993; Peterson et al., 1994).

Race differences in youths' reports of parental behaviors are generally consistent with those reported by parents (Peterson et al., 1994). It should be noted that despite Black parents' ostensibly more authoritarian parenting styles, relative to White youth, Black youth report more intimate relationships with their parents and they also report less family conflict (Giordano et al., 1993). Race differences in the reasons that youth give for not using drugs are consistent with these findings.

For example, Black youths' closeness to their parents is reflected in the fact that they are more likely than White youth to report parental disapproval as a reason for them not to use drugs (Ringwalt & Palmer, 1990). Consistent with Black parents' greater likelihood to use physical punishment, Black youth report a significantly higher fear of being punished as a reason for their not using drugs than do White youth. Interestingly, a recent study found that while physical punishment was related to an increase in negative behavior among White children, such was not the case for Black youth (Deater-Deckard, Dodge, Bates, & Pettit, 1996). In fact, the relationship was in the opposite direction, a point that suggests that the process by which physical discipline relates to behavior may differ for Black and White youth.

As young people pass through adolescence into young adulthood, parental discipline, monitoring, and general ability to know, control, and buffer the impact of the environments to which adolescents are exposed decreases. For many youth, the transition to adulthood involves leaving home, going to college, or full-time employment. Along with these transitions away from the parental home there is often an increase in drug use among young people, regardless of race (Bachman et al., 1997), with the prevalence of drug use reaching its peak, among White youth, during this period. Within three to seven years after adolescence, drug prevalence rates begin to decline significantly among White young adults but continue to increase among Black young adults. Although the reason for this difference has yet to be adequately addressed empirically, the ecological model developed here hypothesizes that the continued increase in drug use prevalence among some Black young adults may be related to the fact that important life transitions that lead to reduced alcohol and other drug use, like stable employment and strong marital relationships (Sampson &

Laub, 1993), do not happen until later in life for many Black Americans, if they happen at all (Bennett & Bloom 1989). And so, for many Black young adults, continued and increasing levels of drug use may reflect their response to the harshness of the racialized social system from which their parents had previously shielded them.

The relationship that adolescents have with their parents has important implications for the other relationships that are important during adolescence, namely, the relationship that adolescents have with their peers. Research on race differences in peer relationships indicate that relative to White youth, Black youth are more parent- versus peer-oriented, score significantly lower in the need for similarity as the basis for friendship choices, consider it less important to associate with a group of friends, score lower on measures of peer intimacy, experience lower levels of peer pressure, and indicate lower levels of need for approval from peers (Cernkovich & Giordano, 1992; Giordano & Cernkovich, 1986; Giordano et al., 1993). Given the strong relationship between peer drug use and adolescents' own drug use, it would be expected that youth who are more strongly peer oriented (i.e., White youth) would be more likely to use drugs than those who are less strongly peer oriented (i.e., Black youth). In fact, not only are White youth more likely than Black youth to use drugs, researchers consistently find a statistical interaction between peer use and race indicating that the strength of the relationship between peer drug use and adolescents' own drug use is higher for White youth than for Black youth (Barnes & Farrell, 1994; Newcomb & Bentler, 1986; Wallace, 1991).

Individual Influences. If the theoretical framework is correct in its assertion that the individual level factors that place young people at risk for drug use are shaped by the societal, community, and interpersonal contexts in which Black and White youth are nested, the research discussed in the various sections above suggests that Black youth should, on average, exhibit less individual level risk for drug use than do White youth. With the exception of those risk factors that strongly relate to family income and education (e.g., school grades), past research generally supports this hypothesis (Wallace & Bachman, 1991).

For example, relative to White youth, Black youth initiate the use of most substances later, they have more negative attitudes to drugs, they are less likely to expect to use drugs as an adult, they are less oriented toward risk taking and sensation seeking, they perceive greater risk in the use of drugs, they express greater disapproval of drug use, they perceive greater disapproval of their using drugs by their friends, and they express equal or higher commitment to school (Cernkovich & Giordano, 1992; Gilmore et al., 1990; Kurtz & Zuckerman, 1978; Peterson et al., 1994; Prendergast et al., 1989; Wallace & Bachman, 1991).

LIMITATIONS AND DIRECTIONS FOR FUTURE RESEARCH

For the sake of conceptual clarity, the racialized social systems model of race differences in adolescent and young adult drug use described herein highlights the key *differences* that characterize the community, interpersonal, and individual level contexts and experiences of White and Black youth. In reality, there is considerable within-race heterogeneity as well as considerable overlap in the ways in which Black and White parents seek to raise their children, in the nature of Black and White youths' peer relationships, and in the various other individual, interpersonal, and community level factors that increase young people's risk for drug use and that protect them from using drugs. The theoretical focus of the framework on race differences aside, an important strength of the model is its emphasis upon the complex way in which individual, interpersonal, community, and societal (i.e., micro and macro) influences impact adolescent's drug use, independent of their race.

Although it has long been recognized that adolescent problem behaviors like drug use can only be understood by considering both the micro and macro contexts in which they occur (see Shaw, 1929), many current theories continue to focus almost exclusively on proximate individual level psychological and motivational characteristics as the key explanators for adolescent problem behaviors. More sophisticated frameworks, however, have begun to look not only at characteristics of individuals but also at the ways in which adolescent problem behavior is influenced by the interpersonal (e.g., family and peer) processes and environments in which adolescents are nested. The most enlightened theoretical perspectives have begun to incorporate not only individual and interpersonal level characteristics into their models, but they have also included broader structural (i.e., community level) contexts as explicit components of their models (see, for example, Sampson & Laub, 1994; Catalano & Hawkins, 1996; Thornberry, 1987).

Although the specific proximal and distal mechanisms hypothesized to account for variation in adolescent problem behaviors differ across ecological theoretical paradigms, the basic model that underlies them is that the social contexts influence interpersonal relationships which in turn influence the behavior of young people. Despite the conceptual insight provided by these paradigms and despite the scientific appeal of "multipurpose" universal models that are able to explain why young people use drugs *and* why there are race differences in these behaviors, current theoretical perspectives that ignore "race" altogether or that treat race as exogenous to the theoretical model (e.g., Catalano & Hawkins, 1996) are limited in their ability to fully (versus just statistically) explain race differences in drug use outcomes, developmental processes, or antecedent mean levels on key influences.

The absence of comprehensive theoretical explanations for race differences in drug use (and other outcomes) may be the result of researchers' failure to recognize that it is possible to *statistically* explain race difference in some outcome and still provide minimal theoretical or empirical insight into the *true* explanation for the disparity. For example, researchers (Williams & Collins, 1994) often attribute race differences in outcomes to race differences in socioeconomic status (SES). Assuming that past research has found that drug use is significantly higher among people with low SES, a researcher might hypothesize that higher levels of drug use among Black adults results from the fact that Black people are more likely than White people to have low incomes. In order to empirically test this hypothesis the researcher might regress drug use on race and income. If the coefficient for the race variable were statistically insignificant when income is controlled, the researcher would conclude that race differences in drug use were "explained" by race differences in SES.

Despite the parsimony of this statistical model and its apparent ability to account for the race difference in drug use, it is limited in its ability to fully (versus just statistically) explain the nature of the relationship between drug use and race. Specifically, there are at least two key problems with the model. First, the model assumes that the way in which SES relates to drug use is the same for Black people and White people. Second, the model fails to provide any insight into why there are race differences in SES in the first place. It is possible that SES is simply a proximate "surface cause" or mediator of a theoretically more distal variable that is the root cause of the race disparity in drug use.

The theoretical framework developed here argues that the root cause of race differences in drug use and other behaviors lies in American society as a racialized social system comprised of social structures and a culture in which racialized practices and racialized ideologies are inherent. The model argues that while many of the predictors and processes that underlie the relationships between societal, community, interpersonal, and individual factors and drug use are the same for Black and White people, some are not, because of the nature of racialized social systems and their impact on behavior.

For example, research among Black and White men reveals that the relationship between income and alcohol is not racially invariant. Specifically, the prevalence of alcohol use has been found to increase among White men as income increases; among Black men, however, the prevalence of alcohol use is lower among those with higher incomes than among those with less money (Herd, 1990). This income by race interaction suggests that alcohol use may have different meanings and different purposes for Black and White men, depending upon their economic circumstances. In light of these findings, and in light of the substantial race disparities in income, a thorough explanation for race differences in alcohol use would seek to explain not only why income differentially relates to alcohol use for Black and White men, but it would also seek to identify the source(s) of the race differences in income.

The distinctly racial nature of persisting race differences in economic well-being is highlighted by the fact that among Black Americans, skin color recently has been empirically demonstrated to be a significant predictor of occupational status and income (Keith & Herring, 1991). More specifically, lighter skinned Black people have been found to have higher status jobs and higher incomes than their darker skinned counterparts. This finding is important in that it suggests that within the American racialized social system there is a quantifiable economic "tax" that Black people pay the further their phenotypic appearance deviates from that of the superordinate group. The finding is also important in that it demonstrates that race and SES are not confounded, as often suggested by researchers who attribute race differences in outcomes to SES differences. Rather, race, as determined by skin color, is actually a *cause* of SES.

Future investigations on race differences in drug use will require that researchers move beyond simplistic single variable explanations for race differences in drug use toward more comprehensive multilevel conceptual frameworks. More specifically, the model presented in this paper argues that in order for researchers to fully understand race differences in drug use, they must fully understand the complex ways in which social systems influence individual, interpersonal, and community level risk and protective mechanisms that are linked to race, and which in turn, are responsible for racial variation in drug-related outcomes.

REFERENCES

Bachman, J. G., Wallace, J. M., O'Malley, P. M., Johnston, L. D., Kurth, C. L., & Neighbors, H. W. (1991). Racial/ethnic differences in smoking, drinking, and illicit drug use among American high school seniors, 1976-89. *American Journal of Public Health, 81*, 372-377.

Bachman, J., Wadsworth, K., O'Malley, P., Johnston, L., & Schulenberg, J. (1997). *Smoking, drinking, and drug use in young adulthood: The impacts of new freedoms and new responsibilities.* Mahwah, NJ: Lawrence Earlbaum Associates.

Baldwin, A., Baldwin, C., & Cole, R. (1990). Stress-resistant families and stress resilient children. In J. Rolf, A. S. Masten, D. Cicchetti, K. H. Nuechterlein, & S. Weintraub (Eds.), *Risk and protective factors in the development of psychopathology.* Cambridge: Cambridge University Press.

Barnes, G., Farrell, M., & Banerjee, S. (1994). Family influences on alcohol abuse and other problem behaviors among Black and White adolescents in a general population sample. *Journal of Research on Adolescence, 4*, 183-201.

Barnes, G. M., & Welte, J. W. (1986). Adolescent alcohol abuse: Subgroup differences and relationships to other problem behaviors. *Journal of Adolescent Research, 1*, 179-94.

Bonilla-Silva, E. (In press). Rethinking racism: Toward a structural interpretation. *American Sociological Review.*

Burston, B.W., Jones, D., & Robertson-Saunders, P. (1995). Drug use and African Americans: Myth versus reality. *Journal of Alcohol and Drug Education, 40*, 19-39.

Boyle, J. M., & Brunswick, A. F. (1980). What happened in Harlem? Analysis of a decline in heroin use among a generation unit of urban Black youth. *Journal of Drug Issues, 10*, 109-130.

Cernkovich, S., & Giordano, P. (1987). Family relationships and delinquency. *Criminology, 25*, 295-319.

Cernkovich, S., & Giordano, P., (1992). School bonding, race, and delinquency. *Criminology, 30* 261-291.

Chansnoff, I. J., Landress, H. J., & Barret, M. E. (1990). The prevalence of illicit-drug or alcohol use during pregnancy and discrepancies in mandatory reporting in Pinellas County, Florida. *New England Journal of Medicine, 322*, 1202-1206.

Cheung, Y. W. (1990-91). Ethnicity and alcohol/drug use revisited: A framework for future research. *International Journal of the Addictions, 25*, 581-605.

Deater-Deckard, K., Dodge, K., Bates, J., & Pettit, G. (1996). Physical discipline among African American and European American mothers: Links to children's externalizing behaviors. *Developmental Psychology, 23*(6), 1065-1072.

Farley, R., & Allen, W. (1987). *The color line and the quality of life in America.* New York: Russell Sage Foundation.

Gary, L., & Berry, G. (1984). Some determinants of attitudes toward substance use in an urban ethnic community. *Psychological Reports, 54*, 539-545.

Gillmore, M., Catalano, R., Morrison, D., Wells, E., Iritani, B., & Hawkins, J. (1990). Racial differences in acceptability and availability of drugs and early initiation of substance use. *American Journal of Drug and Alcohol Abuse, 16*, 185-206.

Giordano, P., Cernkovich, S., & Demaris, A. (1993). The family and peer relations of Black adolescents. *Journal of Marriage and the Family, 55*, 277-287.

Giordano, P., & Cernkovich, S. (1986). Friendships and delinquency. *American Journal of Sociology, 91*(5), 1170-1202.

Goddard, L. L. (1993). *An African-centered model of prevention for African-American youth at risk* (CSAP Technical Report 6). Rockville, MD: USHHS.

Hawkins, D., Catalano, R., & Miller, J. (1992). Risk and protective factors for alcohol and other drug problems in adolescence and early adulthood: Implications for substance abuse prevention. *Psychological Bulletin, 112*, 64-105.

House, J. (1981). Social structure and personality. In M. Rosenberg & R. H. Turner (Eds)., *Social psychology: Sociological perspectives* (pp. 525-561). New York: Basic Books Inc.

Hacker, A. G., Collins, R., & Jacobson, M. (1987). *Marketing booze to Blacks.* Washington, DC: Center for Science in the Public Interest.

Herd, D. (1990). Subgroup differences in drinking patterns among Black and White men: Results from a national survey. *Journal of Studies on Alcohol, 51*, 221-232.

Herd, D. (1994). Predicting drinking problems among Black and White men: Results from a national survey. *Journal of Studies on Alcohol, 55*, 61-71.

Keith, V. M., & Herring, C. (1991). Skin tone and stratification in the Black community. *American Journal of Sociology, 97*, 760-778.

Kurtz, J. & Zuckerman, M. (1978). Race and sex differences on the sensation seeking scales. *Psychological Reports, 43*, 529-530.

Landrine, H., Klonoff, E., & Alcaraz, R. (1997). Racial discrimination in minors access to tobacco. *Journal of Black Psychology, 23*, 135-147.

Lillie-Blanton, M., Anthony, J. C., & Schuster, C. R. (1993). Probing the meaning of racial/ethnic group comparisons in crack cocaine smoking. *JAMA, 269*, 993-997.

Macdonald S., & Whitehead, P. C. (1983). Availability of outlets and consumption of alcoholic beverages. *Journal of Drug Issues, 13,* 477-486.

Massey, D. S., & Denton, N. A. (1993). American apartheid: Segregation and the making of the underclass. Cambridge, MA: Harvard University Press.

Moore, D., Williams, J., & Qualls, W. (1996). Target marketing of tobacco and alcohol-related products to ethnic minority groups in the United States. *Ethnicity & Disease, 6*, 83-98.

National Institute on Drug Abuse (1995). *Drug use among racial/ethnic minorities* (NIH Publication No. 95-3888). Rockville, MD: NIDA.

Neuspiel, D. R. (1996). Racism and perinatal addiction. *Ethnicity & Disease, 6*, 47-55.

Newcomb, M. D., Maddahian, E., & Bentler, P. M. (1987). Substance abuse and psychological risk factors among teenagers: Associations with sex, age, ethnicity, and type of school. *American Journal of Drug and Alcohol Abuse, 13*, 413-433.

Omi, M., & Winant, H. (1994) *Racial formation in the United States from the 1960s to the 1990s* (2nd ed.). New York: Routledge.

Oliver, M. L., & Shapiro (1995). *Black wealth/white wealth: A new perspective on racial inequality.* New York: Routledge.

Peterson, P., Hawkins, J., Abbot, R., & Catalano, R. (1994). Disentangling the effects of parental drinking, family management, and parental alcohol norms on current drinking by African American and European American Adolescents. *Journal of Research on Adolescents, 4,* 203-227.

Prendergast, M. L., Austin, G. A., Maton, K., & Baker, R. (1989) Substance abuse among Black youth. *Prevention Research Update, 4,* 1-27.

Ringwalt, C., & Palmer, J. (1990). Differences between White and Black youth who drink heavily. *Addictive Behaviors, 15,* 455-460.

Sampson, R., & Laub, J. (1990). Crime and deviance over the lifecourse: The salience of adult social bonds. *American Sociological Review, 55,* 609-627.

Sampson, R., & Laub, J. (1994). Urban poverty and the family context of delinquency: A new look at structure and process in a classic study. *Child Development, 65,* 523-540.

Sampson, R. & Wilson, W. (1995). *Toward a theory of race, crime, and urban inequality, in crime and inequality.* Stanford, CA: Stanford University Press.

Shaw, C. R. (1929). *Delinquency areas: A study of the geographic distribution of school truants, juvenile delinquents, and adult offenders in Chicago.* Chicago: The University of Chicago.

Scott, B., Denniston, R., & Magruder, K. (1992). Alcohol advertising in the African American Community. *Journal of Drug Issues, 22,* 455-469.

Thornton, M. C., Chatters, L. M., Taylor, R. J., & Allen, W. R. (1990). Sociodemographic and environmental correlates of racial socialization by Black parents. *Child Development, 61,* 401-409.

Thomas, M. E., Herring, C., & Horton, H. D. (1995). In G. E. Thomas (Ed.), *Race and ethnicity in America.* Bristol, PA: Taylor and Francis.

Thornberry, T. (1987). Toward an interactional theory of delinquency. *Criminology, 75,* 1222-1245.

Welte, J. W., & Barnes, G. M. (1987). Alcohol use among adolescent minority groups. *Journal of Studies on Alcohol, 48,* 329-336.

Wallace, J. M., & Bachman, J. G. (1991). Explaining racial/ethnic differences in drug use: The impact of background and lifestyle. *Social Problems, 38,* 333-357.

Wallace, J., Bachman, J., O'Malley, P., & Johnston, L. (1995). Racial/ethnic differences in adolescent drug use. In G. Botvin, S. Schinke, & M. Orlandi (Eds.), *Drug abuse prevention with multiethnic youth.* Thousand Oaks, CA: Sage.

Wells, E., Morrison, D., Gillmore, M., & Catalano, R. (1992) Race differences in antisocial behaviors and attitudes and early initiation of substance use. *Journal of Drug Education, 22,* 115-130.

Williams D. R. (in press). Race and health: Basic questions, emerging directions. *Annals of Epidemiology.*

Williams, D. R., & Collins, C. (1995) U.S. socioeconomic and racial differences in health: Patterns and explanations. *Annual Review of Sociology, 21,* 349-386.

Wilson, W. J. (1987). *The truly disadvantaged: Inner city, the underclass, and public policy.* Chicago, IL: University of Chicago Press.

Stress and Coping
as a Conceptual Framework
for Studying Alcohol and Drug Use
Among Asian American Adolescents

S. Susan Su, PhD

SUMMARY. Researchers have conducted very few studies on substance use among Asian American youths, and current etiological studies have suffered from a number of methodological shortcomings: They employ small sample sizes; they define "Asian" race/ethnicity so broadly that they do not distinguish among different Asian American subpopulations; they do not distinguish between U.S.-born Asian Americans and recent immigrants; they employ only a cross-sectional research design; they do not control for factors that may be confounded with race/ethnicity; and they do not consider cultural differences in self-reports of alcohol and drug use. Moreover, these studies lack adequate theoretical frameworks and have several conceptual limitations, including their failure to identify sa-

S. Susan Su is Senior Research Scientist, National Opinion Research Center, University of Chicago.

This research was partially supported by grant number DA05617 from the National Institute on Drug Abuse (NIDA). The views expressed in this paper are those of the author and do not necessarily reflect the views of the NIDA.

This paper was presented at the Conference on Drug Abuse Research with Minority Populations: Methodological and Theoretical Issues and Concerns, Washington, DC, September 26-27, 1996.

[Haworth co-indexing entry note]: "Stress and Coping as a Conceptual Framework for Studying Alcohol and Drug Use Among Asian American Adolescents." Su, S. Susan. Co-published simultaneously in *Drugs & Society* (The Haworth Press, Inc.) Vol. 14, No. 1/2, 1999, pp. 37-56; and: *Conducting Drug Abuse Research with Minority Populations: Advances and Issues* (ed: Mario R. De La Rosa, Bernard Segal, and Richard Lopez) The Haworth Press, Inc., 1999, pp. 37-56. Single or multiple copies of this article are available for a fee from The Haworth Document Delivery Service [1-800-342-9678, 9:00 a.m. - 5:00 p.m. (EST). E-mail address: getinfo@haworthpressinc.com].

© 1999 by The Haworth Press, Inc. All rights reserved.   *37*

lient components of race/ethnicity as risk or protective factors, their lack of attention to the role of the family in the adaptation process, and their failure to consider the interactive and mediating effects of contextual factors between race/ethnicity and alcohol and drug use. To address these methodological and conceptual limitations, this paper proposes a new conceptual model, one which incorporates a family-risk paradigm and stress-coping perspectives. The paper also discusses the methodological considerations for applying this model successfully. *[Article copies available for a fee from The Haworth Document Delivery Service: 1-800-342-9678. E-mail address: getinfo@haworthpressinc. com]*

INTRODUCTION

The literature documenting alcohol and drug use among Asian American youths is noticeably scant–mostly because of a persisting stereotype that Asian Americans are the "model minority," with few social problems in general, and still fewer problems with alcohol and drug use (Austin, 1989; Joe, 1996). Data from existing studies have confronted the stereotypical perception of Asian Americans as alcohol and drug-free (National Institute on Drug Abuse, 1995; Su, Larison, Ghadialy, Rhode, & Johnson, 1997; Wallace & Bachman, 1993). Little research, however, has examined whether factors affecting alcohol and drug use among Asian Americans differ from those among non-Asian Americans. Little is also known about the processes and mechanisms that explain the linkages between Asian race/ethnicity and alcohol and drug use. This paper first reviews the methodological and conceptual limitations of the existing etiological studies on alcohol and drug use among Asian American adolescents. It then proposes a conceptual framework for studying the developmental and etiologic pathways to alcohol and drug use among Asian American youths. Following the discussion of key concepts for research on Asian American adolescents in general, it clarifies several key concepts that are important to better understand alcohol and drug use among Asian American adolescents. Finally, it discusses the methodological considerations and future application of this conceptual framework.

RESEARCH ON ALCOHOL AND DRUG USE
AMONG ASIAN AMERICAN YOUTHS

The limited existing research has reported that fewer Asian Americans than non-Asians use alcohol and drugs, and that the observed racial/ethnic differences in alcohol and drug use are due to differences in the distribution of risk factors. Gillmore et al. (1990) and Maddahian, Newcomb, and Bentler (1986) indicated that Asian American students in general reported the least access to alcohol and drugs, and suggested that the lower rates of substance use among Asian American students may result from the differential availability of substances and having fewer friends who drink.

Similarly, Catalano et al. (1992) indicated that family risk factors of alcohol and drug use varied with an adolescent's race/ethnicity: Although Asian American students were more likely to report that their parents revoked privileges for misbehavior than non-Asian American students, family management practices were not associated with a lower rate of drug initiation among Asian American students. Instead, the absence of a drug-using sibling, living with both parents, perceived parental disapproval of their alcohol use, and female gender accounted for lower substance initiation rates among Asian American students. In contrast, the parents' ability to revoke privileges, the absence of a deviant sibling, proactive family management practices, and the parents' disapproval of an adolescent's alcohol use affected lower substance initiation for non-Hispanic whites; attachment to parents and parents' supervision were related to lower rates of substance initiation for African Americans.

Furthermore, Wells et al. (1992) observed that self-reported delinquency was a more powerful predictor of substance initiation for Asian American students than for African American students, even though Asian American students scored lower on measures of problem behaviors (Wells et al., 1992). Similarly, Barnes and Welte (1986) noted that the relationship between misconduct and alcohol use was stronger for Asian American students than for non-Asian American students.

Bankston (1995), who studied Vietnamese high school students without comparison groups, concluded that involvement in a Vietnamese ethnic community, characterized by use of the Vietnamese language, ethnic friendship networks, and Vietnamese church attendance, appeared to protect Vietnamese students from using alcohol and drugs. Bankston controlled for the effects of family structure and parental involvement in the ethnic community.

Methodological Shortcomings of Existing Studies

Although these studies provide an important foundation for understanding the differences in risk factors for substance use between Asian Americans and non-Asian Americans, they share a number of methodological shortcomings that may limit the usefulness of these research findings.

First, most relied primarily on student samples of younger adolescents, thus excluding older adolescents and young adults, who may be more involved in alcohol and illicit drug use. A great majority of the samples were drawn in the 1970s and early 1980s and therefore included mostly Chinese and Japanese respondents. Those groups do not necessarily represent the current diverse Asian population's ethnic origins, cultures, languages, history of immigration, level of acculturation, and socioeconomic status. In fact, studies in the 1970s and 1980s did not include those subgroups that today are both the fastest growing and the most at-risk, such as southeast Asian refugees, Koreans, and Filipinos (Zane & Sasao, 1992). Also, specific Asian American subgroups were almost never identified or differentiated from one another–most of the researchers did not even acknowledge the heterogeneity of Asian Americans in terms of national heritage and extent of acculturation–so it is unclear which of the Asian groups are represented in their findings. Second, none of the studies used a prospective longitudinal design to study the adaptation processes and mechanisms that explain the linkage between Asian race/ethnicity and substance use. Third, the same measures of risk factors were used across various racial/ethnic groups, without consideration for the possible differences in the meanings of these measures between Asian Americans and non-Asian Americans. For instance, considerable differences may exist between Asian American adolescents and non-Asian American adolescents in their definition of "authoritative parenting styles." Fourth, the studies seldom controlled for socioeconomic and other demographic differences that may be confounded with race/ethnicity. Finally, these studies did not account for cultural differences that may affect self-reporting or self-disclosure with respect to substance use and abuse (Zane & Sasao, 1992).

CONCEPTUAL LIMITATIONS OF PREVIOUS RESEARCH

In addition to the methodological limitations discussed above, previous studies on alcohol and drug use in Asian American youths have conceptual limitations that hamper our understanding of the processes and mechanisms that may lead to the youths' alcohol and drug use. First, instead of identifying the salient components of Asian race/ethnicity that account for the observed racial/ethnic variations in risk factors and prevalence of substance use, these previous studies focused on the distribution of risk factors across various racial/ethnic groups (Adlaf, Smart, & Tan, 1989; Wallace & Bachman, 1991). Similarly, although these previous etiological studies generally reported a lower prevalence of alcohol and drug use among Asian American youths relative to other racial/ethnic groups, and reported that some cultural factors seem to inhibit or protect Asian Americans from using drugs, these studies made no attempt to identify these factors.

Moreover, none of these previous studies distinguished recent immigrants from native-born Asian Americans, even though 61% of all Asians, 91% of Vietnamese, and 82% of Koreans in the United States in 1980 were foreign-born, compared to 29% of Hispanics, 5% of non-Hispanic whites, and 3% of African Americans (Barringer, Gardner, & Levin, 1993). Research empirically has supported that recent Asian immigrants differ significantly from native-born Asian Americans, even if they are of the same ethnicity, in demographic characteristics, geographical residence, family and household composition, occupational status, income levels, perceived discrimination, and degree of intergenerational conflict (Barringer, Gardner, & Levin, 1993; Coll & Magnuson, 1997; Rumbaut, 1997). As a result, correlates of alcohol and drug use among adolescent children of recent Asian immigrants may be different from those of native-born Asian American adolescents. Additionally, these studies did not differentiate southeast Asian refugees from voluntary Asian immigrants. Southeast Asian refugees generally display characteristics that are more typical of socially and economically disadvantaged minorities, such as Hispanics, African Americans, and Native Americans: poor education, marginal occupation, and poverty (Barringer, Gardner, & Levin, 1993). They are at higher risk for alcohol and drug use because of their experience of traumatic events, such as violence, loss, and severe deprivation, during their flight from war-torn countries, and because of their experience of undesirable life changes as the result of economic hardship in the United States.

Except for Catalano et al. (1992), researchers also failed to recognize the centrality of the family among Asian Americans. For Asian Americans, the family is not only an important aspect of one's cultural identity, but also the primary social control agent through its demands for duty, obligations, and obedience (Sodosky & Lai, 1997). Further, previous research on alcohol and drug use among Asian Americans did not examine the interactive and mediating effects of educational attainment on the relationship between race/ethnicity and alcohol and drug use.

And finally, the etiological studies of Asian Americans' substance use lacked adequate theoretical frameworks and mostly documented the distribution of the prevalence and correlates of substance use among Asian Americans relative to other racial/ethnic groups. What has been missing is a test of specific hypotheses, and an examination, based on the integration of general theories of deviance and the culturally-specific theories of alcohol and drug use, of the fitness of models.

THE CONCEPTUAL MODEL FOR RESEARCH ON DRUG USE AMONG ASIAN AMERICAN YOUTHS

In order to address all the methodological and conceptual limitations of previous etiological studies of substance use among Asian American adolescents, a conceptual model is proposed in this section to investigate the processes and mechanisms that explain the linkages between Asian race/ethnicity and alcohol and drug use. This model integrates a high-risk family paradigm from epidemiology with stress-coping theory. Stress includes negative life events, chronic strain, and acculturation strain, as experienced by adolescents, their parents, and their families as a whole. Susceptibility to alcohol and drug use is considered to be a function of an adolescent's *psychological response* to stress, and not simply a result of mere exposure to stress. The model adapts and integrates important concepts from both general and culturally-specific theories of deviance, including social learning theory, control theory of deviance, strain theory, developmental psychopathology, social network theory, and acculturation theory. The model seeks to explain the mediating effect of protective factors on the relationship between stress and alcohol and drug use in adolescents.

The model begins with stress associated with Asian race/ethnicity and family immigration processes as predisposing factors that affect susceptibility to substance use in adolescents. At the same time, it considers childhood and adolescence adjustment, including depression, conduct behavior, learning difficulties. Further, this model incorporates several mediating factors that may serve to attenuate or exacerbate the risk for alcohol and drug use–understanding that all of this is taking place in the context of already high stress levels associated with being a part of an ethnic minority group and, where relevant, an immigrant.

These mediating factors include parental acculturation and parental psychopathology; family processes, such as parent-child relations and parental supervision and discipline; family cohesion; family structure; living arrangements; and sibling drug use. Mediating factors also include peer's influences and school influences, such as school attachment, educational attainment, and school environment. Finally, mediating factors include personal resources, such as self-esteem and mastery, positive ethnic identity, and biculturalism; social support; and neighborhood characteristics.

The model's outcome variables are alcohol and drug use and abuse, depression and other psychiatric disorders, and delinquency. Figure 1 provides a map of how the proposed measures are related spatially and temporally. Some of the relationships displayed as unidirectional may in fact be reciprocal; for instance, the effect of the relationship between individual stressful life events on the one hand and drug use on the other can be mutual.

KEY CONSTRUCTS FOR RESEARCH ON SUBSTANCE USE AMONG ASIAN AMERICANS

This section explores ways in which key constructs adapted for the conceptual model proposed above can be clarified and broadened to con-

FIGURE 1. Conceptual Model for the Study of Substance Use Among Asian American Youth

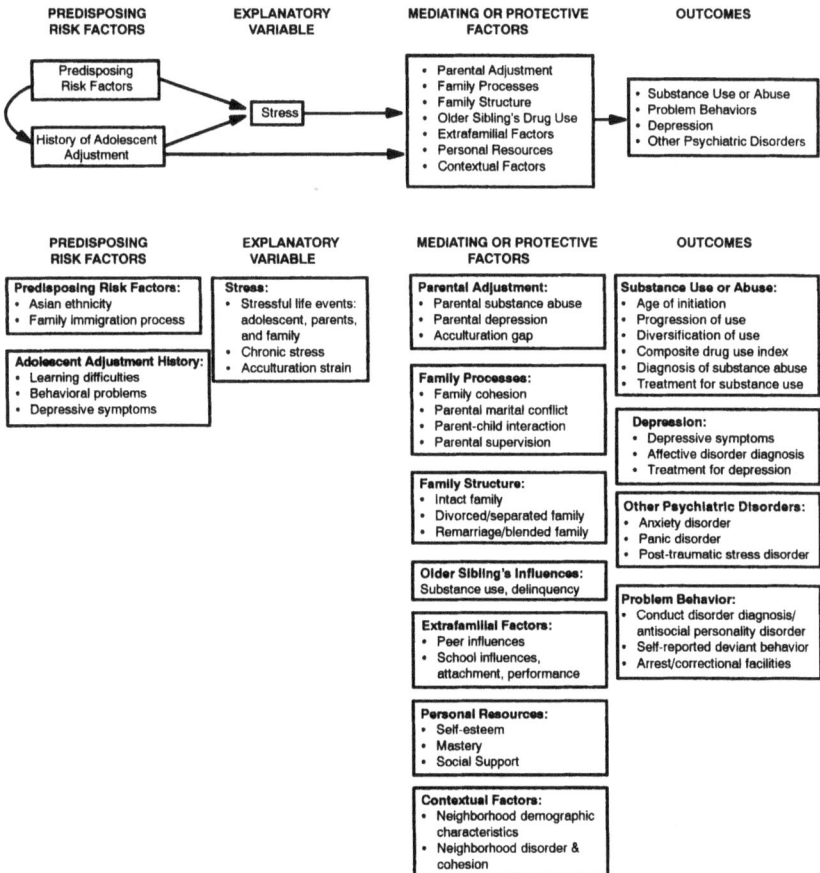

tribute to our understanding of the etiology of substance use among minority youths. Specifically, it discusses the empirical support for and importance of five constructs for studies of alcohol and drug use in Asian American adolescents.

Identifying Salient Components of Asian Race/Ethnicity as Risk or Protective Factors

Current literature indicates that Asian race/ethnicity, as self-identified by the study respondents, is important as an indicator to mark differences among groups in the prevalence and correlates of alcohol and drug use. Little research has moved toward identifying components in Asian race/ethnicity that may explain these observed differences. Such components include disadvantaged minority status, ethnic identity, acculturation strain, and lifestyle or cultural values.

Disadvantaged minority status. A number of researchers have suggested that racial/ethnic differences in adolescent drug use may be due to racial/ethnic differences in other socio-demographic characteristics. For instance, Lillie-Blanton, Anthony, and Schuster (1993) demonstrated that neighborhood crime and poverty rates accounted for the reported racial/ethnic differences in illicit drug use. Other researchers indicated that disadvantaged minority status, that is, marginality, is a significant stressor (Vega & Rumbaut, 1991), as ethnic youths are more likely to encounter discrimination and racial/ethnic prejudices (Gonzales & Cauce, 1995; Vega, Khoury, Zimmerman, Gil, & Warheit, 1995). The problems of the Asian communities to which these youth belong can aggravate the stress that marginality causes; these problems include lack of status, political power, and economic opportunity. These problems convince youths that American society is not open, does not afford equal opportunity, and does not provide a viable set of norms or values upon which to formulate their own identities (Ogbu, 1987).

Empirical studies suggest that youth and adults in disadvantaged racial/ethnic minority groups are more likely to be exposed to stressful life events and chronic strains than whites (see Neff, 1985; Barrera, Li, & Chassin, 1995). A number of studies have further indicated that individuals of lower socioeconomic status, regardless of ethnic group, are exposed to more stressors and consequently show more symptoms of distress (see Ulbrich, Warheit, & Zimmerman, 1989; Neff, 1985; Dornbusch, Mont-Reynaud, Ritter, Chen, & Steinberg, 1991). But these studies have mostly examined the stressful life events and chronic strains in African Americans and Hispanics; little is known about the differences in stressors between Asian and non-Asian Americans. For all these reasons, understanding the stressful life events and chronic life stresses that are unique to southeast Asian refugees, recent voluntary Asian immigrants, and native-born Asian Americans, and how these stressors contribute to substance use and other adaptation outcomes, should be a high priority for future research.

Ethnic identity. Studies have demonstrated that ethnicity is a salient component of self-identity for Asian American adolescents (see Phinney & Alipuria, 1990). Researchers concerned with ethnic identity have suggested that positive ethnic identity or biculturalism–a sense of connection to and pride in one's ethnicity–is an important resource for combating the negative implications for the self that may frequently accompany stressful events (Oetting, 1993; Gonzales & Cauce, 1995). Specifically, positive ethnic identity leads to high self-esteem (Oetting & Beauvais, 1990-1991; Oetting, 1993), which is an important moderator of the negative effects of stressors (Mirowsky & Ross, 1989; Pearlin, 1989). A high level of self-esteem is presumed to stimulate greater flexibility and social adjustment, and make negative coping strategies such as drug use less attractive (Mirowsky & Ross, 1986; Gonzales & Cauce, 1995). In contrast, individuals who have negative feelings about their ethnic identity can find adversity unmanageable and therefore begin using alcohol and/or drugs.

Rodriguez, Adrados, and De La Rosa (1993) extended previous studies to examine the effect of both acculturation and biculturalism on adolescent substance use. They found that Hispanic youths who were more acculturated (i.e., those who had more adherence to American culture) were more likely to use drugs than those who were less acculturated. In addition, acculturation and biculturalism had strong effects on Hispanic adolescent drug use because they weakened family ties and strengthened ties to deviant peers. Little, however, is known about the salience of ethnic identity on alcohol and drug use among Asian American youths. Future research, using sensitive measures of ethnic identity, acculturation, biculturalism, and self-esteem, should help us understand important dimensions of Asian race/ethnicity in their effects on adolescent substance use and abuse.

Acculturation strain. Other researchers have attempted to explain alcohol and drug use as resulting from cultural conflicts. The pressures of adapting to two cultures simultaneously are most pronounced for immigrant youths, and for youth whose parents were immigrants. These youths may experience daily conflict and stress as they discover that their cultural values and behaviors at home are not recognized or valued among peers or at school, and as they encounter among their peers a wide range of values and cultural orientations that may conflict with and challenge the values and expectations of their parents (Gonzales & Cauce, 1995). As a result, these youths may feel stress related to their English-speaking ability, unfamiliarity with school rules and expectations, and variant learning styles which they, as immigrant adolescents, must adapt to styles prevalent in the wider culture (Berry & Kim, 1988).

Vega, Zimmerman, Gil, Warheit, and Apospori (1993) were among the first to study the relationship between acculturation strain and drug use. They defined acculturation strain as language-related conflicts, strain related to intergenerational acculturation gaps, discrimination-related conflicts, and conflicts related to perceptions of the United States as a closed society. They reported that among foreign-born Hispanic adolescents, those who had high acculturation strain tended to report more language-related conflicts. Among native-born Hispanic adolescents, those with high acculturation strain were more likely than their counterparts to rate high on language conflicts, perceived discrimination, and stresses related to the perception of a closed society (Vega et al., 1995). Further, both native-born and foreign-born Hispanic adolescents who had higher acculturation stress were more likely to have higher scores for problem behavior. These acculturation strain measures represent one of a few important advances in research on substance use among racial/ethnic minorities and should serve as a useful tool to study the effect of acculturation strain among Asian American youths.

Lifestyle or cultural values. Wallace and Bachman (1991) suggested that lifestyle factors, such as time spent in educationally-oriented versus peer-oriented activities, may contribute to differences in alcohol and drug use between Asian Americans and whites. It will be important to identify additional lifestyle or cultural value factors that either expose Asian American youths to risk for alcohol and/or drug use or protect them from risk of using alcohol and/or drugs.

Understanding Origins and Dimensions of Stress

The role of stress in explaining alcohol and drug use has received much attention in recent research. Previous research based on predominantly white adolescent samples generally defined stress as negative or uncontrollable life events, and found that adolescents who experienced more stressful life events were prone to substance use (e.g., Bruns & Geist, 1984; Newcomb & Harlow, 1986; Agnew & White, 1992; Hoffmann & Su, 1997). In contrast, research on the relationship between stress and substance use among racial/ethnic minority youth has primarily relied on acculturation strain (Vega et al., 1993; Vega et al., 1995). However, although acculturation strain theory captures an important origin and dimension of the stress that racial/ethnic minorities experience, this theory illuminates only one small aspect of the universe of social stressors.

According to Pearlin and Lieberman (1979), the major precursor of emotional distress is exposure to chronic stress. The sources of chronic stress, which tend to be somewhat interrelated, have been identified as including barriers to the achievement of life goals, inadequate rewards relative to invested effort or qualifications, frustration of role expectations, resource deprivation (Wheaton, 1983). Others have suggested the sources of chronic stress include discrepancy between aspirations and achievements (Dressler, 1988), disjunction between economic goals and educational means (Farnworth & Lieber, 1989), and social and economic hardship including poverty, crime, violence, and overcrowding (Pearlin & Lieberman, 1979). These chronic stresses appear to be especially prevalent among racial/ethnic minorities and individuals of low socioeconomic status. For this reason, in investigating the relationship between stress and substance use among Asian American youths, it is important to include and differentiate among the various separate dimensions of stress, specifically, acculturation strain, stressful life events, and chronic strain. And it is also crucial to take account of not only the youths' own life stresses but also the concurrent levels of stress experienced by their parents and their families, since there is considerable empirical evidence that stress among adolescents is strongly influenced by stress among their parents and other family members (Banez & Compas, 1990). Further, research has suggested that parental psychological well-being mediates the relationship between stressors and adolescent adjustment and competence, through parenting practices (Taylor, 1997).

Understanding Stress and Adaptation in the Family Context

The family is central for understanding the dynamics of adaptation processes among recent Asian immigrants and native-born Asian Americans (Rumbaut, 1997). On the one hand, the family may be an important source of support or buffer from life strains from outside the family (Pearlin, 1982). Similarly, the demands, values, and structure of Asian American families may protect against substance use. On the other hand, the primary ties of affection, loyalties, and obligation embedded in Asian families, can serve as a significant source of stress. Especially among immigrant families moving from one socio-cultural environment to another, gender and generational role dissonance in rapidly changing marital and parental-child relationships can amplify and intensify conflicts (see Rumbaut, 1997). Sung (1985) suggested that intergenerational acculturation gaps can occur between adolescents and their parents, often leading to conflicts about behavioral expectations that in turn contribute to adjustment problems. Further, the discrepancy between the parents' and adolescents' level of acculturation may cause conflict for the adolescents and lead them to bond more strongly with their peers. Research to date, however, has not provided empirical support for these hypotheses. Moreover, the roles of family stress and of parental stress are not fully understood in etiological research on adolescent substance use, even though researchers have acknowledged that the stressful events the individuals experience often concern family members (Hammen, 1992).

Understanding Ethnic/Racial Minorities in Their Environmental Context

Many Asian Americans, particularly southeast Asian refugees, are concentrated in inner-city areas that are physically deteriorated and have high rates of families on welfare, population mobility, drug use, and violent crime. Here they are exposed to a wide range of stressors like reduced personal safety; limited access to mainstream social, economic, and educational opportunities; and less access to successful peer or adult role models. Nevertheless, research on substance use among Asian American adolescents has not studied Asian American adolescents and families in the context of their neighborhoods. Research grounded in the "Chicago School" of sociology shows that the neighborhood characteristics, such as poverty, prevalence of minority residents, migration patterns, and proportion of single-parent homes, affect both family-level variables and individual rates of delinquency, drug use, and educational attainment. Moreover, these neighborhood variables explain much of the variance in racial/ethnic and social-status differences among these interrelated phenomena (e.g., Sampson & Groves, 1989; Brewster, 1994; Peeples & Loeber, 1994).

Examining the Effects of Ethnic-Oriented Peer Groups

Rotheram-Borus (1993) noted that ethnic identity in younger adolescents is strongly related to their choice of an "ethnically-oriented peer reference group." Empirical studies suggest that race/ethnicity is one of the most consistent categories, after age and gender, upon which the formation of adolescent friendship is based. As the predominant structure of adolescent friendship becomes established, the peer reference group provides a set of guidelines for identity development, behavior, attitudes, role models, and affiliation with other groups. It also provides social pressures to conform to group expectations. And during adolescence, individuals become capable of actively reshaping their concept of self.

Unfortunately, little is understood about the process by which adolescents choose friends and thereby derive a sense of belonging and personal meaning from their peer group. Previous studies have, however, demonstrated the clear importance of association with deviant peers for explaining both alcohol and drug use (Aseltine, 1995; Krohn, Lizotte, Thornberry, Smith, & McDowall, 1996). Research on adolescent alcohol and drug use generally concludes that peers exert a greater influence than family or parent-child relations (Aseltine, 1995). But at the same time, there is evidence that family variables significantly influence adolescent drug use and delinquency *through* their effects on adolescent peer choices (Su, 1996). Family characteristics that act in this manner include low family cohesion, non-intact family structure, and low parental supervision. Similarly, solid family relations limit deviant peer choices, and thus restrict exposure to drug-using peers (Steinberg, 1987).

Additionally, prior research has demonstrated that friendship networks of African Americans and Hispanics have a different structure than those of white youths (Krohn & Thornberry, 1993). There is also evidence that the family exerts a greater influence than peers for African American and Hispanic youths (Becerra, 1988; De La Rosa, 1988). Little, however, is known about the structure of friendship networks of Asian Americans, and the relative importance of peer and family influences for Asian Americans.

Application of the Conceptual Model

This theoretically guided conceptual model is promising for understanding the processes and mechanisms linking Asian ethnicity and substance use. Specifically, it takes into consideration the heterogeneity of the Asian American population in the United States by including several salient components of Asian race/ethnicity and differences in the sources of stress; it also acknowledges the centrality of the family in Asian culture by using a family-based design; it considers the variables mediating the effects of stress associated with Asian race/ethnicity and the immigration process. However, in order to apply this model successfully, four methodological issues must be addressed.

Sampling design. The first methodological issue confronting researchers is to select a sample of Asian American youths that is both large enough and representative of the specific Asian subgroups of interest. Because Asian Americans still consist of a relatively small percentage of the American population, probability sampling of the general population will be difficult and expensive, if not impossible. Innovative sampling design strategies with greater efficiency will need to be developed. Regardless of the sampling strategies used, both foreign-born and native-born Asian Americans need to be included and compared in order to control for the effects of generation status and associated characteristics.

Additionally, comparison groups of youths in other racial/ethnic groups should be included in order to determine whether certain risk or protective factors are unique to or inherent in Asian cultures. Finally, both low- and high-socioeconomic-status youths should be represented in the sample to disentangle the effects of Asian race/ethnicity from those of neighborhoods and socioeconomic status.

Research design. The second methodological challenge concerns the research design that is required for the proposed conceptual model.

1. This model requires using a "high-risk research" paradigm, in order to help clarify the dimensions of vulnerability related to race/ethnicity and to study the dynamic interplay of factors that determine whether and how adolescents will use alcohol and/or drugs. Although the high-risk research paradigm has been used extensively to test general theories of deviance (e.g., poverty and parental psychopathology), it has not yet been used with theories that define risk on the basis of race/ethnicity.
2. The model requires a longitudinal, prospective design, rather than a cross-sectional one, in order to illuminate properly the causal relations between stressors and substance use among young Asian Americans, and to identify these youths' etiological and developmental pathways to substance use and abuse. Although previous research found a link between stressors and substance use, these findings were mostly based on cross-sectional research, and consequently the mediational mechanism linking these two variables is still poorly understood.
3. Finally, the model will require a family-based research design, because previous studies have suggested that adolescents' self-reported stressful events are associated with the level of stress experienced by their parents as well as with the adolescents' own emotional problems or substance use (Benez & Compas, 1990).

Measure development. Researchers must also develop comprehensive measures of stressors that are sensitive to the contexts of Asian American adolescents and their parents, and which at the same time permit systematic comparisons between Asian Americans and various other racial/ethnic populations. It has been argued that previous efforts to measure stressors, in particular stressful events and chronic stressors, generally failed to provide a full representation of the forms and sources of stress; and that this could lead to a misspecification of exposure, thereby weakening tests of the effect of stressors on alcohol and drug use. Efforts to understand how certain factors may mediate between stressors and substance use are further constrained by the absence of suitable personal, familial, and extra-familial measures. Such measures would include cultural identity, acculturation, biculturalism, self-esteem, parental adjustment, family influences, neighborhood environment, and social support. These measures are either not yet developed or are difficult to assess because they are more subjective in nature.

When attempting to collect data for these measures, it is important to gain *a priori* familiarity with the life experiences of Asian Americans to frame appropriate questions. Ethnography, a research method used to study a culture or social group from the perspective of its members (Feldman, Agar, & Beschner, 1979), is a useful tool for understanding the complex set of factors that influence the lives of both native-born and foreign-born Asian Americans. Although ethnography has been extensively used by drug researchers to study injection drug users and other "hidden populations," it has not yet been used in combination with epidemiological methods to study the etiology of substance use among racial/ethnic minority youths. The techniques of ethnography can provide rich cultural and social contextual information that would help to develop meaningful epidemiologic interview instruments.

Data analysis examining gender differences. Research has shown significantly higher prevalence rates of alcohol and illicit drug use among Asian American males than females. Studies have also demonstrated that stress has negative effects on both genders but may show itself differently in men than in women (Aneshensel, 1992). For instance, a number of studies noted a stronger association between stress and distress among women than among men–possibly because women's greater sensitivity creates differences in perceived interpersonal contexts that affect both available social support and the types of interpersonal events that are perceived as stressful (Gore, Aseltine, & Colten 1993). Other research, however, has provided evidence that males and females are similarly affected by the level of negative life events endured by the family (Attar, Guerra, & Tolan, 1994; Hoffmann & Su, 1997). Recent work in developmental psychopathology suggests that the etiological pathways to adolescent substance use may be gender-specific, and the difference in pathways may be the result of differential vulnerabilities between males and females to interpersonal depressive experiences, experiences that often stem from negative life events involving the self and/or others (Hops, 1995; Leadbeater, Blatt, & Quinlan, 1995). For all these reasons, when applying this conceptual model, the data need to be analyzed separately for males and females in order to examine potential gender differences in exposure to stress, vulnerability to stress, and underlying mechanisms linking stressors and substance use among Asian American youths.

CONCLUSIONS

Research on substance use among Asian Americans has lagged behind research on other racial/ethnic groups. As a result, our current understanding of the processes and mechanisms that explain linkages between Asian race/ethnicity and alcohol and drug use is limited. The major difficulties with studying the etiology of alcohol and drug use among Asian Americans involve selecting a sufficient number of Asian Americans who are representative of Asian Americans in specific subgroups, and dealing with the heterogeneity of the Asian American population in the United States.

Moreover, in order to understand the etiological and developmental pathways to substance use among Asian Americans, we need data from prospective longitudinal studies that incorporate recent advances in both general and culturally-specific theories of deviance. These theoretically guided investigations must be strategic in their use of research and sampling designs, measures, and analysis, so that we can test the power of the theoretical explanation against the actual data and see if alternative explanations appear more plausible. The results of these studies would increase our understanding of the bases for differences in vulnerability to substance abuse in Asian Americans relative to other racial/ethnic groups. This would in turn offer considerable promise for improving the efficacy of substance use prevention programs for Asians Americans and for other racial/ethnic groups as well.

REFERENCES

Adlaf, E. M., Smart, R. G., & Tan, S. H. (1989). Ethnicity and drug use: A critical look. *International Journal of the Addictions, 24*, 1-18.

Agnew, R., & White, H. R. (1992). An empirical test of general strain theory. *Criminology, 30*, 475-499.

Aseltine, R. H., Jr. (1995). A reconsideration of parental and peer influences on adolescent deviance. *Journal of Health and Social Behavior, 36*, 103-121.

Attar, B. K., Guerra, N. G., & Tolan, P. H. (1994). Neighborhood disadvantages, stressful life events, and adjustment in urban elementary-school children. *Journal of Clinical Child Psychology, 23*, 391-400.

Austin, G., Pendergast, M., & Lee, H. (1989). Substance use among Asian American youth. *Prevention Research Update No. 5*. Winter. Portland, OR: Western Regional Center, Drug Free Schools and Communities.

Banez, G. A., & Compas, B. E. (1990). Children's and parents' daily stressful events and psychological symptoms. *Journal of Abnormal Child Psychology, 18*, 591-605.

Bankston, C. L., III. (1995). Vietnamese ethnicity and adolescent substance abuse: Evidence for a community-level approach. *Deviant Behavior, 16*, 59-80.

Barnes, G. M., & Welte, J. W. (1986). Patterns and predictors of alcohol use among 7-12 grade students in New York State. *Journal of Studies on Alcohol, 47,* 53-62.

Barrera, M., Jr., Li, S. A., & Chassin, L. (1995). Effects of parental alcoholism and life stress on Hispanic and non-Hispanic Caucasian adolescents: A prospective study. *American Journal of Community Psychology, 23,* 479-507.

Barringer, H., Gardner, R. W., and Levin, M. J. (1993). *Asians and Pacific Islanders in the United States.* New York, NY: Russell Sage Foundation.

Becerra, R. M. (1988). The Mexican American family. In C. H. Mindel, R. W. Habenstein, & R. Wright, Jr. (Eds.), *Ethnic families in America* (pp. 141-159). New York, NY: Elsevier.

Berry, J., & Kim, U. (1988). Acculturation and mental health. In P. R. Dasen, J. W. Berry, & N. Sartorius (Eds.), *Health and cross cultural psychology,* Vol. 10. Newbury Park, CA: Sage.

Brewster, K. L. (1994). Race difference in sexual activity among adolescent women: The role of neighborhood characteristics. *American Sociological Review, 59,* 408-424.

Bruns, C., & C. S. Geist. (1984). Stressful life events and drug use among adolescents. *Journal of Human Stress, 10,* 135-139.

Catalino, R. F., Morrison, D. M., Wells, A., Gillmore, M. R., Iritani, B., & Hawkins, J. D. (1992). Ethnic differences in family factors related to early drug initiation. *Journal of Studies on Alcohol, 53,* 208-217.

Coll, C. G., & Magnuson, K. (1997). The psychological experience of immigration: A developmental perspective. In A. Booth, A. C. Crouter, & N. Landale (Eds.), *Immigration and the family: Research and policy on U.S. immigrants* (pp. 91-131). Mahwah, NJ: Lawrence Erlbaum Associates.

De La Rosa, M. R. (1988). Natural support systems of Hispanics: A key dimension for their well-being. *Health and Social Work, 15,* 181-190.

Dornbusch, S. M., Mont-Reynaud, R., Ritter, P. L., Chen, Z., & Steinberg, L. (1991). Stressful events and their correlates among adolescents of diverse background. In M. E. Colten & S. Gore (Eds.), *Adolescent Stress: Causes and Consequences* (pp. 111-130). New York: Aldine De Gruyter.

Dressler, W. W. (1988). Social consistency and psychological distress. *Journal of Health and Social Behavior, 29,* 79-91.

Farnworth, M., & Leiber, M. J. (1989). Strain theory revisited: Economic goals, educational means, and delinquency. *American Sociological Review, 54,* 263-274.

Feldman, H. W., Agar, M. H., & Beschner, G. (1979). *Angel dust: An ethnographic study of PCP users.* Lexington, MA: Lexington Books.

Gillmore, M. R., Catalina, R. F., Morrison, D. M., Wells, E. A., Iritani, B., & Hawkins, J. D. (1990). Racial differences in acceptability and availability of drugs and early initiation of substance use. *American Journal of Drug and Alcohol Abuse, 16,* 185-206.

Gonzales, N. A., & Cauce, A. M. (1995). Ethnic identity and multicultural competence: Dilemmas and challenges for minority youth. In W. D. Hawley & S. W.

Jackson (Eds.), *Toward a common destiny: Improving race and ethnic relations in America* (pp. 131-162). San Francisco, CA: Jossey-Bass Inc.

Gore, S., Aseltine, R. H., Jr., & Colten, M. E. (1993). Gender, social-relational involvement, and depression. *Journal of Research on Adolescence, 3*, 101-125.

Hammen, C. (1992). *Depression runs in families: Children of depressed mothers.* New York, NY: Springer-Verlag.

Hoffmann, J. P., & Su, S. S. (1997). The conditional effects of stress on delinquency and drug use: A strain theory assessment of sex differences. *Journal of Research in Crime and Delinquency, 34*, 46-78.

Hops, H. (1995). Age- and gender-specific effects of parental depression: A commentary. *Developmental Psychology, 31*, 428-431.

Joe, K. (1996). The lives and times of Asian-Pacific American women drug users: An ethnographic study of their methamphetamine use. *Journal of Drug Issues, 26*, 199-218.

Krohn, M. D., & Thornberry, T. P. (1993). Network theory: A model for understanding drug abuse among African-American and Hispanic youth. In M. R. De La Rosa & J. R. Adrados (Eds.), *Drug abuse among minority youth: Advances in research and methodology* (NIDA Research Monograph 130, pp. 102-127). Rockville, MD: National Institute on Drug Abuse.

Krohn, M. D., Lizotte, A. J., Thornberry, T. P., Smith, C., & McDowall, D. (1996). Reciprocal causal relationships among drug use, peers, and beliefs: A five-wave panel model. *Journal of Drug Issues, 26*, 405-428.

Leadbeater, B. J., Blatt, S. J., & Quinlan, D. M. (1995). Gender-linked vulnerabilities to depressive symptoms, stress, and problem behaviors in adolescents. *Journal of Research on Adolescence, 5*, 1-29.

Lillie-Blanton, M., Anthony, J. C., & Schuster, C. R. (1993). Probing the meaning of racial/ethnic group comparisons in crack cocaine smoking. *Journal of American Medical Association, 269*, 993-997.

Maddahian, E., Newcomb, M. D., & Bentler, P. M. (1986). Adolescents' substance use: Impact of ethnicity, income, and availability. *Advances in Alcohol and Substance Abuse, 5*, 68-80.

Mirowsky, J., & Ross, C. E. (1986). Social patterns of distress. *Annual Review of Sociology, 12*, 23-45.

Mirowsky, J., & Ross, C. E. (1989). *Social sources of psychological stress.* New York, NY: Aldine de Gruyter.

National Institute on Drug Abuse. (1995). *Drug use among racial/ethnic minorities.* U.S. Department of Health and Human Services, Public Health Service, National Institute of Health. Rockville, MD: National Institute on Drug Abuse.

Neff, J. A. (1985). Race and vulnerability to stress: An examination of differential vulnerability. *Journal of Personality and Social Psychology, 49*, 481-491.

Newcomb, M. D., & Harlow, L. L. (1986). Life events and substance use among adolescents: Mediating effects of perceived loss of control and meaninglessness in life. *Journal of Personality and Social Psychology, 51*, 564-577.

Oetting, E. R., & Beauvais, F. (1990-91). Orthogonal cultural identification theory: The cultural identification of minority adolescents. *International Journal of Addiction, 25*, 655-685.

Oetting, E. R. (1993). Orthogonal cultural identification: Theoretical links between cultural identification and substance use. In M. R. De La Rosa & J. R. Adrados (Eds.), *Drug abuse among minority youth: Advances in research and methodology* (NIDA Research Monograph 130, pp. 32-56). Rockville, MD: National Institute on Drug Abuse.

Ogbu, J. U. (1987). Variability in minority school performance: A problem in search of an explanation. *Anthropology and Education Quarterly, 18*, 312-334.

Peeples, F., & Loeber, R. (1994). Do individual factors and neighborhood context explain ethnic differences in juvenile delinquency? *Journal of Quantitative Criminology, 10*, 141-157.

Pearlin, L. I. (1982). The social context of stress. In L. Goldberger & S. Breznitz (Eds.), *Handbook of stress: Theoretical and clinical aspects.* New York: The Free Press.

Pearlin, L. I., & Lieberman, M. A. (1979). Social sources of emotional distress. *Research in Community Mental Health, 1*, 217-48.

Phinney, J. S., & Alipuria, L. (1990). Ethnic identity development in older adolescents from four ethnic groups. *Journal of Adolescence, 13*, 271-281.

Rodriguez, O., Adrados, K. R., & De La Rosa, M. (1993). Integrating mainstream and subcultural explanations of drug use among Puerto Rican youth. In M. R. De La Rosa & J. R. Adrados (Eds.), *Drug abuse among minority youth: Advances in research and methodology* (NIDA Research Monograph 130, pp. 8-31). Rockville, MD: National Institute on Drug Abuse.

Rotheram-Borus, M. J. (1993). Biculturalism among adolescents. In M. E. Bernal & G. P. Knight (Eds.), *Ethnic identity: Formation and transmission among Hispanic and other minorities* (pp. 81-102). Albany, NY: SUNY Press.

Rumbaut, R. G. (1997). Ties that bind: Immigration and immigrant families in the United States. In A. Booth, A. C. Crouter, & N. Landale (Eds.), *Immigration and the family: Research and policy on U.S. immigrants* (pp. 3-46). Mahwah, NJ: Lawrence Erlbaum Associates.

Sampson, R. J., & Groves, W. B. (1989). Community structure and crime: Testing social-disorganization theory. *American Journal of Sociology, 94*, 774-802.

Sodowsky, G. R., & Lai, E. W. (1997). Asian immigrant variables and structural models of cross-cultural distress. In A. Booth, A. C. Crouter, & N. Landale (Eds.), *Immigration and the family: Research and policy on U.S. immigrants* (pp. 211-236). Mahwah, NJ: Lawrence Erlbaum Associates.

Steinberg, L. (1987). Single parents, stepparents, and the susceptibility of adolescents to antisocial peer pressure. *Child Development, 58*, 269-275.

Su, S. S. (1996, November). *Characteristics of adolescent friendship and delinquency.* Paper presented at the 48th annual meeting of the American Society of Criminology, Chicago.

Su, S. S., Larison, C., Ghadialy, R., Rhode, F., & Johnson, R. A. (1997). *Substance use and abuse among women in the United States.* Rockville, MD: Substance Abuse and Mental Health Services Administration.

Sung, B. L. (1985). Bicultural conflicts in Chinese immigrant children. *Journal of Comparative Family Studies, 26*, 255-269.

Taylor, R. D. (1997). The effects of economic and social stressors on parenting and adolescent adjustment in African-American families. In R. D. Taylor & M. C. Wang (Eds.), *Social and emotional adjustment and family relations in ethnic minority families*. Mahwah, NJ: Lawrence Erlbaum Associates.

Ulbrich, P. M., Warheit, G. J., & Zimmerman, R. S. (1989). Race, socioeconomic status, and psychological distress: An examination of differential vulnerability. *Journal of Health and Social Behavior, 30*, 131-146.

Vega, W. A. & Rumbaut, R. G. (1991). Ethnic minorities and mental health. *Annual Review of Sociology, 17*, 351-383.

Vega, W. A., Khoury, E. L., Zimmerman, R. S., Gil, A. G., & Warheit, G. J. (1995). Cultural conflicts and problem behaviors of Latino adolescents in home and school environments. *Journal of Community Psychology, 23*, 167-179.

Vega, W. A., Zimmerman, R., Gil, A., Warheit, G. J., & Apospori, E. (1993). Acculturation strain theory: Its application in explaining drug use behavior among Cuban and other Hispanic youth. In M. R. De La Rosa & J. R. Adrados (Eds.), *Drug abuse among minority youth: Advances in research and methodology* (NIDA Research Monograph 130, pp. 144-166). Rockville, MD: National Institute on Drug Abuse.

Wallace, J. M., & Bachman, J. G. (1991). Explaining racial/ethnic differences in adolescent drug use: The impact of background and lifestyle. *Social Problems, 38*, 333-357.

Wallace, J. M., & Bachman, J. G. (1993). Validity of self-reports in student-based studies on minority populations: Issues and concerns. In M. R. De La Rosa & J. R. Adrados (Eds.), *Drug Abuse Among Minority Youth: Advances in Research and Methodology* (NIDA Research Monograph 130, pp. 167-200). Rockville, MD: National Institute on Drug Abuse.

Wells, E. A., Morrison, D. M., Gillmore, M. R., Catalina, R. F., Iritani, B., & Hawkins, J. D. (1992). Race differences in antisocial behaviors and attitudes and early initiation of substance use. *Journal of Drug Education, 22*, 115-130.

Wheaton, B. (1983). Stress, coping resources, and psychiatric symptoms: An investigation of interactive models. *Journal of Health and Social Behavior, 24*, 208-229.

Zane, N., & Sasao, T. (1992). Research on drug abuse among Asian Pacific Americans. *Drugs & Society, 6*, 181-210.

A Model for Explaining Drug Use Behavior Among Hispanic Adolescents

William A. Vega, PhD
Andres G. Gil, PhD

SUMMARY. This paper presents an integrative framework for etiological research about Hispanic adolescent drug use. The integrative framework provides a logical, theoretically grounded approach for linking immigrant and native born Hispanic adolescents and their parents to social environments, and describes the contingencies of social psychological adaptation that occur within these environments. Substantive findings from previous research are presented to support the integrative framework. The integrative framework provides a rational basis for organizing complex concepts and synthe-

William A. Vega is Professor of Public Health, School of Public Health, University of California, Berkeley, CA. Andres G. Gil is Assistant Professor and Associate Director for Research, School of Social Work, Florida International University, Miami, FL.

Address correspondence to: William A. Vega, School of Public Health, 320 Warren Hall, University of California, Berkeley, CA 94720.

The authors wish to express their appreciation to Superintendent OctavioVisiedo, Dr. James Mennes, Dr. Sylvia Rothfarb, and the principals, assistant principals, teachers and students of the Dade County, Florida public schools whose cooperation made the conduct of this research possible.

This research was supported by a grant from the National Institute on Drug Abuse, R01 DA 05192, William A. Vega, PhD, Principal Investigator.

[Haworth co-indexing entry note]: "A Model for Explaining Drug Use Behavior Among Hispanic Adolescents." Vega, William A., and Andres G. Gil. Co-published simultaneously in *Drugs & Society* (The Haworth Press, Inc.) Vol. 14, No. 1/2, 1999, pp. 57-74; and: *Conducting Drug Abuse Research with Minority Populations: Advances and Issues* (ed: Mario R. De La Rosa, Bernard Segal, and Richard Lopez) The Haworth Press, Inc., 1999, pp. 57-74. Single or multiple copies of this article are available for a fee from The Haworth Document Delivery Service [1-800-342-9678, 9:00 a.m. - 5:00 p.m. (EST). E-mail address: getinfo@haworthpressinc.com].

sizing fragmentary or competing theoretical approaches, and for empirically testing derived hypotheses using quantitative and qualitative methods. *[Article copies available for a fee from The Haworth Document Delivery Service: 1-800-342-9678. E-mail address: getinfo@ haworthpressinc.com]*

INTRODUCTION

This paper presents an integrative framework to explain drug use behavior among Hispanic adolescents. There are now about 28 million Hispanics in the United States, and lifetime drug use rates for Hispanic adolescents have been increasing and are now among the highest in the nation (NIDA, 1994). Nevertheless, the substance use literature about adolescent drug use has only recently begun to consider the social and cultural differences in American society, and the factors and processes that are unique to Hispanic adolescent development and drug use etiology. As a consequence, there are knowledge gaps about causal processes, social contexts, and the epidemiology of drug use among Hispanics over the life course.

There is a need for integrative models that explain adolescent drug use in diverse ethnic groups, locations, and social classes. In addition to inter-ethnic differences in rates of drug use (Bachman et al., 1991), there are inter- and intra-ethnic variations in the environmental conditions and risk factors that are associated with drug use behaviors (Vega, Zimmerman, Warheit, Apospori, & Gil, 1993), deviant behaviors, and deviant peer associations among adolescents (Apospori, Vega, Zimmerman, Warheit, & Gil, 1995). Attempts at assessing or preventing drug use among ethnic groups, such as Hispanics, have been hampered by a lack of conceptual models that address factors associated with drug use behaviors in this ethnic group. This article examines theoretical and empirical issues relevant to the etiology and social context of drug using behavior among Hispanic adolescents.

INTEGRATIVE FRAMEWORK
OF HISPANIC ADOLESCENT DRUG USE

The proposed framework for the explanation of drug use behavior among Hispanic adolescents is social and ecological. An assumption is made that drug use among immigrant and U.S.-born Hispanic adolescents is affected by their socialization experiences, and the experiences of other family members, within their new environments. A core supposition is that acculturation simultaneously evolves in various critical arenas that include, for immigrants, the context of exit from their nation of origin and entrance into the U.S. (Fabrega, 1969). These experiences can threaten the viability of families, and the relationships between family members. For both immigrants and U.S.-born Hispanics, acculturation is a discontinuous and idiosyncratic process, rather than a monolithic one, aptly described as segmented assimilation by Portes and Zhou (1993). Figure 1 presents the proposed acculturative framework for drug use behavior that will be discussed throughout this paper.

Immigrant Experience: Contexts of Exit and Entrance

In the proposed model, social and developmental factors in the context of emigration are critically important components. Thus, the experiences of preparing for separation from a native land, a process inevitably fraught with social implications, emotional meaning, and financial complications, or actual flight under the extreme duress of a refugee situation, have important implications for the ultimate adjustment of immigrants (Vega & Rumbaut, 1991).

Developmental stage, or age at the time of immigration, are also paramount for the adjustment of immigrant children. For example, those who migrate during mid- or late adolescence have very different socialization experiences when contrasted with young children. Having grown-up within a consistent socio-cultural context in the country of birth allows older immigrant children to have developed a firmer sense of self-identity before entering the U.S. environment. On the other hand, second generation children may be reared in an environment of social and cultural conflicts and competition between the traditional values of their parents and that of their peers in the new society (Portes & Rumbaut, 1993; Rumbaut, 1995, 1996).

The model in Figure 1 is applicable to immigrant and U.S.-born children and adolescents. However, the stages that apply to U.S.-born children are limited to the context of U.S. society. That is, the context of exit does not directly apply to Hispanic adolescents born in the U.S. However, inasmuch as parental and family history affects children and subsequent generations, the full model applies to U.S.-born Hispanic children to the extent that their parents are affected by their own context of exit (Rumbaut, 1996).

The immigrant experiences of entrance into U.S. society have important consequences for the adaptation and adjustment of families. However, the influences of these experiences on the acculturation stress and drug use behaviors of children and adolescents take place through the diverse paths of families engaging in the process of social and economic incorporation into American society. Acculturation involves resocialization about drug use for immigrant parents, including increased exposure to both the dan-

FIGURE 1. Acculturative Model of Immigrant and U.S. Born Hispanic Adolescent Drug Use*

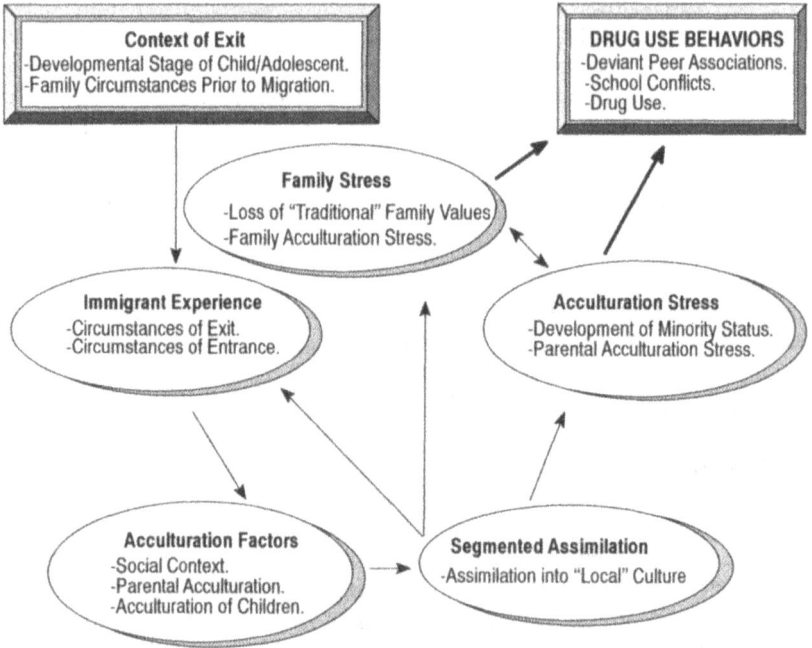

*NOTE: The full model applies to immigrant adolescents. For U.S. born, the full model applies to parents, but for the adolescents the model begins with "Acculturation Factors."

gers of drug use, and the norms and social networks supporting regular alcohol use and the easier availability of illicit drugs.

Acculturation stress occurs through the combination of adaptive experiences of exit from nations of origin, and entrance into U.S. society. The assimilation of new immigrants is mediated by local and national environments that are socially and structurally diverse, featuring important differences in degrees of anti-immigrant resistance and hostility. This is the reason for the lack of direct paths in Figure 1 between immigrant experience and acculturation stress in the model. Portes and Zhou (1991) described three dominant outcomes of the segmented assimilation process that are dependent on the characteristics of social areas: assimilation into an underclass low-income minority community, cultural assimilation into the dominant culture where mediating institutions and social norms exist to facilitate this process, or participation in a dual cultural society of stabilized cultural differences where maintenance of one's language and culture of origin is possible and functional. In complex environments, all three adaptations may be occurring simultaneously to some extent. In cities like Miami, Florida, where a significant Hispanic social, cultural, and business enclave already exists, the dual society is more likely to flourish and provide the primary determinants of adolescent socialization. However, even in this type of environment, personal and group characteristics will interact with environmental factors to produce different types of adaptation, for example, segmented assimilation.

Acculturation Factors Among Parents and Children

The next component of the model demonstrates that environmental factors that provide a context for acculturation experiences for both parents and adolescents will ultimately control both the level of acculturative stress and exposure to the social learning required for early drug experimentation. That is, the paths of both parental or adolescent acculturation directly and indirectly influence the comprehensiveness or modality of assimilation, and the likelihood and consequences of exposures to drug use, including progression to abuse and drug using lifestyles.

The model in Figure 1 emphasizes the larger social context in which both the parents and their adolescent children are situated. Our research indicated that language conflicts and acculturation conflicts experienced by immigrant parents and their adolescent children explained 58% of variance in parent-child cultural conflicts among Nicaraguans, and 53% among Cubans in Miami (Gil & Vega, 1996). Therefore, it is clear that environments created family stress that had important consequences for adolescent cognitive and emotional functioning. However, we (Vega, Gil, & Zimmerman, 1993), and other researchers as well (Amaro, Whitaker, Coffman, & Heeren, 1990), have found that even small changes in parental and adolescent acculturation increases drug use. Therefore, acculturation in our model is positioned as an exogenous factor that causes segmented assimilation. In turn, segmented assimilation produces family stress and adolescent stressors, and interacts (historically) with the immigrant experience because it conditions the environment for new immigrants.

Acculturation stress is created by the acculturative process of acculturation factors and segmented assimilation. It reinforces the effects of acculturation on drug use, albeit somewhat differently for immigrants and U.S.-born adolescents. This double vulnerability occurs because acculturation increases exposure to drugs and drug use, and unmediated acculturation stress increases negative self-concept and low perceived efficacy among Hispanic adolescents. Acculturation, operating through segmented assimilation, increases family stress by weakening Hispanic familism (Gil, Vega, & Dimas, 1994). Sustained adolescent and parent acculturation stressors and family stress, when experienced longitudinally, will increase drug use behaviors. This occurs because psychological vulnerability is created among both adolescents and parents, and simultaneously, family cohesiveness is decreased and family conflicts are increased, thus lowering the protective value of family values and norms. However, birthplace (e.g., nativity) and acculturation make differential contributions to intermediary factors in the model, and will have differential importance (i.e., as path co-efficients) in contributing to drug use behaviors.

The Social Context of Minority Status Acquisition: Segmented Assimilation

The current wave of American immigration is predominantly non-white and originating from impoverished Hispanic American and Asian nations with marginal educational systems, and is predominantly destined for California, Texas, New York, Illinois, and Florida. On the face of it, immigrant poverty does not appear to be a radical departure from the immigrant profile of the early 20th century immigration that was centered in the Northeast. The new immigration is more regionally dispersed. This fact alone creates important environmental differences in immigrant adaptation and accommodation linked to local conditions. This lack of uniformity suggests that, at least for some immigrants, conditions have improved because ethnic enclaves have developed to anchor and incorporate them. Regrettably, in other sites, conditions have worsened (Gans, 1992).

Many immigrants are moving into deteriorating inner-city areas with long histories of violence, poor educational systems, few ladders of opportunity, and where intensive drug distribution and sales, gang activity, and other forms of criminal deviance are rampant. This situation poses two fundamental questions: (1) Will the social and economic integration of new immigrants, and their children, result in segregation and the creation of a caste-like minority status as has occurred for many African Americans, or consistent intergenerational social integration and social mobility as occurred earlier with European immigrants? and (2) will factors extrinsic to immigration *per se,* such as nation of origin, long-standing minority group status, and skin color produce differential outcomes for immigrants that will ultimately affect their drug using behavior? While these questions are not primary determinants in our model, they are important contextual factors (Abramson, 1991).

For these reasons, a critical element of the model is the influence of segmented assimilation as an outcome of local acculturative experiences. In this instance, social context, especially neighborhood, plays an important role in shaping acculturation experiences generally, and exposures to drug use specifically. Social context affects the types of schools that children attend, exposure level to drug use and gang activity, as well as the regularity and quality of employment that parents are able to obtain. Thus, the social order constrains both parental and adolescent educational or occupational aspirations and attainments. American society is highly segregated by social class, and race/ethnicity (Gordon, 1964). Low-income Hispanics are assimilated into subcultures that differ drastically from those experienced by co-ethnics in corresponding suburban middle-class neighborhoods.

How are immigrant and minority statuses similar or different in terms of their consequences for healthy adolescent development, identity formation, and drug abuse? Gibson and Ogbu (1991) distinguished immigrant status from "involuntary" minority status. The difference rests in power relationships and "different historical experiences which lead to different adaptive responses." Immigrants and other ethnic groups who have non-oppositional experiences and no history of previous conflicts or domination by U.S. ethnic groups have a basis for positively evaluating present conditions compared to past circumstances in a nation of origin, and are more likely to believe they have personally benefitted from cultural change. As a result, they are not as likely to be socialized into, or to have psychologically internalized, a minority group frame of reference. If individuals believe their ethnic group (e.g., African Americans, Chicanos, Puerto Ricans) is exploited and discriminated against overtly and covertly, they are more likely to perceive themselves as oppositional, resisting discrimination, and occupying minority statuses in American society. Although this process can be seen as separable from acculturative stress, if the process of acculturation involves socialization into involuntary minority status, it is virtually impossible to distinguish between stress attributable to change of culture or perceptions of discrimination. Both would seem to emerge from the same intertwined social experiences.

Anecdotal and indirect evidence of how this process is experienced by individuals can be gleaned from contemporary research in California. Rumbaut (1995) reported that among Mexican American immigrant children, performance test scores improve over time, demonstrating rapid acquisition of the English language (Rumbaut, 1996). However, immigrant children's grades and educational aspirations actually decrease with the amount of time spent in the United States, reflecting the social environment of peers in the schools and neighborhoods they enter, and perhaps more importantly, the weakening of families and traditional values. The protective effects of Hispanic culture are weakened even more among low-income U.S.-born adolescents. These adolescents are far more likely to believe they have limited personal opportunity and are the subjects of discrimination. A recent study of human services workers involved in prevention activities with Hispanic adolescents throughout California identified five primary problems facing these youth: (1) societal invalidation, that is, a perception that no one cares; (2) lack of economic opportunity; (3) low educational expectations; (4) lack of personal safety and significant health risks; and (5) parents unable to understand or advocate for adolescents (Vega & Barnett, 1995).

The construct of involuntary minority status is a logical extension of segmented assimilation. Both are useful for understanding Hispanic adolescent drug use. They provide an analytical approach for assessing the importance of "local" social contexts encountered by immigrant adolescents and their families. And they help to explain the level and course of individual and group drug use among adolescents in differing regional, urban-rural, or inter-group situations. Portes (1995) identified three key factors that interact in the segmented assimilation process: color, location, and opportunity structure. American society is highly segregated and stratified by ethnicity and income. This fact alone produces great variability in the social contexts of substance use and a differential likelihood that experimental drug use will proceed to serious abuse and addiction. Although it is a reasonable assumption that experimental drug use is ubiquitous in American society, drug addiction and its sequelae (e.g., crime, incarceration, HIV/AIDS, etc.) are not randomly distributed, but tend to concentrate among the poorest Americans, including Hispanics. This situation is compounded by recent laws and policies that scapegoat and marginalize both U.S.-born and immigrant Hispanics.

It is important to reiterate that the complex effects of segmented assimilation are taking place at both the individual and group level, and that our conceptual model (Figure 1) offers a framework for conceptualization and measurement at both levels.

The Family Context of Hispanic Drug Use

Although there is great divergence in the historical origins and immigration histories of Hispanic cultural groups, the family is uniformly a primary source of identity and meaning in the Hispanic value system. Our own research has demonstrated unique protective and risk effects of familism in Hispanic culture (Vega, Zimmerman et al., 1993; Gil et al., 1994). Immigrants use family networks in the migratory process, and use them to facilitate the acquisition of residential shelter and employment information after resettlement (Portes, & Bach, 1985; Chavez, 1988; Vega, 1990).

Among immigrants, and perhaps less so for the U.S.-born Hispanics, the values of familism (e.g., cohesiveness, frequent face-to-face interaction, reciprocity, pride, and respect) serve as the foremost source of nurturance, guidance, and support for adolescents (Vega, 1990). The challenge for immigrants, and especially for second-generation Hispanic adolescents, is that too often economic hardships and marginal living conditions, and the stressors and dislocations embedded in that situation, undermine family structure, cohesion, process, and social roles to a degree that interferes with effectively socializing adolescents (Gil & Vega, 1996). When the Hispanic family is less effective in high risk, disorganized communities, the essential protective factor contributing to positive adolescent identity, resiliency, and adaptability is compromised (Baca-Zinn, 1995). As researchers and preventionists, we have discovered that a central source in the prevention of delinquent and drug using behaviors among Hispanic children and adolescents, the family, is frequently the first "victim" of Americanization for a sizable group of Hispanic immigrants (Gil & Vega, 1996). Moreover, as the family is exposed to the cumulative conditions of disorganized inner-city *barrios,* it is evident that preventive interventions that focus solely on family dynamics will prove to be inadequate and ineffective at a population level.

DISCUSSION AND CONCLUSION

The proposed integrative model recognizes that the path toward drug use behavior for Hispanic children travels through their social environment and their family. Based on immigration histories, the pathways differ in importance for immigrant children and adolescents, as contrasted with second-generation Hispanics. This fact is illustrated by prior findings which show marked differences in the epidemiology of drug use among U.S.- and foreign-born Hispanics (Vega, Gil, & Zimmerman, 1993; Warheit, Biafora, Zimmerman et al., 1996), as well as important differences in the distributions of acculturative stress, and familism (Gil et al., 1994; Gil & Vega, 1996).

Unquestionably, the process of acculturation is complex and idiosyncratic. Nevertheless, it is patterned in fundamental ways. One important element in this pattern is the personal and developmental histories of immigrant children, who to some extent may benefit from early socialization in a more culturally integrated society in their nation of origin. As a result the experiences of immigrant and first-generation Hispanic children and adolescents represent different developmental trajectories. The immigrant adolescent is confronted with the problem of social transplantation, cultural changes, and acquiring a new language. The U.S.-born Hispanic adolescent is presented with the challenge of growing up in a complex social milieu in which traditional Hispanic family values are perceived as anachronistic by adolescents, and poorly suited for confronting crime and gang ridden neighborhoods, inadequate schools, limited job opportunities, and anti-Hispanic prejudices. These conditions undermine adolescent perceptions of self-worth. Our findings indicate that these intra-group differences have important consequences for the healthy development of Hispanic adolescents.

This paper presented an integrative model for the explanation of drug use behavior among Hispanic adolescents. The results of our previous studies point to the importance of linking acculturative stress theory (Vega, Gil, Warheit, Zimmerman, & Apospori, 1993) to gateway and risk factor models (Newcomb, 1995; Kandel, 1975; 1980; 1983); self-esteem enhancement, differential association, and structured strain theories (Kaplan, Martin, & Johnson, 1986; Sutherland, 1939; Merton, 1938) and family process models (Olsen, McCubbin, Barnes, Larsen, Muxen, & Wilson, 1983; Elkind, 1994), in order to derive explanations and prevention schema about Hispanic adolescent drug use. Cultural factors have a formidable role in shaping attitudes and behaviors that decrease the likelihood of drug use among Hispanics; however, these factors are intersected by the social milieu. The traditional values of family and active familistic behaviors constitute important protective factors. However, these protective characteristics will erode over time when undermined by aversive social-environmental conditions.

Acculturation affects both risk and protective factors differentially among immigrant or native born Hispanic adolescents. Therefore, theory and empirical models should reflect this basic finding. In this light, Figure 1 can be understood as a heuristic strategy linking general deviance models to contemporary assimilation and acculturative stress theories in an explanatory framework for Hispanic adolescent drug use. It is not intended to be a falsifiable theory; it is a blueprint for developing testable theory. Although it is broad in scope, it can be partitioned into sub-models for basic or applied studies. The model is useful at an exploratory stage in *quantitative and qualitative* studies, especially when both methodologies are used, simultaneously or sequentially, to provide convergent observations and rich detail about causal processes.

Qualitative methods are especially useful for discovering subtle differences linked to nativity, acculturation, and culture change. It is our experience that complex quantitative path models, such as those based on latent constructs, share common limitations that are overcome by qualitative research. For example, using only one path model to test complex theory, it is difficult to adequately contrast differences in factorial relationships, such as differential contributions to path loadings, by sub-groups (e.g., immigrants vs. U.S.-born, Cubans vs. Nicaraguans, etc.). This problem can be overcome by partitioning sub-groups into separate models in order to identify differences in path coefficients. However, explaining differential path coefficients requires examining the structure of the data (e.g., decomposition) and, optimally, information derived from qualitative studies. Using mixed methodologies is useful for both initial pilot studies and full scale field studies.

Our model can be adopted to studies in which one or more theoretically salient dimensions are being compared: (1) migration contexts, such as studies of acculturation and acculturative stress effects of drug use among migrants (e.g., Puerto Ricans) as contrasted with co-ethnic non-migrants (e.g., Puerto Ricans born and reared in the continental U.S.), and immigrants (e.g., Dominicans); (2) regional contexts, such as opportunity structures and inter-group relations (e.g., contrasting Hispanic adolescents in South Florida and Southern California); or (3) neighborhood contexts, such as racially/ethnically mixed or homogeneous areas, or social areas with varying levels of deterioration, social cohesion, delinquency, and organized criminal activity. One of the most challenging and high yield areas of research is whether subjective or objective measures are better suited for measuring model parameters. This point has both theoretical and empirical importance. Theoretically, subjective assessments of adolescents may have more predictive value for deviance and drug use than objective assessments. However, having both types of measurements makes it possible to determine whether environmental conditions are truly shaping behaviors, or whether behaviors are being justified by subjective perceptions that are not validated by objective assessments, thereby enabling testing and refinement of model components.

Figure 2 presents some suggested measured variables that correspond to the constructs in Figure 1. The literature contains numerous possibilities for specific scales, indexes, and indicators that could be adapted for this type of research. Nevertheless, we include a appendix of some recommended scales of acculturative stress and acculturation that have proven useful in our own research.

This model is applicable to other ethnic groups that have a substantial immigrant sector within their population, especially when there is a gradient in cultural assimilation and social incorporation, including subculture formation, and a historical background of minority status in the United States (e.g., Chinese), or problematic social integration of adolescents because of basic socio-cultural disjunctures (e.g., Cambodians or Laotians). Particular attention should be paid to the process we (and others) refer to as the "internalization of minority status." This is not a self-evident or uniform process. It is an intra-psychic process with yet undefined temporal-developmental characteristics. However, it does seem evident

FIGURE 2. Manifest Variables of Acculturative Model for Hispanic Adolescent Drug Use

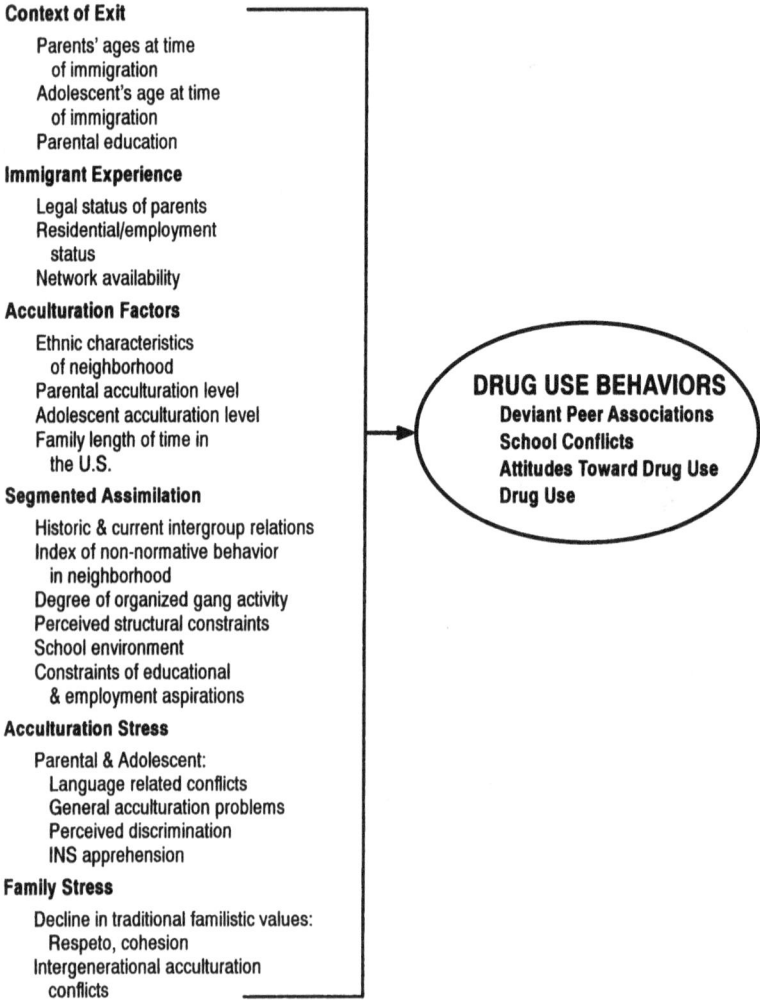

Context of Exit

    Parents' ages at time
      of immigration
    Adolescent's age at time
      of immigration
    Parental education

Immigrant Experience

    Legal status of parents
    Residential/employment
      status
    Network availability

Acculturation Factors

    Ethnic characteristics
      of neighborhood
    Parental acculturation level
    Adolescent acculturation level
    Family length of time in
      the U.S.

Segmented Assimilation

    Historic & current intergroup relations
    Index of non-normative behavior
      in neighborhood
    Degree of organized gang activity
    Perceived structural constraints
    School environment
    Constraints of educational
      & employment aspirations

Acculturation Stress

    Parental & Adolescent:
      Language related conflicts
      General acculturation problems
      Perceived discrimination
      INS apprehension

Family Stress

    Decline in traditional familistic values:
      Respeto, cohesion
    Intergenerational acculturation
      conflicts

DRUG USE BEHAVIORS
Deviant Peer Associations
School Conflicts
Attitudes Toward Drug Use
Drug Use

that during adolescence, boys and girls become aware that they are members of an ethnic group. When this involves minority status, some individuals will come to believe that their own future treatment in society is at least partially conditioned by membership in a marginalized subgroup. We believe this process begins in earnest in early adolescence, and increases vulnerability to drug experimentation through increasing personal distress. However, greater vulnerability to internalized minority status occurs in later adolescence during peer subculture formation. At this point there is an isolation and detachment from conventional norms, and peer groups act as an incubator for learning the repertoire of behaviors needed for launching drug abuse careers. Whether this process is widespread and has a consistent causal connection among minority groups to adolescent nonnormative behavior or drug abuse is an empirical question. Our own research has convinced us that constructs such as internalized minority status are not easily or uniformly measured, and constitute a quasi-independent arena of inter-cultural research.

For those concerned with prevention of drug use in the Hispanic population, we point out that person- or family-centered interventions are inadequate at a population level in the absence of community-wide mobilization, advocacy, and the recognition of the multi-sectoral coordination required to redress the intimate relationships between social and ecological factors and the availability, sale, and use of both licit and illicit drugs. Most school prevention programs have been based on the premise of rational behavior and social skills development among adolescents, and have not proven effective in consistently reducing drug use. More importantly, attempts at reducing drug use among Hispanics have been hampered by a lack of conceptual models that address the internal variance in cultural adjustment and risk patterns associated with drug use behaviors. Our proposed model is only a starting place, and additional theoretical work on this topic is required, but implicit in the model are several critical factors that must be examined in studies attempting to explore or determine factors associated with drug use among Hispanic adolescents. These include the distinction between immigrant and U.S.-born, the importance of local environments, including Hispanic social and political influence, and how they affect segmented assimilation, familial stress, and the formulation of minority status.

REFERENCES

Abramson, H. J. (1981). *Assimilation and pluralism*, In S. Thernstrom (Ed.), Harvard encyclopedia of American ethnic groups. Cambridge, MA: Harvard University Press, pps. 150-160.
Apospori, E. A., Vega, W. A., Zimmerman, R. S., Warheit, G. J., & Gil, A. G.

(1995). A longitudinal study of the conditional effects of deviant behavior on drug use among three racial/ethnic groups of adolescents. In H. B. Kaplan (Ed.), *Drugs, crime, and other deviant adaptations: Longitudinal studies*. New York: Plenum Press.

Amaro, H., Whitaker, R., Coffman, G., & Heeren, T. (1990). Acculturation and marijuana and cocaine use: Findings from HHANES 1982-1984. *American Journal of Public Health, 80,* (Suppl), 54-60.

Baca Zinn, M. (1995). Social science theorizing for Latino families in the age of diversity. In R. E. Zambrana (Ed.), *Understanding Latino families: Scholarship, policy, and practice*. Thousand Oaks, CA: Sage Publications.

Bachman, J. G., Wallace, J. M., O'Malley, P. M., Johnston, L. D., Kurth, C. L., & Neighbors, H. W. (1991). Racial/ethnic differences in smoking, drinking, and illicit drug use among American high school seniors, 1976-1989. *American Journal of Public Health, 81,* 372-377.

Chavez, L. (1988). Settlers and sojourners: The case of Mexicans in the United States. *Human Organization, 47,* 95-108.

Cuellar, I., Harris, L. C., & Jasso, R. (1980). An acculturation scale for Mexican American normal and clinical populations. *Hispanic Journal of Behavioral Science, 2,* 199-217.

Elkind, D. (1994) *The ties that stress: The new family imbalance*. Cambridge, MA: Harvard University Press.

Fabrega, H. (1969). Social psychiatric aspects of acculturation and migration. *Comprehensive Psychiatry, 10,* 314-329.

Gans, H. J. (1992). Second generation decline: Scenarios for the economic and ethnic futures of the post-1965 American immigrants. *Ethnic and Racial Studies, 15,* 173-192.

Gibson, M. A., & Ogbu, J. U. (1991). *Minority status and schooling: A comparative study of immigrant and involuntary minorities*. New York: Garland Publishing.

Gil, A. G., Vega, W. A., & Dimas, J. M. (1994). Acculturative stress and personal adjustment among Hispanic adolescent boys. *Journal of Community Psychology, 22,* 43-54.

Gil, A. G., & Vega, W. A. (1996). Two different worlds: Acculturation stress and adaptation among Cuban and Nicaraguan families. *Journal of Social and Personal Relationships, 13,* 435-456.

Gordon, M. (1964). *Assimilation in American life*. New York: Oxford University Press.

Kandel, D. B. (1975). Stages of adolescent involvement in drug use. *Science, 190,* 912-914.

Kandel, D. B. (1980). Drug and drinking behavior among youth. *Annual Review of Sociology, 6,* 235-285.

Kandel, D. B. (1983). Socialization and adolescent drinking. *Child Health, 2,* 66-75.

Kaplan, H. B., Martin, S. S., & Johnson, R. J. (1986). Self-rejection and the explanation of deviance: Specification of the structure among latent constructs. *American Journal of Sociology, 92,* 384-411.

Kaplan, H. B., Johnson, R. J., & Bailey, C. A. (1986). Self-rejection and the explanation of deviance: Refinement and elaboration of a latent structure. *Social Psychological Quarterly, 49,* 110-128.

Merton, R. K. (1938). Social structure and anomie. *American Sociological Review, 3,* 672-682.

National Institute of Drug Abuse. (1994). *The monitoring the future study; 1975-1994.* December, 1994. Rockville, MD: National Institute of Drug Abuse.

Newcomb, M. D. (1995). Drug use etiology among ethnic minority adolescents: Risk and protective factors. In G. J. Botvin, S. Schinke, & M. A. Orlandi, (Eds.), *Drug use prevention with multiethnic youth.* Thousand Oaks, CA: Sage Publications.

Olson, D. H. (1989). Circumplex model of family systems VIII: Family assessment and intervention. In D. H. Olson, C. S. Russell, & D. H. Sprenkle (Eds.), *Circumplex model: Systematic assessment and treatment of families.* New York: The Haworth Press, Inc.

Olson, D. H., McCubbin, H. I., Barnes, H., Larsen, A. S., Muxen, M. J., & Wilson, M. A. (1983). *Families: What makes them work.* Beverly Hills, CA: Sage Publications.

Portes, A. (1995). Segmented assimilation among new immigrant youth: A conceptual framework, (pp. 72-76). In Center for U.S.-Mexican Studies, *California's immigrant children; Theory, research, and implications for educational policy.* San Diego, CA: University of California, San Diego.

Portes, A., & Bach, R. L. (1985). *Latin journey: Cuban and Mexican American immigrants in the United States.* Berkeley, CA: University of California Press.

Portes, A., & Rumbaut, R. (1993). *Immigrant America.* Berkeley, CA: University of California Press.

Portes, A., & Zhou, M. (1993). The new second generation: Segmented assimilation and its variants. *The Annal of the American Academy of Political and Social Sciences, 530,* 74-96.

Rumbaut, R. (1996). The crucible within: Ethnic identity, self-esteem, and segmented assimilation among children of immigrants. *International Migration Review, 18,* 748-794.

Rumbaut, R. (1995) New Californians: Comparative research findings on the educational progress of immigrant children (pp. 16-69). In Center for U.S.-Mexico Studies, *California's immigrant children: Theory, research, and implications for educational policy.* San Diego, CA: University of California, San Diego.

Sutherland, E. H. (1939). *Principles of criminology.* Philadelphia: Lippincott.

Szapocznik, J., Scopetta, M., Kurtines, W., & Arnalde, M. (1978). Theory and measurement of acculturation. *Interamerican Journal of Psychology, 12,* 113-130.

Vega, W. A. (1990). Hispanic families in the 1980s: A decade of research. *Journal of Marriage and the Family, 52*, 1015-1024.

Vega, W. A., & Rumbaut, R. (1991). Ethnic minorities and mental health. *Annual Review of Sociology, 17*, 351-83.

Vega, W. A., & Barnett, K. (1995). *Community-based health promotion/disease prevention programs for Latina/Latino youth in California.* Berkeley, CA: Chicano/Latino Policy Project, University of California.

Vega, W. A., Gil, A. G., Warheit, G. J., Zimmerman, R. S., & Apospori, E. (1993). Acculturation and delinquent behavior among Cuban American adolescents: Toward an empirical model. *American Journal of Community Psychology*, 1993.

Vega, W. A., Gil, A. G., & Zimmerman, R. S. (1993). Patterns of drug use among Cuban American, African American, and white non-Hispanic boys. *American Journal of Public Health, 83*, 257-259.

Vega, W. A., Zimmerman, R. S., Warheit, G. J., Apospori, E., & Gil, A. G. (1993). Risk factors for early adolescent drug use in four ethnic and racial groups. *American Journal of Public Health, 83*, 185-189.

Warheit, G. J., Biafora, F. A., Zimmerman, R. S., Gil, A. G., & Apospori, E. (1995). Self-rejection/derogation, peer factors, and alcohol, drug, and cigarette use among a sample of Hispanic, African American, and white non-Hispanic adolescents. *The International Journal of the Addictions, 30*, 97-116.

APPENDIX*

Acculturation Level[1] (Alphas: Time 1 = .83, Time 2 = .89)

What language do you prefer to speak?
What language do you speak at home?
What language do you speak at school?
What language do you speak with friends?
What language are the magazines you read?
In general, in what language are the movies, T.V., and radio programs you like to watch and listen the most?
What kind of music do you like to listen to?

Language Conflicts[2] (Alphas: Time 1 = .63, Time 2 = .67, Time 3 = .70)

How often has it been hard for you to get along with others because you don't speak English well?
How often has it been hard to get good grades because of problems in understanding English?

Acculturation Conflicts

Perceived Discrimination[1] (Alphas: Time 1 = .58, Time 2 = .63, Time 3 = .68)

How often do people dislike you because you are Latin?
How often are you treated unfairly because you are Latin?
How often have you seen friends treated badly because they are Latin?

Conflicts from Acculturation[1] (Alphas: Time 1 = .61, Time 2 = .66, Time 3 = .70)

How often have you had problems with your family because you prefer American customs?
How often do you feel that you would rather be more American if you had a choice?
How often do you get upset at your parents because they don't know American ways?
How often do you feel uncomfortable having to choose between non-Latin and Latin ways of doing things?

Familism[3] (Alphas: Time 1 = .86, Time 2 = .89, Time 3 = .91)

Family members respect one another.
We share similar values and beliefs as a family.
Things work out well for us as a family.
We really do trust and confide in each other.
Family members feel loyal to the family.
We are proud of our family.
We can express our feelings with our family.

Disposition to Deviance[4] (Alphas: Time 1 = .62, Time 2 = .78, Time 3 = .79)

It is O.K. to sneak into a movie or ball game without paying.
It is OK to steal a bicycle if one can do it without getting caught.
It is important to pay for all things taken from a store.
It is important to try to follow rules and obey the law.
I don't care about other people's feelings.
I would like to quit school as soon as possible.
I would like to leave home.

The kids who mess around with the law seem to be better off than those who always follow the law.

*The alphas for these scales are based on a longitudinal study of Hispanic adolescents in middle school conducted in South Florida.

[1] Sources for this scale are Cuellar, Harris & Jasso (1980), and Szapocznik et al. (1978).
[2] Source for this scale is Cuellar, Harris & Jasso (1980).
[3] Source for this scale is Olson (1989), and has been described as family pride.
[4] Source for this scale is Kaplan, Johnson & Bailey (1986).

COMMUNITY INVOLVEMENT: ADVANCES AND ISSUES

This section focuses on the involvement of the community in the research process. Common themes which emerge from this section include: (1) the importance of community involvement to develop strong, trusting, and respectful relationships between researchers and people in the community; (2) the critical role that people in the community play to provide information to researchers to identify barriers that could jeopardize their research; (3) using community advisory boards and gatekeepers as primary agents to involve the community in the research process; and (4) the disadvantages and advantages of the community's involvement in the research process. Included in this section are papers by Baldwin, Delgado, and Sterk.

Baldwin discusses in detail the development of a model for data collection with American Indian populations who live on reservations. She suggests a model that will involve the community in all aspects of the research process. Baldwin argues for the involvement of American Indian communities as active participants in the research process and not just passive or supportive associates to researchers in the conduct of drug abuse research. Delgado proposes a model to access community involvement in Hispanic populations. This model calls for development of a process that seeks to involve the community in the research through advisory councils, employment of community residents, and co-sponsorship of projects by community-based organizations. This model presumes that communities are generally more of an asset than a hindrance to researchers in their conduct of their research. Sterk reports on the development of a community involvement model that encourages the incorporation of African-Americans in the research process. She discusses the importance of advisory community boards as a way to gain access to African-American communities.

75

Conducting
Drug Abuse Prevention Research
in Partnership
with Native American Communities:
Meeting Challenges
Through Collaborative Approaches

Julie A. Baldwin, PhD

SUMMARY. Many prior drug abuse studies conducted in Native American communities have been almost exclusively directed by

---

Julie A. Baldwin is Associate Professor, Northern Arizona University.

Address correspondence to: Julie A. Baldwin, PhD, Associate Professor, Health Education, Northern Arizona University, NAU P.O. Box 15095, Flagstaff, AZ 86011.

This project was made possible through the active participation of several local schools, community-based organizations, and tribal agencies. The author wishes to express her deepest gratitude to all of the Native American Prevention Project Against AIDS and Substance Abuse (NAPPASA) staff and consultants, as well as the many youth, parents, teachers, and community members whose creative ideas, encouragements, energies, and logistical resources enabled this project to be successfully developed, implemented, and evaluated.

This article was funded in part from the National Institute on Drug Abuse (NIDA) Grant # U01-DA09965. Points of view and opinions expressed in the manuscript are not those of NIDA. NAPPASA was supported with a grant from the NIAAA Prevention Research Branch (R01 AA08578) with additional support from a Maternal and Child Health Bureau Training Grant to the Department of MCH, Johns Hopkins University School of Hygiene and Public Health.

[Haworth co-indexing entry note]: "Conducting Drug Abuse Prevention Research in Partnership with Native American Communities: Meeting Challenges Through Collaborative Approaches." Baldwin, Julie A. Co-published simultaneously in *Drugs & Society* (The Haworth Press, Inc.) Vol. 14, No. 1/2, 1999, pp. 77-92; and: *Conducting Drug Abuse Research with Minority Populations: Advances and Issues* (ed: Mario R. De La Rosa, Bernard Segal, and Richard Lopez) The Haworth Press, Inc., 1999, pp. 77-92. Single or multiple copies of this article are available for a fee from The Haworth Document Delivery Service [1-800-342-9678, 9:00 a.m. - 5:00 p.m. (EST). E-mail address: getinfo@haworthpressinc.com].

researchers with little community input. This paper focuses on the challenges in conducting research in Native American communities and provides a multi-step model for developing, implementing, and evaluating drug abuse prevention programs in partnership with Native American communities. Key steps in the model include: building collaborative relationships with community members, developing interventions to fit local culture and norms, training indigenous staff to implement the program(s), and obtaining on-going feedback from participants using both qualitative and quantitative methods. A case study, the Native American Prevention Project Against AIDS and Substance Abuse (NAPPASA), serves to illustrate how integrating cultural and community input into the project can lead to empowerment of community members and successful program outcomes. *[Article copies available for a fee from The Haworth Document Delivery Service: 1-800-342-9678. E-mail address: getinfo@haworthpressinc. com]*

INTRODUCTION

At the time of the 1990 census, approximately 1.9 million Native Americans* represented 0.8% of the total population of the United States (U.S. Bureau of the Census, 1991). While the first peoples of North America consisted of diverse populations, certain general observations are possible. The federal government currently recognizes over 500 tribes. While many Native Americans in the Western states live and work off-reservation, these populations, if they do not live on reservation, tend to cluster in border towns near reservations (Hodgkinson, Outtz, & Obarakpor, 1990). The Native American population is young, with a birth rate that is twice that of the U.S. average. In 1987, the crude birth rate for Native Americans was 28.0 per 1,000 compared to 15.7 for the general U.S. population (May, 1995). Although socio-economic indices vary widely from tribe to tribe, with some tribes prospering, Native Americans are disproportionately represented among the nation's disadvantaged. In addition, modern patterns of behavior vary widely from one Native American community to the next based on such factors as the traditional folk culture of the tribal group, and the relative rate of change that has occurred in recent decades (May, 1995). Frequently, the majority culture views Native Americans as a homogenous group; however, Native people are highly diversified with individual and family differences, as well as tribal languages and cultural

---

*This term will be used throughout to refer to members of American Indian and Alaska Native tribes and villages.

differences that vary greatly from location to location. Some Native Americans are very traditional in their beliefs, upholding tribal languages, ceremonies, and customs, while others may be more contemporary, respecting some Native traditions but also demonstrating successful orientation to the non-Native culture.

As noted by Thurman (1995), one similarity shared by all Native Americans is a long history of Federal or governmental control over Tribal/Native issues. Federal actions have included attempts to remove Native Americans from homelands, sterilize women of child-bearing age, relocate populations, suppress various ceremonies and dances, and restrict communication in Native languages. Most states did not grant Native Americans the vote until 1924, and Native Americans in Arizona and New Mexico waited until 1946. Another experience most Native American groups shared was education in the boarding school. Thurman (1995) depicted this ordeal:

> From the late 1800's to the 1960's, church-affiliated boarding schools, in their attempts to successfully assimilate Indian people, literally terrorized many Native children. They were punished, often severely, for speaking their Native language, were humiliated in front of their peers, and received extreme hair cuts in an effort to conform to "White society." (p. 247)

Thurman continues, however, that although the Bureau of Indian Affairs still maintains a number of boarding schools, their efforts to educate Native youth are more sensitive; schools now employ Native American teachers and staff and use a culturally appropriate curriculum.

This sweep of historical events continues to influence the personal, social, political, and cultural environments of Native Americans; they are unavoidable as considerations for researchers in drug abuse in Indian communities. As an underserved population, Native American communities are in need of appropriate and responsive research models, measurement tools, and reliable data on the nature and extent of drug abuse. But the manner in which this research is undertaken has critical implications. This paper describes research challenges, methods, and parameters in conducting alcohol and other drug abuse prevention research in partnership with Native American communities.

RESEARCH CHALLENGES
IN WORKING WITH NATIVE AMERICAN COMMUNITIES

Trimble (1977) described the barriers to building positive collaborative relationships between researchers and Native American communities.

While Trimble's article is 20-years-old, few of the issues he described then are changed now. These research challenges are outlined below.

Challenge 1: There has been little, if any, community or tribal partici-pation in anything other than the data collection process. Without tribal or community input, researchers have directed formidable quantities of re-search into Native American communities; they have expected community members to play only a passive or supportive role. As Beauvais (1995) suggested, this approach's critical flaw is that problems often remain poor-ly understood: Since definitions of problems do not reflect real conditions in the community, little that is helpful can result.

Challenge 2: Research findings that are published only contribute to controversy. Much of what researchers have published about Native Americans has proven more a liability than an asset, and in some cases, research has fostered shame and controversy for Native American com-munities. Because many research programs with Native Americans ex-amine "problem areas," a researcher's failure to proceed carefully may perpetuate negative stereotypes. For instance, May (1994) observed that much of the common understanding about alcohol use among Native Americans is myth or a gross oversimplification, and that unfortunately, researchers frequently enough do not seek facts.

Challenge 3: Many Native American communities view research and researchers with suspicion. Research projects have met with mixed reac-tions in Native American communities over the past few years (see Man-son, 1989). The reasons are varied, but in some cases, researchers have treated the community as a convenient field laboratory. This attitude ob-viously can lead to a sense of exploitation in the community and make it unwilling to participate in future research efforts. As Beauvais and Trimble (1992) noted, many communities report that researchers have "burned" them in the past; this maltreatment has led tribes to establish and enforce restrictions on further research. In some cases, the problem has become sufficiently severe that the community has imposed a complete ban on research (Trimble, 1977, 1988).

Challenge 4: Research projects are viewed as an intrusion. As Beau-vais and Trimble (1992) described, new research projects sometimes give rise to concerns that yet another outsider has arrived to detail what is wrong with the tribe or community. A new program that includes exces-sive participation from outside the community understandably may pro-voke resentment, especially if members of the community already are working to solve the problem.

Challenge 5: Tribes lack policies for research endeavors. Increased con-cern about the intrusion of non-Native researchers has led several Native

American communities in North America to establish guidelines that regulate the research process. Such guidelines may address the need to: (1) ensure that a tribal member monitors the program; (2) establish appropriate procedures for the selection of respondents; (3) have the community review and edit questionnaires, interview schedules, and research reports; (4) determine the ownership of raw data; and (5) select mechanisms to disseminate the findings of the study (Beauvais & Trimble, 1992).

Challenge 6: Results contribute little to program development or problem solving. Although Native American alcohol and other drug (AOD) programs now commonly evaluate their efforts, it is surprising how little use is made of the results. Currently, there is no central source where prior data and reports are available to those designing prevention programs. Unless a professional journal has published the evaluation, there is no access to the findings.

Challenge 7: Researchers view findings in non-Native theoretical frameworks. The explanations of and solutions to alcohol and drug abuse among Native Americans call for innovative preventive strategies. These approaches must account for the impact of both traditional and modern cultures upon the individual and his or her use of drugs (May, 1986). Research has suggested that the better an individual's adaptation to both Native American ways and modern society, the less susceptible that individual is to the misuse of drugs. Those at highest risk for alcohol or drug misuse are marginally adapted to both traditional and modern cultures (May, 1982, 1986; Schinke et al., 1986).

NAPPASA: A CASE EXAMPLE OF A COMMUNITY'S INVOLVEMENT IN THE RESEARCH PROCESS

The Native American Prevention Project Against AIDS and Substance Abuse (NAPPASA) demonstrated methods researchers might use to involve Native American communities in the design and implementation of a drug abuse prevention research project. NAPPASA was a multi-component, in-school, and community outreach program to prevent HIV/AIDS and AOD abuse among youth. As Rolf (1992) described, the project, funded by NIAAA and initiated in 1990, sought to work collaboratively with Native American and neighboring communities in northern Arizona to plan, implement, and evaluate culturally sensitive AOD and HIV/AIDS preventive efforts.

NAPPASA created intensive, multi-component, school-based preventive intervention programs based on Social Action Theory (Ewart, 1991) adapted to the multi-cultural social contexts of the rural southwestern United States. To ensure cultural sensitivity, all NAPPASA programs were developed through partnerships with local Native American educational, health, and other community-based organizations. Therefore, the in-school prevention curriculum and supporting after-school activities emphasized ways for Native youth to build knowledge about health, protective skills, and a sense of self-efficacy.

As Figure 1 illustrates, the first step in the NAPPASA project was to develop collaborative relationships with communities. This step incorporated several components, including: (1) development of access to the community, establishment of the project's credibility, and cultivation of the community's trust; (2) the hiring of indigenous staff and consultants; and (3) the formation of a community advisory board. The second step involved the design of the intervention by: (1) adaptation of theoretical perspectives to local values, beliefs, and norms; (2) use of qualitative methods to garner the reflections of youth and adults in the target communities; and (3) dialogue with key community and national consultants. The next step was to implement the program; implementation entailed training community members to realize the intervention and closely monitor its progress. The final step was to evaluate the program. Evaluation used process and outcome approaches; it emphasized *both* quantitative and qualitative methods. The model suggests that the research process should be a cyclical one with continual input and feedback from community members. The following sections describe the processes inherent in each of these steps.

Step 1: Build Collaborative Relationships

Gain community entry. In general, a researcher must know and use proper channels to gain access to a Native American community. Many Native American communities have developed a certain level of independence, founded on both formal and informal regulatory structures not found in non-Native communities. In the case of NAPPASA, local leaders invited J. Rolf, NAPPASA's Principal Investigator, in 1987 to come to Arizona; the invitation arose when members of a local community school board came to Johns Hopkins University to inquire about the HIV/AIDS epidemic's potential threats to Native American adults and youth. After working directly with the community and obtaining funding from NIAAA, the P. I. and the research team consulted with many local governments in Arizona to sanction the research. It is usually necessary to gain approval for new programs and research from tribal or village councils. In larger tribes, this authority may be delegated to a council or a health

FIGURE 1. Cycles of Input and Feedback in the Research Process

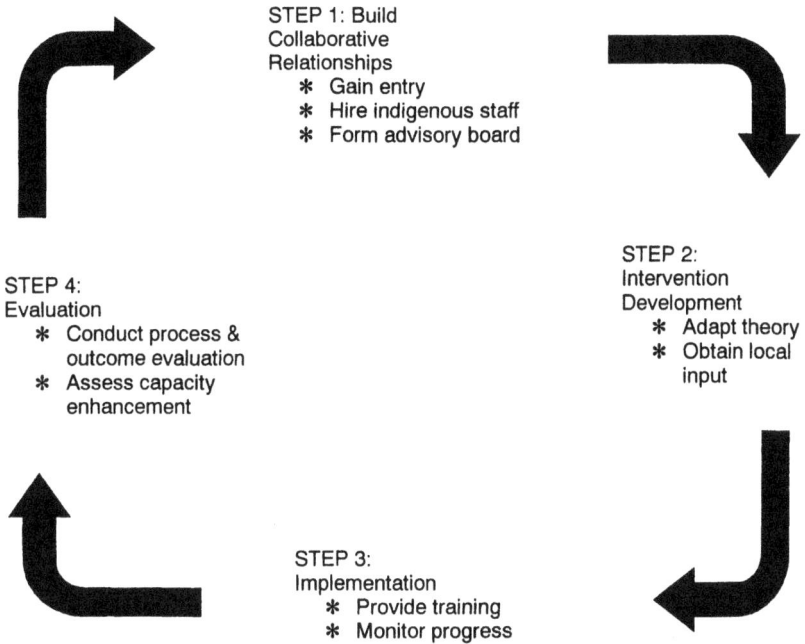

STEP 1: Build
Collaborative
Relationships
  * Gain entry
  * Hire indigenous staff
  * Form advisory board

STEP 2:
Intervention
Development
  * Adapt theory
  * Obtain local
    input

STEP 4:
Evaluation
  * Conduct process &
    outcome evaluation
  * Assess capacity
    enhancement

STEP 3:
Implementation
  * Provide training
  * Monitor progress

committee, or a tribal institutional review board. In addition, community gatekeepers often need to know and consent, if only informally, to new programs and research. The NAPPASA project expended much time to explain to local residents, particularly tribal elders, the program's rationale, content, and evaluation.

Hire indigenous staff and consultants. While working closely with targeted sites on the reservations to initiate the research process, NAPPASA simultaneously recruited specific personnel within the sites for intervention delivery positions. The project was fortunate to recruit as the Community Program Coordinator a culturally traditional woman who was fluent in both the Native language and English, and who was well known within the local education and health services networks. In a role essential to the project, she remained focused on the program's relevance and sensitivity to traditional cultural and community concerns. The project also hired from the community other key staff members, including the administrative assistant, the school health coordinator, interventionists, and curriculum development consultants. As Beauvais (1995) advised, the most effective agents of change are members of the community.

Establish a community advisory board and collaborate with community agencies. As Delgado and Sterk each have suggested in this publication, an advisory board composed of community residents and leaders can contribute significantly to research. NAPPASA found that its active Advisory Board, composed almost exclusively of Native Americans and local residents, kept the project focused on long-term investments and local values. At each successive state, it encouraged the project to gain local input (Rolf, 1995). Regular consultations with the Advisory Board led the staff to develop and implement outreach activities as extensions of the school-based programs.

Step 2: Intervention Development: Integrating Theory with Local and National Input

Adapt theoretical perspectives to fit the local culture. NAPPASA sought to prevent AOD and HIV risk-taking behaviors among Native American adolescents who live on reservations and in border towns in northern Arizona. Trimble and others (e.g., Dinges, Yazzie, & Tollefson, 1974; Manson et al., 1985) already had suggested the relevance of social cognitive theory to preventive interventions with Native American youth. Based on elements of Social Learning/Social Cognitive Theory (Bandura, 1986) and Social Action Theory (Ewart, 1991), NAPPASA began to shape a multi-component approach to AIDS/AOD that: (1) integrated scientific theories of behavior change; (2) was compatible with both indigenous belief systems about holistic health and biomedical views of health and illness; (3) had relevance to the developmental issues of its adolescent target groups; (4) directly addressed the values, beliefs, and attitudes of the recipients within the contexts of Native American socio-cultural systems; (5) enhanced the skills of individuals to incorporate healthy behaviors in day-to-day life; and (6) demonstrated promise as a method to alter existing peer norms (Oetting, 1992; Tarter, 1992).

Obtain local input. NAPPASA used focus groups to obtain community input in the early stages of the development of the curricula and assessment tools. The focus groups sought information from specific groups of adult and youth informants. During the first year of the grant, the project conducted 14 two-hour focus groups. To encourage participation and avoid embarrassment, the project limited groups to six to eight persons and separately interviewed males and females. The compositions of these groups were: (1) eight groups of adults (dorm aides, teachers, parents, etc.), (2) three groups of adolescent females, and (3) three groups of adolescent males. (See Baldwin et al., 1996 for further details about the focus groups.)

The information from these focus groups contributed to a more culturally sensitive prototype of NAPPASA's prevention curriculum. The focus group data enabled the research team to understand better the primary features of culture in the daily life of the project's host communities (Trotter et al., 1993). Fortuitously, the focus groups also served a purpose beyond assisting the development of the prototype curriculum. Focus groups helped to create a sense of cross-cultural partnership in prevention research by forming an important, on-going dialogue regarding HIV/ AIDS among the researchers, school, community groups, and adolescents. This dialogue opened up new channels of communication for local communities to provide valuable input into the very foundation of the project's programs. Furthermore, by allowing communities to define these and other health problems and then incorporate these views into the program, NAPPASA developed culturally congruent prevention messages, activities, and evaluative processes.

Obtain feedback from local and national consultants. The project sought to ensure the selection of appropriate approaches to intervention and assessment that fit the local culture. In addition to the dialogue established with the local community, NAPPASA engaged a panel of local and national consultants who had worked with American Indians and used qualitative research approaches (Beauvais, Oetting, & Edwards, 1985a; Beauvais, Oetting, & Edwards, 1985b; Manson et al., 1985; Schinke et al., 1985; Trotter, 1991). NAPPASA recognized that AOD use/abuse and other risk behaviors are highly complex phenomena in Native American communities: A one-shot and short-term prevention program would not work (Gilchrist, Schinke, Trimble, & Cvetkovich, 1987). So as the literature recommends (Bobo, Snow, Gilchrist, & Schinke, 1985; Carpenter, Lyons, & Miller, 1985), NAPPASA's research team and community partnership embedded its AIDS/AOD programs into the fabric of the daily life of local youth.

Step 3: Implementation

Train community members to implement the intervention. The NAPPASA project's research protocol required high fidelity to a single standard for implementation of its prevention curriculum. This standard included the use of motivated and culturally appropriate interventionists whom NAPPASA recruited from the host schools and communities. NAPPASA trained teachers from local schools and co-instructors, also recruited from the community, to implement the program. When members of the target culture participate as deliverers of the intervention, they are more likely to feel ownership of the study. Using indigenous staff to deliver services also can enhance the intervention's access to the targeted culture (Schinke & Cole, 1995).

The training workshops for instructors devoted considerable time to cultural issues; sensitive topics like sex, local AIDS cases, and abuse; and practice of the curriculum's role playing activities. Workshops oriented instructors to the intervention's rationale, described intervention materials, provided a session-by-session analysis of interventions, and afforded rehearsals of skills for delivering the intervention. NAPPASA staff also provided "in-service" training at the host schools for teachers, administrators, and, where pertinent, dormitory staff.

Monitor the intervention during the implementation phase. During all phases of research, but especially the implementation phase, the NAPPASA research staff in Arizona diligently monitored the project and made site visits. As Beauvais and Trimble (1992) observed, it is not enough to leave the field work to others and assume that original conditions will persist. Researchers must participate more personally in work with American Indian communities (Trimble, 1977); they can learn a tremendous amount by immersion in the culture. A genuine interest and willingness to engage in community-based social and cultural events, such as pow-wows and traditional ceremonies, may not directly address the research agenda, but it demonstrates respect. It is also essential for the researcher to be patient. The political and decision-making processes in many Native American communities are often complex, and their nuances are not always apparent to someone from outside the community. It is often critical to consult with community collaborators to determine when it is appropriate to proceed with certain aspects of the research.

Step 4: Evaluation

Conduct process evaluation. Once NAPPASA had developed and implemented a pilot version of the curriculum, it conducted multiple focus groups with youth and teachers. These focus groups examined the interventions for their cultural responsiveness, curriculum content, and logistical requirements. Native American staff from the community assisted in conducting, recording, and interpreting the focus groups. As a result of cycles of formative and confirmative research methods, always reflecting feedback from the community, the prototype curriculum eventually underwent several rounds of revision.

Process evaluation in the community included repeated focus groups, periodic spot surveys, and interviews with key informants, including the project's Advisory Board and local consultants. These methods yielded data on awareness, understanding, approval, and reported behavioral effects of the project's messages. In 1993, the NAPPASA research team conducted a series of in-depth focus groups and key informant interviews to determine to what degree the program had achieved its goals. These data indicated that, in general, the efforts were well received. However, linkages from school to community varied depending upon the level of intensity of outreach activities in that particular community (Rolf, 1995).

Conduct outcome evaluation. NAPPASA employed a quasi-experimental design. In this design, some schools received the whole intervention and others, a brief, didactic HIV/AIDS and AOD prevention program that the school coordinated. Many intervention studies require a no-intervention control group. Some communities may consider such a group to be unacceptable or unethical, particularly in an HIV/AIDS, alcohol, and other drug abuse prevention program. Distrust can increase when people learn that some members of their community will not receive the intervention. One solution is to offer subjects in the control or comparison group a different, unrelated intervention. Another is to offer subjects in a wait-list control group the same intervention that the other groups have received *after* the completion of the formal study period. It is essential to have the right balance between scientific goals and the targeted community's concerns.

Assess capacity enhancement. NAPPASA primarily sought to measure changes in knowledge, attitudes, and behavior among youth and community members; nevertheless, research in drug abuse prevention within ethnic communities also needs to examine indicators of capacity enhancement. According to Pentz (1995), this examination might seek to observe:

> Changes in community acceptance of the initial problem and social norms for the target health behavior; increased centrality of community leader and interagency communications and cooperation; increased community leader and resident perceptions of empowerment and capacity to empower other leaders and agencies for long-term health initiatives through policy change; and institutionalization of prevention programs in the community. (p. 87)

These issues are relevant to the empowerment of the community and its ownership of the program and its outcomes.

NAPPASA and others (Schinke & Cole, 1995) also have found that when the drug abuse prevention project expires, it must leave behind tangible products for the community. These products may include treatment manuals, curricula, posters, videotapes, and reports summarizing the results of the study. Hopefully, field staff from the targeted communities, schools, and community-based organizations will continue to use, update, and enhance the materials. One potential risk is that the community may misinterpret the purpose of the research, confusing research with actual service delivery. This confusion can lead to problems both during and at the end of the project. Review of the project's goals and objectives with key community members in the early stages of the project may circumvent this problem.

CONCLUSIONS AND IMPLICATIONS
FOR FURTHER RESEARCH

This paper has argued for the involvement of Native Americans in the whole process of research, from conceptualization of the research issue, to the refinement of the methodological approach, to data collection, and to analysis, interpretation, and dissemination of results. The content of alcohol and drug abuse prevention research programs in Native American communities must reflect tribal culture. Research efforts must facilitate the empowerment of the tribe (Beauvais & LaBoueff, 1985). Empowerment-based approaches emphasize that solutions to substance abuse and other community issues should be sought within the indigenous community and not imposed from the outside (Mail, 1992). In fact, the most successful prevention models in Native American communities are, as Fleming (1992) described, those that "promote self-determination (i.e., they are not prescriptive and do not try to tell communities what to do), interdependence (recognize that each individual and agency is affected by actions or inactions of another), and social responsibility" (p. 85). Researchers from outside, working with tribal members and leaders, can initiate programs, but individuals within the local community must conduct the activities.

A need continues for well-trained ethnic/racial researchers, who have worked with Native American populations, to serve as principal investigators, advisors, reviewers, advocates, and mentors. Some funding institutions have recognized this need and established several commendable programs. In 1986, the National Institute on Drug Abuse introduced the Minority Research Development Seminar Series with the mission to provide training opportunities to ethnic minorities. Minority supplemental grants are also available for pre- and post-doctoral minority researchers. However, additional scholarships and funding for undergraduate or graduate minority students should be included in future grants. The inclusion of more Native American high school students, their teachers, and parents in designing research projects could begin to provide the needed skills and motivation for more Native Americans to become involved in drug abuse prevention research.

Finally, the need to adapt preventive intervention approaches to Native American cultures has been a recurrent theme. Programs should be made relevant to local norms, values, and conditions through particular culturally sensitive adaptations. Research on the effectiveness of culturally competent drug abuse treatment programs indicates that treatment programs that reflect Native American culture and incorporate Native religious beliefs are more successful than those that do not incorporate such cultural components (Mail & McDonald, 1980; Stubben, 1995). Funding for research on the impact of the integration of traditional Native American prevention modalities into community-based prevention programs needs to be a priority in drug abuse prevention research. As May (1992b) explained:

> We must move forward in a positive vein with great expectations. We should assist in solutions. All the while we must acknowledge that there are many paths to alcohol (and drug) problems, and therefore, that many solutions are possible. No one paradigm approach will do unless it allows for embracing a multitude of directed influences. (p. 131)

REFERENCES

Baldwin, J., Rolf, J. E., Johnson, J., Bowers, J., Benally, C., & Trotter, R. T. (1996). Developing culturally sensitive HIV/AIDS and substance abuse prevention curricula for Native American youth. *Journal of School Health, 66*(9), 322-327.

Bandura, A. (1986). *Social foundations of thought and action: A social cognitive theory.* Englewood, NJ: Prentice.

Beauvais, F. (1995). Ethnic communities and research: Building a new alliance. *The Challenge of Participatory Research: Preventing Alcohol-related Problems in Ethnic Communities* (pp. 105-128). Special Collaborative NIAAA/CSAP Monograph Based on a NIAAA Conference. U.S. Department of Health and Human Services.

Beauvais, F., & LaBoueff, S. (1985). Drug and alcohol abuse intervention in American Indian communities. *International Journal of Addictions, 20,* 139-171.

Beauvais, F., Oetting, E. R., & Edwards, R.W. (1985a). Trends in the use of inhalants among American Indian adolescents. *White Cloud Journal, 3*(4), 3-11.

Beauvais, F., Oetting, E. R., & Edwards, R.W. (1985b). Trends in drug use of Indian adolescents living on reservations: 1975-1983. *Amer J Drug Alcohol Abuse, 11*(3 & 4), 209-230.

Beauvais, F., & Trimble, J. E. (1992). The role of the researcher in evaluating

American Indian alcohol and other drug abuse prevention programs. In M. Orlandi, R. Westin, & L. G. Epstein (Eds.), *Cultural competence for evaluators: A guide for alcohol and other drug abuse prevention practitioners working with ethnic/racial communities* (pp. 173-201). U.S. Department of Health and Human Services.

Bobo, J. K., Snow, W. H., Gilchrist, L. D., & Schinke, S. P. (1985). Assessment of refusal skill in minority youth. *Psychol Rep, 58*(3 Pt 2), 1187-91.

Carpenter, R. A., Lyons, C. A., & Miller, W. R. (1985). Peer-managed self-control program for prevention of alcohol abuse in American Indian high school students: A pilot evaluation study. *International Journal of Addictions, 20*(2), 299-310.

Dinges, N., Yazzie, M., Tollefson, G. (1974). Developmental intervention for Navajo families in mental health. *Personnel and Guidance Journal, 52*, 390-395.

Ewart, C. (1991). Social action theory for a public health psychology. *American Psychologist, 46*(9), 931-946.

Fleming, C. M. (1992). The next twenty years of prevention in Indian country: Visionary, complex, and practical. *American Indian and Alaska Native Mental Health Research, 4*(3), 85-88.

Gilchrist, L. D., Schinke, S. P., Trimble, J. E., Cvetkovich, G. T. (1987). Skills enhancement to prevent substance abuse among American Indian adolescents. *Int J Addict, 22*(9):869-879.

Hodgkinson, H. L., Outtz, J. H. & Obarakpor, A. M. (1990). *The demographics of American Indians: One percent of the people; 50% of the diversity.* Washington, DC: Institute for Educational Leadership.

Mail, P. D. (1992). Do we care enough to attempt change in American Indian alcohol policy? *American Indian and Alaska Native Mental Health Research, 4*(3), 105-111.

Mail, P. D., & McDonald, D. R. (1980). *Tulapai to Tokay: A bibliography of alcohol use and abuse among Native Americans of North America.* New Haven: HRAF Press.

Manson, S. (1989). *American Indian and Alaska Native Mental Health Research, 2*(3): Entire issue.

Manson, S., Shore, J., Bloom, J., Keepers, G., & Neligh, G. (1985). Alcohol abuse and major affective disorders: Advances in epidemiologic research among Native Americans. In *Alcohol use among U.S. ethnic minorities* (pp. 291-300). NIAAA Research Monograph 18, DHHS (ADM).

May, P. A. (1995). The prevention of alcohol and other drug abuse among American Indians: A review and analysis of the literature. *The challenge of participatory research: Preventing alcohol-related problems in ethnic communities* (pp. 183-244). Special Collaborative NIAAA/CSAP Monograph Based on a NIAAA Conference. U.S. Department of Health and Human Services.

May, P. A. (1994). The epidemiology of alcohol abuse among American Indians: The mythical and real properties. *American Indian Culture and Research Journal, 18*(2), 121-143.

May, P. A. (1992a). Alcohol policy considerations for Indian reservations and bordertown communities. *American Indian and Alaska Native Mental Health Research, 4*(3), 5-59.

May, P. A. (1992b). Let the debate, study, and action continue: Response to twelve critiques. *American Indian and Alaska Native Mental Health Research, 4*(3), 126-132.

May, P. A. (1986). Alcohol and drug misuse. Prevention programs for American Indians: Needs and Opportunities. *Journal of Studies of Alcohol, 47*, 187-195.

May, P. A., (1982). Substance abuse and American Indians: Prevalence and susceptibility. *International Journal on the Addictions, 17*, 1185-1209.

Oetting, E. (1992). Planning programs for prevention of deviant behavior: A psychosocial model. In J. E. Trimble, C. E. Bolek, & S. J. Niemcryk (Eds.): *Ethnic and multi-cultural drug abuse: Perspectives on current research.* NY: The Haworth Press, Inc.

Pentz, M. A. (1995). Alternative models of community prevention research in ethnically and culturally diverse communities. *The challenge of participatory research: Preventing alcohol-related problems in ethnic communities* (pp. 67-104). Special Collaborative NIAAA/CSAP Monograph Based on a NIAAA Conference. U.S. Department of Health and Human Services.

Rolf, J. (1995). Methods to create and sustain cross-cultural prevention research partnership: The NAPPASA Project's American Indian-Anglo American Example. *The challenge of participatory research: Preventing alcohol-related problems in ethnic communities* (pp. 149-182). Special Collaborative NIAAA/CSAP Monograph Based on a NIAAA Conference. U.S. Department of Health and Human Services.

Rolf, J. (1992). *The 1992 NAPPASA Project Annual Report for NIAAA RO1-08578.* Baltimore, MD: Johns Hopkins University, Department of Maternal and Child Health.

Schinke, S. P., Botvin, G. J., Trimble, J. E., Orlandi, M. A., Gilchrist, L. D., & Locklear, V. S. (1986). Preventing substance abuse among American Indian adolescents: A bicultural competence skills approach. *Journal of Counseling Psychology, 35*, 87-90.

Schinke, S. P., & Cole, K. C. (1995). Methodological issues in conducting alcohol abuse prevention research in ethnic communities. *The challenge of participatory research: Preventing alcohol-related problems in ethnic communities* (pp. 129-148). Special Collaborative NIAAA/CSAP Monograph Based on a NIAAA Conference. U.S. Department of Health and Human Services.

Schinke, S. P., Gilchrist, L. D., Schilling, R. F., II, Walker, R. D., Kirkham, M. A., Bobo, J. K., Trimble, J. E., Cvetkovich, G. T., & Richardson, S. S. (1985). Strategies for preventing substance abuse with American Indian youth. *White Cloud Journal, 3*(4), 1-7.

Stubben, J. D. (1995). Discussion Paper: American Indian alcohol prevention research: A community advocate's perspective. *The challenge of participatory research: Preventing alcohol-related problems in ethnic communities* (pp. 259-278). Special Collaborative NIAAA/CSAP Monograph Based on a NIAAA Conference. U.S. Department of Health and Human Services.

Tarter, R. E. (1992). Prevention of drug abuse: Theory and application. *Am J Addict, 1*, 3-20.

Thurman, P. J. (1995). Native American community alcohol prevention research. *The challenge of participatory research: Preventing alcohol-related problems in ethnic communities* (pp. 245-258). Special Collaborative NIAAA/CSAP Monograph Based on a NIAAA Conference. U.S. Department of Health and Human Services.

Trimble, J. (1994). A cognitive-behavioral approach to drug abuse prevention and intervention with American Indian youth. In L. A. Vargas & J. D. Doss-Chioino (Eds.), *Working with culture: Psychotherapeutic interventions with ethnic minority children and adolescents.* San Francisco: Jossey-Bass Publishers.

Trimble, J. (1988). Putting the ethic to work: Applying social-psychological principles in cross-cultural settings. In M. Bond (Ed.), *The cross-cultural challenge to social psychology*, Newbury Park, CA: Sage Publications.

Trimble, J. (1977). The sojourner in the American Indian community: Methodological concerns and issues. *Journal of Social Issues, 33*, 159-174.

Trimble, J., & Hayes, S. (1984). Mental health intervention in the psychosocial contexts of American Indian communities. In W. O'Conner, & B. Lubin (Eds.), *Ecological approaches to clinical and community psychology* (pp. 293-321). New York: Wiley.

Trotter, R., Rolf, J., Quintero, G., Alexander, C., & Baldwin, J. (1993). *Cultural models of alcohol, drug abuse and AIDS on the Navajo reservation: Navajo youth at risk.* Unpublished manuscript.

Trotter, R. T. (1991). Ethnographic research methods for applied medical anthropology. In C.E. Hill (Ed.), *Training manual in applied medical anthropology.* American Anthropological Association Special Publication, No. 27. Washington, DC: American Anthropological Association.

U.S. Bureau of Census. (1991). *American Indian and Alaska Native areas: 1990.* Washington, DC: U.S. Government Printing Office.

Involvement of the Hispanic Community in ATOD Research

Melvin Delgado, PhD

SUMMARY. Alcohol, tobacco, and other drugs (ATOD) have had a devastating impact on Hispanic communities in the United States. This population historically has not had access to culturally competent services to address the effect of drugs in their lives. There is little debate in the field of ATOD about the need to develop strategies to involve communities in research and service to ensure quality services. This paper identifies issues and challenges for researchers wishing to engage Hispanic communities in the research process. *[Article copies available for a fee from The Haworth Document Delivery Service: 1-800-342-9678. E-mail address: getinfo@haworthpressinc.com]*

INTRODUCTION

The impact of alcohol, tobacco, and other drugs (ATOD) on communities-of-color in the United States has been devastating (Davis & Lurigio, 1996). These communities, nevertheless, have generally not had access to culturally competent services to address the impact of drugs on their lives (Brisbane, 1995; Delgado, in press, a). When services have been available, they have not been based on community involvement, capacity enhance-

---

Melvin Delgado is Professor of Social Work and Chair of Macro-Practice, Boston University School of Social Work, 264 Bay State Road, Boston, MA 02215.

[Haworth co-indexing entry note]: "Involvement of the Hispanic Community in ATOD Research." Delgado, Melvin. Co-published simultaneously in *Drugs & Society* (The Haworth Press, Inc.) Vol. 14, No. 1/2, 1999, pp. 93-105; and: *Conducting Drug Abuse Research with Minority Populations: Advances and Issues* (ed: Mario R. De La Rosa, Bernard Segal, and Richard Lopez) The Haworth Press, Inc., 1999, pp. 93-105. Single or multiple copies of this article are available for a fee from The Haworth Document Delivery Service [1-800-342-9678, 9:00 a.m. - 5:00 p.m. (EST). E-mail address: getinfo@ haworthpressinc.com].

ment, or empowerment or asset principles that actively seek to involve the community.

There is little debate in the field of ATOD, or other fields, about the need to develop strategies that involve the communities being studied or served (Delgado, 1996a, 1996b; NIDA, 1993; Pettiway, 1993). Stanfield (1993a) addressed this concern when he commented, ". . . (T)here is a great need for epistemological traditions such as participatory research strategies that would assist research subjects in improving their quality of life, as opposed to the interpersonal, exploitive conventions of logical positivism" (p. 35).

Involvement, however, can be conceptualized as a continuum with minimal (advisory) input from the community at one end, to meaningful and active involvement in all facets of the project, at the other end, be it service or research focused (Becerra & Zambrana, 1985; Marin & Marin, 1991). This paper provides an overview of the issues and challenges that face researchers who seek to involve Puerto Rican and other Hispanic communities in the research process. In addition, this paper presents examples of various techniques to operationalize this approach, along with the considerations researchers must weigh in deciding the most useful methodology.

REVIEW OF LITERATURE

The impact of ATOD on communities-of-color is widely recognized in all circles ranging from the academic/researcher, to providers, communities, and consumers. The lack of culture group-specific data has complicated the process of developing treatment and service models that take into account contextual factors in order to ensure quality, culturally-competent services (Segal, 1995; Soriano, 1994). As a result, there is a tremendous need for culturally-specific research to help inform service planning and delivery (Collins, 1992).

Barriers to Community Involvement

Researchers have generally avoided the involvement of communities-of-color in the research process. Stanfield (1993a) observed that people-of-color have historically been excluded as researchers, as subjects of research, and from key decision-making roles in research projects.

Exclusion may be the result from any one or combination of the following reasons: (1) concern about how local politics will influence the research process; (2) a belief that the community does not have the resources (personnel, knowledge of local issues, understanding of research, or the interest) to warrant involvement with a research project; (3) lack of willingness to invest resources in the community; and (4) lack of knowledge on how to involve the community.

Concerns of researchers about how local politics may influence research are not uncommon (Debro & Conley, 1993). Researchers, in all likelihood, do not live in the communities they are studying, and will rarely be willing to relocate to those communities during the research period (Bourgois, 1995). Thus, a limited knowledge of community-level politics often results in researchers going to great pains to avoid virtually any form of involvement with a community.

Most researchers have not been exposed to an asset/strength perspective in graduate studies. If they do not belong to the ethnic/racial group being studied or reside in the community, their knowledge of Hispanic communities may be limited to a deficit perspective–namely, Puerto Ricans and other Hispanics have no indigenous resources. This perspective, unfortunately, does not permit researchers and funders to identify community resources to employ or to consult at various stages of the research.

A lack of willingness to invest resources in the community seriously limits any efforts at community capacity enhancement. Many researchers do not want to invest time, energy, and resources to train and supervise locals as field interviewers, contract with local businesses, and so on. A paucity of knowledge and awareness of how to enter a community from an asset perspective may also account for lack of community participation. Few researchers have had extensive studies focused on Hispanics, or had professors with such experience. Thus, they have not had the role models, or the skills and knowledge for analysis and interaction, to venture into this "unknown area."

Advantages of Community Involvement

One method of increasing the specificity and relevance of the research is to involve the ultimate beneficiaries of the process: the community. This can be accomplished by stressing the importance of community participation in all aspects of program design and implementation and the provision of opportunities for meaningful involvement.

Becerra and Zambrana (1985) have outlined three basic approaches to involve the community. The first approach, that is, to always involve the community in some fashion, is without a doubt the preferred approach for ATOD research. The manner and degree of involvement, however, are dependent upon a series of factors: (1) duration and complexity of the project (longer and more difficult to implement projects will offer more opportunities for involvement when compared with short-term and relatively simple projects); (2) the amount and flexibility of the budget (generous budgets provide more opportunities for hiring community residents and contracting with community institutions); and (3) the previous experiences senior project personnel have had with community involvement (those with extensive histories will, in all likelihood, be more comfortable with community participation).

Access to Hispanic and other communities-of-color has increased in difficulty over the past decades because of local concerns about how the research will be used to harm them (Andranovich & Riposa, 1993). According to Debros and Conley (1993), these communities require researchers to demonstrate commitment of resources or strong statements of how the community will benefit. In addition, some communities will only allow investigators of similar racial and ethnic backgrounds to enter. Marin and Marin (1991), raising similar considerations to those of Debros and Conley (1993) regarding research and Hispanics, focused on the suspicions Hispanics may have of other racial and ethnic groups. Hispanics are concerned about what happens to the personal information they provide once it leaves their homes.

Research in Hispanic communities, as a result, will present researchers and their sponsoring organizations with significant challenges. Methodological issues (Pentz & Trebow, 1991) such as obtaining samples and developing measures may pale by comparison with the political resistance that can result when the community does not perceive that the research meets its best interests. Community involvement in the research process can help researchers with the following activities: (1) framing research questions (Humm-Delgado & Delgado, 1983); (2) questionnaire back translation when applicable (Lindholm & Lopez, 1980; Marin & Marin, 1991); (3) selection and development of measures (Collins, 1992; Marin & Marin, 1991); (4) sample selection (Finlinson, Robles, Colon, & Page, 1993; Wiebel, 1990); and (5) interpretation of findings (Delgado, 1996b; Humm-Delgado, 1983).

Funders, researchers, and the community have raised the question of whether or not to pay community participants. Those who argue to not pay community members stress that payment may compromise participation by having participants give "socially appropriate" answers; those who argue to pay community members stress that participants provide "expertise" that should be rewarded.

Delgado (1996), commenting on remuneration of advisory committee members, suggested, "Finally, members should be compensated for their participation in the form of a gift certificate or stipend. Payment conveys a sense of respect for . . . knowledge and time" (p. 408). In addition, communities-of-color tend to have a high percentage of residents living below the poverty level, and the money for services rendered can be put to good use.

GUIDING PRINCIPLES

A set of principles to help researchers develop strategies and techniques to involve communities-of-color must guide community participation in ATOD research. Principles invariably consist of values and beliefs that can be translated into methods and procedures. The following three principles are highly interrelated and serve to both guide researchers and "send a message" to the community concerning their value and expected contributions to the research process.

Use of an asset paradigm. An asset or strength paradigm identifies and uses indigenous resources, cultural and otherwise, that can mobilize a community to address internal needs and issues. Research premised on an asset paradigm must first, and foremost, seek to identify the kind of resources (financial, physical, and personal) a community possesses (Kretzmann & McKnight, 1993; Saleebey, 1992). Once research has identified these resources and coping mechanisms, the focus shifts to understanding better why ATOD represents a challenge for the community, and how assets can be used to address identified concerns.

ATOD researchers need to remain conscious that the vast majority of people-of-color do not use or abuse alcohol, tobacco, and other drugs. These individuals possess resiliencies that need more study and better understanding. An asset paradigm not only addresses research questions, methodology, and implementation strategies, but also guides researchers on how best to work with a community in the process. In essence, an asset "stance" should permeate all aspects of a research process.

Empowerment. The concept of empowerment is no longer restricted to the provision of services but also is applicable to research (Florin & Wandersman, 1990; Swift, 1992). Empowerment can be defined as a process where individuals and communities are provided with opportunities and tools to take control over decisions impacting on their lives.

ATOD research, as a result, must not only seek to answer critical questions but also provide an avenue for community participation and empowerment. The empowerment process takes hold when the community is expected to play an important role in the making and implementation of decisions.

Community capacity enhancement. Capacity enhancement is a strategy to develop further a community's ability to address internal needs and concerns. The concept of capacity enhancement is applicable to individuals, organizations, and communities. The goals of enhancement, as a result, are to build upon and use resources that are indigenous to a community (Davis & Lurigio, 1996; Delgado, 1995; Florin & Wandersman, 1990). Opportunities must be developed to use a community's capacity to help itself. Institutional resources, as a result, must be strategically used to not only achieve research goals but also enhance a community's capacity to help itself in the present and future. Two products will complete a research project: (1) a report with answers to critical research questions; and (2) a community's enhanced skills and knowledge about ATOD.

Culturally-competent research. The three principles outlined above help both researchers and communities to better comprehend ATOD trends, issues, and needs. These principles minimize, but do not totally eliminate, challenges to achieving culturally-competent research. Nevertheless, the implementation of these principles will go a long way towards all parties (funders, policy makers, providers, researchers, and community) benefitting from the research.

Methods for Involving Community

No one institution or individual can provide complete access to a community. Thus, it is necessary to seek assistance from multiple institutions, formal as well as informal, and from individuals. Humm-Delgado and Delgado (1986) have identified a multifaceted set of approaches to maximize community access and participation: (1) development of interagency collaborations with community-based organizations; (2) contact with and involvement of natural support systems (individual and institution-based); (3) active community involvement throughout all phases of a project through an advisory committee and the hire of local interviewers; (4) use of local radio, television, and print; and (5) use of multiple qualitative and quantitative research methods to allow community residents, leaders, and other key individuals to provide input into the research process.

Development of an advisory committee. A number of researchers have recommended the development and use of a research advisory committee (Delgado, 1996b; Humm-Delgado & Delgado, 1986; Soriano, 1994; see also Baldwin and Sterk in this publication). An advisory committee composed of community residents, gatekeepers, and leaders can play an influential role in increasing the relevance of the research and in all aspects of the research process.

Mart-Costa and Serrano-Garcia (1995) strongly recommended the development of a "core" group of influential community residents that has responsibility for planning, coordination, and evaluation of a research project. This group not only provides input into major discussions, but also access to the community. Humm-Delgado and Delgado (1983) suggested use of an advisory committee and identified 10 facets of the research process for advisory community input: (1) posing general research questions; (2) defining the population; (3) selecting the methodology; (4) selecting the sample; (5) gaining entry and support/publicity; (6) selecting and pretesting instruments; (7) selecting and training staff; (8) interpreting findings; (9) presenting findings; and (10) using and disseminating findings.

Delgado (1996b) suggested the development of two advisory committees based upon his experience in implementing a study of elders of color in a New England community. One committee consisted of local professional gatekeepers, while the other consisted of potential research respondents. Delgado (1996b) described the following functions of this latter committee:

> (1) Planning–input on key questions to be included in questionnaire development; reactions to key informant comments on demographic changes, including dispersal patterns within the city; identification of Puerto Rican religious, civic, and social institutions serving elders; (2) Publicity–identification of sources for publicity on the project and assistance in disseminating information about the study within key organizations that they attend; (3) Problem-Solving–assistance in obtaining subjects using snowballing techniques and identification of institutions to help locate Puerto Rican elders; (4) Data Analysis–review of findings and assistance with interpretations, recommendations, etc.; and (5) Dissemination of Findings–assistance with the identification of, and access to, the best local sources for dissemination of study findings. (p. 407)

Hiring community residents. To minimize social distance, individuals of the same ethnic/racial background as the communities they are studying whenever possible should conduct ATOD research (Anderson, 1992). The literature has reported on numerous successful efforts at carrying out community-based research by employing residents as field interviewers (Bloom & Studying, 1979; Delgado, 1981, 1995, 1996a; Finlinson, Robles, Colon, & Page, 1993; Perez et al., 1980; Wiebel, 1990).

Several researchers have stressed the importance of hiring community residents in recovery; they not only have access to the community in general, but also to individuals who may be actively using drugs (Koester,

1994; Singer, Gonzalez, Vega, Centeno, & Davison, 1994; Vazquez, 1994). Hiring individuals familiar with treatment also will aid the development of treatment and policy recommendations. Hiring community residents in other arenas is also highly recommended. Delgado (1995) presented a case study that involved Puerto Rican adolescents as interviewers in a community asset study in a New England city.

The employment of residents serves to ensure that research subjects meet the eligibility requirements (Pettiway, 1993) and is a mechanism to provide employment in communities with high levels of unemployment.

Interagency collaboration. Research utilizing interagency collaboration takes on added significance when one or more of the agencies are based in the community (Florin & Wandersman, 1990). Bastian (1995) noted that collaboration with these institutions should be attempted because they enjoy the trust and goodwill of their communities and are sensitive to the prevalent cultural values and mores of their communities.

Interagency collaboration also increases the chances that research questions are relevant to both residents and agencies that serve their needs. It also is one means of sharing costs. Collaboration with community agencies takes on a variety of forms. It includes using staff as interviewers, meeting space, newsletters to inform potential subjects, and so on. In essence, collaboration can very well result in a "win-win" situation for all parties.

Local institutional co-sponsorship of research. Researchers should initiate activities with community sponsorship. A local institutional co-sponsor provides a research project with institutional legitimacy (Delgado, 1996a; Marin & Marin, 1991). Marin and Marin (1991) suggested the sponsorship of a community leader or organization as the means to achieve the necessary community sanction. They also suggested that studies that address particularly sensitive topics may benefit from such sponsorship.

The greater the number of co-sponsors, the higher the likelihood a project will encounter minimal resistance from the community being studied. A word of caution, however, is in order. Thorough background research on institutions and leaders is particularly critical. No research project should seek the sponsorship of an organization or individual who is controversial, or has a less than stellar reputation in the community. The "wrong" sponsorship will have deleterious consequences for a project.

Contracting local businesses. Researchers should use local businesses whenever possible. This strategy develops local contacts and community capacity; it funnels badly needed funds into the community; and it provides a research project with important visibility beyond the sample population and gatekeepers. There are numerous opportunities to use local businesses: food for functions, travel arrangements, supplies, repairs of equipment, office maintenance, rental of vehicles, and so on. Involvement of local businesses, in turn, increases the number of avenues for a project to inform the community and obtain the necessary research subjects. Accessibility, it must be remembered, is earned; it is not a right in Hispanic and other communities-of-color. Thus, it makes good business, research, and political sense to "buy" from the community.

Community base. Having a community base as a field site is of particular importance to gain access to the community. Residents know where they can go to get information. Goldstein, Spunt, Miller, and Bellucci (1990) argued that the research process starts with locating a field-based site, thus facilitating project personnel establishing a street presence in an area and developing street contacts to informally discuss issues to be studied.

Having the administrative offices geographically located within a community is one means of reassuring residents. In addition, it also reduces travel time for interviewers. Space permitting, office space also can be made available for community meetings and other events, minimizing distance between staff and community. Hours of operation, in turn, must facilitate access. Research personnel cannot expect to gather data 9 to 5, Monday through Friday. Operational and geographical accessibility must go hand-in-hand and are critical precursors to psychological comfort and cultural (values and beliefs) accessibility.

Use of qualitative methods. A narrow methodological focus on gathering data severely limits the possibilities for community involvement in the research process. The use of qualitative methods, such as key informants, focus groups, and community forums, opens up endless possibilities for community involvement (Williams, 1993).

Delgado (in press, b) described the use of community forums consisting of research respondents as an excellent way to assist with the interpretation of unexpected data. The forum, for example, is then followed by key informant interviews and use of focus groups. This three-prong approach provides researchers with important community input into data analysis and interpretation. The use of qualitative methods, too, lends themselves to empowerment and capacity enhancement (Delgado, in press, c; Williams, 1993).

CONCLUSION

Community involvement in the research process serves a multitude of important functions to ensure ATOD research addresses the needs of community residents. Participation, in turn, can take on a variety of manifestations depending upon project goals, funding, and comfort level of staff with community involvement. Participation, however, is a question of degree rather than whether-or-not it will take place. Communities-of-color have tremendous needs that result from the impact of alcohol, tobacco, and other drugs. Consequently, that research that targets their communities needs to be relevant and beneficial to them. This article has identified a series of facilitating and hindering factors to achieve Hispanic community participation in ATOD research; in addition, this paper has presented a series of principles and approaches to help bring the goal of meaningful participation to fruition. These principles and approaches do not have to compromise "scientific validity" in order to involve communities. However, communities-of-color no longer will tolerate research as "business as usual."

REFERENCES

Adler, P. (1990). Ethnographic research on hidden populations: Penetrating the drug world. In E. Y. Lambert (Ed.), *The collection and interpretation of data from hidden populations* (NIDA Research Monograph 98, pp. 96-112). Rockville, MD.: National Institute on Drug Abuse.

Anderson, M. L. (1992). Studying across difference: Race, class and gender in qualitative research. In J. H. Stanfield II & R. M. Dennis (Eds.), *Race and ethnicity in research methods* (pp. 39-52). Newbury Park, CA: Sage Publications.

Andranovich, G. D., & Riposa, G. (1993). *Doing urban research.* Newbury Park, CA: Sage Publications.

Bastien, A. (1995). HIV in the inner cities: Epidemiologic trends and their influence on policy-making decisions. *Journal of Community Health, 20,* 177-181.

Beauvais, F. (1992). *Reconciling the requirements of science and community in cross-cultural research.* Paper presented at the NIAAA Working Group on Alcohol Prevention Research in Ethnic Minority Communities Conference, Washington, DC.

Becerra, R., & Zambrana, R. E. (1985). Methodological approaches to research on Hispanics. *Social Work Research & Abstracts, 4,* 42-49.

Bloom, D., & Studying, A. M. (1979). A peer interviewer model in conducting surveys among Mexican-American youth. *Journal of Community Psychology, 7,* 129-136.

Bourgois, P. (1995). *In search of respect: Selling crack in El Barrio.* New York: Cambridge University Press.

Brisbane, F. L. (1995). Introduction. In J. Philleo, F. L. Brisbane, & L. G. Epstein (Eds.), *Cultural competence for social workers: A guide for alcohol and other drug abuse prevention professionals working with ethnic/racial communities* (pp. ix-xiv). Rockville, MD: Center on Substance Abuse Prevention.

Collins, R. L. (1992). Methodological issues in conducting substance abuse research on ethnic minority populations. *Drugs & Society, 6,* 59-77.

Davis, R. C., & Lurigio, A. J. (1996). *Fighting back: Neighborhood antidrug strategies.* Thousand Oaks, CA: Sage Publications.

Debro, J., & Conley, D. J. School and community politics: Issues, concerns, and implications when conducting research in African-American communities. In M. R. De La Rosa & J. L. R. Adrados (Eds.), *Drug abuse among minority youth: Advances in research and methodology* (pp. 258-279). Rockville, MD: National Institute of Drug Abuse.

Delgado, M. (in press, a). Cultural competence and the field of ATOD: Latinos as a case example. *Alcoholism Treatment Quarterly.*

Delgado, M. (in press, b). Interpretation of Puerto Rican elder research findings: A community forum of research respondents. *Journal of Applied Gerontology.*

Delgado, M. (in press, c). Puerto Rican elders and gerontological research: Avenues for empowerment and participation. *Activities, Adaptation & Aging.*

Delgado, M. (1996a). Community asset assessments by Latino youths. *Social Work in Education, 18,* 169-178.

Delgado, M. (1996b). Aging research and the Puerto Rican community: The use of an advisory committee of intended respondents. *The Gerontologist, 36,* 406-408.

Delgado, M. (1995). Community asset assessment and substance abuse prevention: A case study involving the Puerto Rican community. *Journal of Child & Adolescent Substance Abuse, 4,* 57-77.

Delgado, M. (1981). Using Hispanic adolescents to assess community needs. *Social Casework: The Journal of Contemporary Social Work, 62,* 607-613.

Finlinson, H. A., Robles, R. R., Colon, H. M., & Page, J. B. (1993). Recruiting and retaining out-of-treatment injecting drug users in the Puerto Rico AIDS prevention project. *Human Organization, 52,* 169-175.

Florin P., & Wandersman, A. (1992). An introduction to community participation, voluntary organizations, and community development: Insights for empowerment through research. *American Journal of Community Psychology, 18,* 41-54.

Goldstein, P. J., Spunt, B. J., Miller, T., & Bellucci, P. (1990). Ethnographic field stations. In E. Y. Lambert (Ed.), *The collection and interpretation of data from hidden populations* (NIDA Research Monograph 98, pp. 80-95). Rockville, MD: National Institute on Drug Abuse.

Hess, P. M., & Mullen, E. J. (1995). *Practitioner-researcher partnerships: Building knowledge from, in, and for practice.* Washington, DC: National Association of Social Workers.

Humm-Delgado, D., & Delgado, M. (1985). Gaining community entree to assess service needs of Hispanics. *Social Casework: The Journal of Contemporary Social Work, 67,* 80-89.

Humm-Delgado, D., & Delgado, M. (1983). Assessing Hispanic mental health needs: Issues and recommendations. *Journal of Community Psychology, 11,* 363-375.

Kerr, K. (1995). Action research as empowering practice. *Journal of Progressive Human Services, 6,* 45-58.

Koester, S. (1994). Applying ethnography to AIDS prevention among IV drug users and social policy. In J. P. Van Vught (Ed.), *AIDS prevention and services: Community based research* (pp. 35-57). Westport, CT: Bergin & Garvey.

Kretzmann, J. P., & McKnight, J. L. (1993). *Building communities from the inside out.* Evanston, IL: Center for Urban and Policy research, Northwestern University.

Lindholm, M. G., & Lopez, R. (1980). *Fundamentals of proposal writing: A guide for minority researchers.* Rockville, MD: National Institute of Mental Health, Center for Minority Group Mental Health Programs.

Marin, G., & Marin, B. V. (1991). *Research with Hispanic populations.* Newbury Park, CA: Sage Publications.

Marti-Costa, S., & Serrano-Garcia, I. (1995). Needs assessment and community development: An ideological perspective. In F. M. Cox, J. L. Erlich, J. Rothman, & J. E. Tropman (Eds.), *Strategies of community organization* (pp. 257-267). Itasca, IL: F. E. Peacock Publishers, Inc.

National Institute on Drug Abuse. (1993). *The indigenous leader outreach model: Intervention manual.* Rockville, MD: U. S. Department of Health and Human Services.

Studying, E. R., Studying, A. M., Ramirez, A., Morales, A., & Olmeda, E. L. (1990). Inhalant, marijuana, and alcohol abuse among barrio children and adolescents. *International Journal of the Addictions, 17,* 945-964.

Pentz, M. A., & Trebow, E. (1991). Implementation issues in drug abuse prevention research. In C. G. Leukefeld & W. J. Bukoski (Eds.), *Drug abuse prevention intervention research: Methodological issues* (NIDA Monograph Series 107, pp. 123-139). Rockville, MD: National Institute on Drug Abuse.

Perez, R., Studying, A. M., Ramirez, A., Ramirez, R., & Rodriguez, M. (1980). Correlates and changes over time in drug and alcohol abuse within a barrio population. *American Journal of Community Psychology, 8,* 621-636.

Pettiway, L. E. (1993). Identifying, gaining access to, and collecting data on African-American drug addicts. In M. R. De La Rosa & J. L. R. Adrados (Eds.), *Drug abuse among minority youth: Advances in research and methodology* (pp. 258-279). Rockville, MD: National Institute on Drug Abuse.

Saleebey, D. S. (Ed.), (1992). *The strengths perspective in social work practice.* New York, NY: Longman Publishing Co.

Segal, B. (1995). Prevention and culture: A theoretical perspective. In C. G. Leukefeld & R. R. Clayton (Eds.), *Prevention practice in substance abuse* (pp. 139-147). New York: The Haworth Press, Inc.

Singer, M., Gonzalez, W., Vega, E., Centeno, I., & Davison, L. (1994). Implementing a community based AIDS prevention program for ethnic minorities. In J. P. Van Vught (Ed.), *AIDS prevention and services: Community based research* (pp. 59-92). Westport, CT: Bergin & Garvey.

Soriano, F. I. (1994). The Latino perspective: A sociocultural portrait. In J. U.

Gordon (Ed.), *Managing multiculturalism in substance abuse services* (pp. 117-147). Thousand Oaks, CA: Sage Publications.

Stanfield, J. H., II. (1993a). Epistemological considerations. In J. H. Stanfield, II & R. M. Dennis (Eds.), *Race and ethnicity in research methods* (pp. 16-36). Newbury Park, CA: Sage Publications.

Stanfield, J. H., II. (1993b). Methodological reflections: An introduction. In J. H. Stanfield, II & R. M. Dennis (Eds.), *Race and ethnicity in research methods* (pp. 3-15). Newbury Park, CA: Sage Publications.

Swift, C. F. (1992). Empowerment: The Greening of prevention. In M. Kessler, S. E. Golston, & J. M. Joffe (Eds.), *The present and future of prevention* (pp. 99-109). Newbury Park, CA: Sage Publications.

Vazquez, B. (1994). St. Ann's corner of harm reduction. *Centro de Estudios Puertorriquenos, VI*, 193-204.

Wiebel, W. W. (1990). Identifying and gaining access to hidden populations. In E. Y. Lambert (Ed.), *The collection and interpretation of data from hidden populations* (pp. 4-11). NIDA Research Monograph 98. Rockville, MD: National Institute on Drug Abuse.

Williams, M. D. (1993). Urban ethnography: Another look. In J. H. Stanfield II & R. M. Dennis (Eds.), *Race and ethnicity in research methods* (pp. 135-156). Newbury Park, CA: Sage Publications.

Building Bridges: Community Involvement in Drug and HIV Research Among Minority Populations

Claire E. Sterk, PhD

SUMMARY. This paper describes community involvement in substance abuse and HIV research. The paper is based on 6 years of research among female prostitutes and drug users in two major metropolitan areas in the United States. The central focus of the paper is on the notion of community involvement and the dynamics involved in research that assume a close collaboration with communities. This is particularly important when studying hard-to-reach populations such as drug users and prostitutes. Based on the previous research, a

---

Claire E. Sterk is Associate Professor, Rollins School of Public Health, Emory University.

Address correspondence to: Claire E. Sterk, Rollins School of Public Health, Emory University, 1518 Clifton Road NE, Atlanta, GA 30322 (E-mail: csterk@sph.emory.edu).

The author is grateful to Kirk Elifson, Stephani Hatch, Lee Jenkins, Yvonne Medina, and Tanya Sharp for their assistance in the data collection and their insightful feedback concerning the manuscript.

Support for this study was provided by the National Institute on Drug Abuse (NIDA), grant number 1 R29 DA07406, R01 DA09819, Claire E. Sterk and Kirk Elifson, Co-Principle Investigators. The opinions expressed in this paper are solely those of the author and do not represent the funding institutions.

[Haworth co-indexing entry note]: "Building Bridges: Community Involvement in Drug and HIV Research Among Minority Populations." Sterk, Claire E. Co-published simultaneously in *Drugs & Society* (The Haworth Press, Inc.) Vol. 14, No. 1/2, 1999, pp. 107-121; and: *Conducting Drug Abuse Research with Minority Populations: Advances and Issues* (ed: Mario R. De La Rosa, Bernard Segal, and Richard Lopez) The Haworth Press, Inc., 1999, pp. 107-121. Single or multiple copies of this article are available for a fee from The Haworth Document Delivery Service [1-800-342-9678, 9:00 a.m. - 5:00 p.m. (EST). E-mail address: getinfo@haworthpressinc.com].

107

model of community development was developed that includes: (1) a community identification stage; (2) the establishment of a community advisory board; and (3) the inclusion of community consultants as research staff. In addition, the findings include a discussion of the main advantages and disadvantages of community involvement in research. Specific attention is paid to issues unique to research that use a qualitative methodology. *[Article copies available for a fee from The Haworth Document Delivery Service: 1-800-342-9678. E-mail address: getinfo@haworthpressinc.com]*

INTRODUCTION

Within society, the awareness of structural racism and its associated poverty as antecedents for drug abuse is increasing. The prevailing public image of drug users is that of poor, urban, minority populations (Anderson, 1990; Reinarman, 1983). The "war on drugs" has been equated with the "war on minorities." Policies regarding drug use often reflect the dominant societal views on race and class. An example of such biased policy is the Comprehensive Crime Control Act (CCCA), the amendment of which provides for a 100:1 enhancement ratio between cocaine hydrochloride (powder) and crack cocaine. While the use of the former, especially intranasal use, is more common among members of the middle class, crack cocaine use appears to be more prevalent among poor, minority, urban populations (Williams, 1992; Sterk, 1996). With the onset of crack–a cocaine derivative available in small units for a price of $5 or less–a new class of consumer became available to drug dealers who began marketing the drug in inner-city neighborhoods.

Throughout the 20th century, numerous prevention and intervention programs have been established to reduce drug use and its consequences (Musto, 1973). However, few of these initiatives have taken the impact of larger social forces such as class and race into consideration (de la Vega, 1990; Flaskerud & Nyamathi, 1989; Robles, Gonzalez, Gonzales, & Mateos, 1990; Singer, 1991; Weeks, Schensul, Williams, Singer, & Grier, 1995). Moreover, very few programs are founded on a culturally sensitive approach. With the emergence of the AIDS epidemic, the interest in culturally specific prevention interventions increased. To date, no biomedical cure to treat HIV or AIDS is available, and behavioral modifications are the main strategy to curtail the spread of the epidemic. Early HIV interventions often had limited success; in course, it became clear that the failure of these interventions, at least in part, was due to the lack of attention to culturally specific issues. For example, interventions to reduce sexual HIV risk showed that women, due to cultural norms and values, often do not propose or insist on condom use. It appeared that the main barriers to behavioral change were not lack of knowledge and motivation (Cochran, 1989; Worth, 1989).

The challenge of developing and implementing culturally sensitive research and programs is related closely to the extent to which researchers and program staff have an understanding of the target population. One way to ensure a culturally specific approach is to involve members of the target population. This notion of community involvement is not new to research in general; but it is only recently that it gained popularity among drug abuse and HIV researchers. The focus of this paper is on community involvement in research among largely African American study populations of drug users and prostitutes. The paper will describe a model of community involvement as well as several advantages and disadvantages of this involvement.

This paper results from 6 years of research in communities with a high prevalence of prostitution and/or drug use in New York City and Atlanta. Researchers employed a qualitative methodology that included participant observation, in-depth interviewing, and focus groups (for more information, see Sterk-Elifson, 1995). Numerous studies have successfully employed these methodologies among drug users (Preble & Casey, 1969; Agar, 1973; Waldorf, 1973; Rosenbaum, 1981; Stephens, 1991; Bourgeois, 1995). Participant observation involves data collection in the subjects' natural setting (Spradley, 1979; Adler, 1993; Agar, 1993). The main stages in participant observation, also referred to as ethnographic mapping, were to gain access, develop a role in the field, identify key respondents, and build trust relationships. Identification of street prostitutes is only the start of the effort; getting them to talk, trust, and share their lives is much more challenging (Sterk, 1995). The main goal of in-depth interviewing was the discovery of the subjects' perspective of their own salient issues. The open-ended structure of the interviews facilitated the development of trust between the interviewer and the subject. Typically, the interviews were not limited to prostitution or drug use, but included discussions of many of the other social roles that the subjects occupied. These roles included being someone's partner, parent, child, relative, neighbor, or colleague.

Prostitutes and drug users are "hidden" and difficult-to-reach populations. They engage in illegal activities that dispose them to be distrustful of outsiders, specifically those who may represent the criminal justice system. Their involvement in illegal activities also has caused most drug users and prostitutes to feel alienated from mainstream society. The involvement of members of the community–drug users, prostitutes, and other community members–enhances access to these hard-to-reach individuals.

The involvement of community members was vital to the research methodology. Members of the community participated in activities such as the ethnographic mapping of the neighborhoods, the recruitment of subjects, the development of the interview guide, and data analysis. Communities were defined physically–geographically defined areas/neighborhoods–as well as socially–the contacts and interactions between people. Drug abuse researchers often refer to the "community of drug users" and define the use of indigenous outreach workers as community involvement (Sterk, 1993). Community involvement, however, should not be limited to members of the target population; rather, it also should include members of the larger community. Community involvement included informing community members of on-going research activities, seeking advice and the community members' endorsement of the research, and hiring community members as project staff.

A MODEL FOR COMMUNITY INVOLVEMENT

One of the potential advantages of community involvement is that it allows researchers to familiarize themselves with the community and to increase their cultural understanding. It also fosters collaboration between researchers and members of the community as well as the collaboration among community members. In addition, such collaboration assists researchers in checking the validity of the data collection instruments and the findings. Finally, it provides a basis for the continuation of activities initiated by the project after completion of the research.

Community involvement is a process that requires mutual commitment from the researchers and the community members. Figure 1 provides an overview of the community involvement process.

Although researchers often limit their focus to members of the study population, community involvement obliges them to place their subjects in the larger social context, which presumes additional information from individuals who know and interact with the subjects.

For example, it became clear that drug using and non-using community members often differed in their perception of the impact of drugs on their community. In several communities, users expected non-using community members not to care about them. However, interviews with the latter indicated that they did care about users, and that they were willing to support research and interventions programs that seek to reduce drug use. While the motivations for support among users and non-users often differed, their ultimate goal–the reduction of drug use and its consequences–tended to be the same.

The process of community involvement familiarizes researchers with their study communities. This familiarity includes knowledge of the community's demographic composition, leadership structure, social interactions, and perceived strengths and weaknesses.

Researchers err to view drug users as a homogeneous group that consists of segments that characteristics such as drug use pattern, age, race and ethnicity, gender, and other demographic characteristics define (Tashima, Crain, O'Reilly, & Sterk, 1996). Ethnographic mapping captures the heterogeneity of the drug using population.

Part of the process of community identification also involved a basic exploration of the perceived community resources and needs. These resources included the economic infrastructure, available educational programs, and health and social services. Our research indicated that subjects often were unaware of the resources available in their community. They often did not use available resources because of structural barriers, such as hours of operation, availability of day care, and geographic location. Pre-

FIGURE 1. Model of Community Involvement

Community Identification

Members	Resources	Needs
• Leaders	Economic	Community level
• Non-drug users	Educational	Household level
• Drug users	Health/medical	Individual level
Drug Use Pattern	Social Services	
Demographics	Housing	
(age, gender, race, etc.)	Other	

Community Advisory Board

represents all segments of the community and its members assist in all stages of the research including the conceptualization and the local utilization of the findings.

Community Consultants

Community members actively involved in the research process as members of the project staff.

vious negative experiences with service providers and negative rumors about the quality of the programs also prevented subjects' use of community resources. One public housing community had a community-based health center on its grounds, but relatively few of the residents used the program. The rumor was that people often were referred for more specialized care provided at a local public hospital. Instead of using the center to receive basic health checks or to get a child immunized, most residents by-passed the center and sought preventive and primary care at the hospital. At the same time, a local interest group was exploring whether to add a drug abuse center to the existing community-based clinic; it was concluding that many residents, in fact, were supportive of transforming the clinic into a drug abuse center. But several residents perceived these plans to change the clinic's mission as a confirmation of their belief that the hospital, and not the community-based health center, would better address their health care needs.

The establishment of a community advisory board is a central feature in community involvement (see Baldwin and Delgado in this publication). Such a board ensures the continued involvement of community members in the research and should consist of a wide cross-section of community members. For our research among African American female drug users, a community board was established in several of the study communities. The community advisory board assisted with the conceptualization as well as the logistics of the research project, including sampling decisions, recruitment strategies, data collection instruments and strategies, data analysis, and the dissemination of findings.

An unanticipated outcome of the establishment of the board was that various parties, who normally did not interact, began to communicate with each other. The prior lack of communication usually resulted from a want of awareness of the other's existence or a perception that representatives of other organizations were fighting different battles. For example, staff from the youth club never had interacted with community HIV outreach workers. Another important barrier to collaboration was financial. Many of the community-based organizations perceived the others to be competitors for the same local dollars. By their involvement on the same community advisory board, they realized that they could work toward the same goal, while sharing resources. Currently, the advisory board members are preparing a proposal to receive funding from the Empowerment Zone budget.

The community consultants are most actively involved in the research, and they are the most likely to experience role strain due to conflicting demands from other project staff and community members (Sterk-Elifson,

1993, 1995). Community consultants differ from advisory board members in that the consultants receive compensation for their services. Since the onset of the AIDS epidemic, numerous research projects among drug users have employed outreach workers, who were indigenous members of the drug use community (Wiebel, 1990). Community consultants differ from outreach workers in that the role of the latter is to provide baseline education, while community consultants participate much more actively in research. Typically, the responsibilities of the community consultants include assisting with instrument development, recruitment of subjects, and data analysis. Community consultants should be excluded from actual interviewing as this breaches the confidentiality of the subjects, all of whom also form a part of the life of the community consultants outside of work.

The community consultants as well as other staff members responsible for data collection should work from an office in the community. This is particularly important as none of the other project staff reside in the community. Not only does such a storefront place the project in the community, it also allows subjects to participate in an interview or focus group in their own community. In addition, we have utilized storefronts for purposes other than data collection, including support groups for HIV positive residents, NA and AA groups, after-school activities for adolescents, and day care for young children. Frequently, these activities were coordinated by the project consultants after consultation with the advisory board. Recently, the project has expanded its activities in the community to include the development of posters with messages derived from the project and images that feature community members, and the distribution of a community newsletter with project findings and related news.

Hiring community members as consultants to the project demonstrates the researchers' intention to collaborate with the community. In our experience, several community consultants have become interested in research as a career and have returned to school. Others have found employment at local community-based organizations and drug treatment centers.

As more research projects involve members of the community, the advantages and disadvantages of such involvement will become clear. In addition, researchers will learn which aspects of the research are most appropriate for community involvement. Specifically in the case of drug abuse research, community involvement appears very appropriate for development of instruments, recruitment of subjects, interpretation of data, and dissemination of findings.

ADVANTAGES AND DISADVANTAGES
OF COMMUNITY INVOLVEMENT

Advantages. Among the main advantages of community involvement is the increased likelihood that the research project will be culturally sensitive, and that it will be supported by the community members, which in the case of drug abuse research includes the users as well as their larger social networks. The alienation from and the distrust of society among community residents is mirrored in their distrust of research projects. Such distrust is further amplified if the topic of the research involves drug use, which frequently is conducted by researchers whose racial or ethnic background differs from the target population (Debro & Conley, 1993). The users themselves resist involvement in the research for the fear someone will identify them as a drug user, which in turn may lead to arrest or mandated drug treatment where they may face experimental therapies. Other community residents may resist drug abuse research since it draws attention to the negative aspects of their community. If researchers present the study plans to the community, the community members may raise questions and provide suggestions. Researchers, on the other hand, fear that the disclosure of the research design may create options for the community members to slow or sabotage the research. Real collaboration requires that researchers not only explain the scientific value of the drug abuse research, but also present its possible benefits to the community. For example, in a recent research project in Atlanta among African American women who use drugs, the research team was unable to provide direct resources to the community. However, the project staff was able to assist the communities to seek funds for a treatment center for women, including pregnant women and women with children.

Frequently, researchers will have identified the major questions of their research prior to contacting community members. For this reason, community involvement is more likely to occur during the implementation stage than in the developmental stage of the project. This involvement may include assistance with: (1) the development of the data collection instruments, including culturally appropriate data collection instruments; (2) the sampling frame, including actual recruitment; and (3) the data analysis.

Most measures and scales used in drug abuse research have been developed for Caucasians and, often in the case of drug users, males. Such measures, however, may not be appropriate for women and non-white populations. While drug abuse researchers have developed measurements for minority populations, the extent to which such measures apply to African American drug users is limited. Community involvement will motivate researchers to include effective measures and to use culturally appropriate language.

Despite the fact that researchers may have developed a sophisticated sampling frame, they may have to modify their procedures if recruitment efforts fail. While community members generally cannot keep researchers out of their community, they do have the option to decide if they want to enroll in a study. Community endorsement of the study is likely to facilitate recruitment efforts. Such efforts improve even further when community members participate actively in the recruitment process. Community members may participate in recruitment either as freelance referral specialists who are paid for subject recruitment or as regular project staff members. Community assistance with the recruitment process also increases the potential to identify less visible drug users. During the study in Atlanta described earlier of African American female drug users, the drug users whom the project first recruited tended to be women who used drugs in relatively public settings, such as the street, shooting galleries, and crack houses. With the assistance of community members, the researchers were able to enroll women who used drugs in more hidden settings, such as their own apartments.

Community involvement also may improve the data analysis process and increase the validity of the data. An effective strategy for community involvement in the data analysis process is through focus groups. These groups may verify the researchers' interpretation of the data. Community feedback through focus groups provides researchers with an additional level of reality construction. Focus groups allow participants to discuss their interpretations with each other, thereby stimulating discussions among the participating community members. The research project among the female drug users used three focus groups, one with community members only, one with project staff only, and another that combined community members and project staff. The mixed group greatly enhanced the internal validity of the interpretation of the findings.

Overall, the main advantages of community involvement to the researchers are the inclusion of culturally appropriate questions, a sampling design that is more reflective of the community, and findings that take the community context into consideration. From the community members' point of view, their involvement may yield personal opportunities such as training and job opportunities for some of the members. In addition, the community's involvement may empower members of the community to reflect on the community's strengths and needs.

Disadvantages. Community involvement can be disadvantageous. Researchers may pose scientifically sound questions that would yield potentially significant findings to the field of drug abuse; however, those questions may be of less interest to the community or to segments of the community. The community may seek short-term outcomes that provide additional community resources, while researchers typically operate in an environment founded on long-term outcomes that may not generate direct benefits to the study community. In the Atlanta study, researchers explained that the study would not yield immediate results. While many of the users were grateful to share their story in a non-judgmental, non-threatening environment, many of the non-using residents complained that researchers lacked commitment to take immediate action.

In addition, community involvement places the researchers in a position in which they have to consider local power dynamics and political battles. In addition to the scientific agenda, they must be cognizant of local issues. It is impossible for community involvement to include all community members; rather, "community involvement" tends to refer to the participation of a select number of community members. Researchers face the question of how to select community members who represent the various segments in the community. In our experience, researchers have needed to negotiate with neighborhood and tenant associations, churches, non-profit organizations, schools, neighborhood planning units, and local politicians. Many leaders in the community had negative perceptions of drug users, while others stressed that drug use would not exist if the local government had stopped drugs from entering the community. Several church leaders referred to drugs in African American communities as genocide, and they supported Jesse Jackson's slogan, "Up with hope; down with dope." Other religious leaders were Black Muslims who were more likely to place personal responsibility on the shoulders of individual drug users and who disapproved of drug use for moral reasons. To seek community endorsement of the study, it is important that researchers contact all local bases. These various community leaders each tend to be familiar with specific segments of the population. Acquiring insight into the community dynamics requires an additional investment from the researchers and may inadvertently jeopardize the project or require modification.

This paper earlier described community involvement as advantageous to the development of an appropriate sampling frame and the recruitment of subjects. At the same time, however, community involvement may compromise the sampling frame. Drug abuse studies that involve outreach workers, such as indigenous members familiar with drug use, have shown that these workers are trusted by and can provide access to drug users. However, outreach workers typically represent a narrow segment of the drug using community (Sterk-Elifson, 1993). For instance, former injection drug users are ideal for studies among injection drug users but are less likely to connect with crack cocaine users.

Furthermore, while community members have the capacity to assist researchers in their recruitment efforts, the referrals made may be biased if individuals only refer those persons with whom they routinely interact. The potential for such bias increases if subjects receive an incentive for their participation. The inclusion of community consultants and outreach workers who represented multiple networks minimized this problem, although a certain level of bias still is likely to have occurred.

Community involvement may lead to less objective data analyses and more subjective interpretations. Findings that challenge community perceptions and which are viewed as negative to the community may be difficult for community members to accept. Community involvement in the data analysis also requires that the researchers develop specific strategies to ensure the confidentiality of the data. The need for such confidentiality also hinders the involvement of community members in the data collection process. The questions asked in drug abuse research often are personal and address topics such as family circumstances, involvement in criminal activities, arrest history, drug use, and drug treatment experiences. It would not be appropriate for one community member to seek such information of a fellow member and it, most likely, would compromise the validity of the data.

COMMUNITY INVOLVEMENT AND STUDY DESIGN

Carefully planned community involvement will yield great benefits for the researchers. In epidemiological and survey studies, including longitudinal and case-control studies and clinical trials, the researchers can gain from community involvement. Community representatives can provide assistance with instrument development and recruitment and provide feedback to the initial findings of the study. Such involvement ensures culturally sensitive research, allowing the findings to be placed in the community context. Community involvement becomes more advantageous to researchers, as the research design becomes more complex. In a case control study, for example, community members should understand the constraints on the sampling process and that the study's sampling design limits study enrollment.

Community involvement is more amenable to qualitative than to quantitative studies. However, qualitative researchers need to be conscious of the often tenuous position of most community members involved in the research. On the one hand, community members were selected because of their role in and knowledge of the community, while on the other hand, they are expected to take an objective stand as project staff. Researchers should be aware of the potential for role strain.

Several years ago, a major Atlanta theater group performed a play about the Tuskegee project, a public health research study in which African American men with syphilis did not receive penicillin so researchers could study the natural history of this sexually transmitted disease (Dalton, 1989; Thomas & Quinn, 1991). A female African American nurse was the only non-white person on the project staff, and she was accused of betraying her community. Outreach workers and community representatives may face similar attitudes.

CONCLUDING REMARKS

As most drug users appear to be poor and members of minority populations and as most researchers have a higher socio-economic status and do not share the racial/ethnic background of their subjects, the need for community involvement is becoming increasingly clear. Such involvement ensures that drug abuse research is appropriate for the community in which it takes place and that all stages of the research process are culturally appropriate.

The historical background of African Americans differs from that of other racial/ethnic groups in the United States and includes oppression that stretches back to the days of slavery. Racism and economic exploitation continued after slavery ended (Staples, 1973, 1978; Hooks, 1981). These larger societal factors are likely to account for the relatively high prevalence of drug use among African Americans and researchers should be aware of this historical context. The history of African Americans in the United States warrants their distrust of researchers, and researchers must demonstrate the integrity of their proposed research.

The awareness of the need for culturally specific research has increased among drug abuse researchers, and community involvement is becoming more common. Differences of opinion may result when researchers focus on scientific merit, and community members, on needed resources. Researchers, while seeking to maintain the validity of the data, face questions about when to compromise their research design, and whom to pay for what activities. While most researchers provide short-term direct incentives by paying subjects, they may want to consider long-term incentives to the community as a whole. Long-term incentives may include assistance in seeking additional funds, fostering collaboration among community organizations, and providing services such as information sessions on drug use, HIV, health in general, and available social and medical services. Ideally, community involvement and the corollary community ownership will foster community empowerment and allow communities to continue and establish activities after the researchers complete their project. The proposed model of community involvement has application beyond the fields of substance abuse and HIV. Just as the community advisory board brought the various community leaders and representatives into contact with each other, the model also has the potential to foster collaboration among researchers and program staff from a wide variety of fields.

REFERENCES

Adler, P. (1993). Ethnography and epidemiology: Building bridges. In *Proceedings of the community epidemiology working group*, December 1992 (pp. 531-543). Rockville, MD: National Institute on Drug Abuse.

Adler, P., & Adler, P. (1986). *Membership roles in field research*. Beverly Hills, CA: Sage.

Agar, M. (1973). *Ripping and running: A formal ethnography of urban heroin users*. Lexington, MA: Lexington Books.

Agar, M. (1993). Ethnography: An Aerial View. In *Proceedings of the community epidemiology working group*, December 1992 (pp. 520-530) Rockville, MD: National Institute on Drug Abuse.

Anderson, E. (1990). *Streetwise: Race, class, and change in an urban community.* Chicago, IL: University of Chicago Press.

Bale, R., van Stone, W., Engelsing, E., & Zarcone, V. (1981). The validity of self-reported heroin use. *International Journal of the Addictions, 17,* 1387-1398.

Bourgois, P. (1995). *In search of respect: Selling crack in el barrio.* New York: Cambridge University Press.

Cochran, S. (1989). Women and HIV infection. In V. Mays, G. Albee, & S. Schneider (Eds.), *Primary prevention of AIDS.* Newbury Park, CA: Sage.

Collins, P. (1990). *Black feminist thought: Knowledge, consciousness, and the politics of empowerment.* New York: Routledge.

Collins, R. (1992). Methodological issues in conducting substance abuse research on ethnic minority populations. *Drugs & Society, 6,* 59-77.

Dalton, H. (1989). AIDS in black face. *Daedalus, Proceedings of the American Academy of Arts and Sciences, 118,* 231-235.

Debro, J., & Conley, D. (1993). School and community politics: Issues, concerns, and implications when conducting research in African American communities. In M. R. De La Rosa & J. Adrados (Eds.), *Drug abuse among minority youth: Advances in research and methodology* (pp. 258-279). Rockville, MD: National Institute on Drug Abuse.

De la Vega, E. (1990). Considerations for reaching the Latino population with sexuality and HIV/AIDS information and education. *SIECUS Report, 18,* 1-8.

Flaskerud, J., & Nyamathi, A. (1989). Black and Latina women's AIDS related knowledge, attitudes, and practices. *Research in Nursing and Health, 12,* 339-346.

Forsyth, B., Lessler, J., & Hubbard, M. (1992). Cognitive evaluation of the questionnaire. In C. Turner, J. Lessler, & J. Gfroerer (Eds.), *Survey measurement of drug use: Methodological studies* (pp. 13-52). Rockville, MD: National Institute on Drug Abuse.

Goldstein, P. (1979). *Prostitution and drugs.* Lexington, MA: Lexington Books.

Health and Human Services, National Institutes of Health, SAMSHA/NIDA. (1996). *National household survey on drug abuse: 1995.* Rockville, MD: National Institute on Drug Abuse.

Hooks, B. (1981). *Ain't I a woman: Black women and feminism.* Boston: South End Press.

Johnston, B., O'Malley, & Bachman. (1994). *National survey results on drug use from the monitoring the future study, 1975-1993, volume 1 secondary school students.* Rockville, MD: U.S. Department of Health and Human Services.

Klein, D. (1983). Ill and against the law. *Journal of Drug Issues, 13,* 31-55.

Mensch, B., & Kandel, D. (1988). Underreporting of substance use in a national longitudinal youth cohort. *Public Opinion Quarterly, 52,* 100-124.

Musto, D. (1973). *The American disease: Origins of narcotic control.* New York: Yale University Press.

Preble, E., & Casey, J. (1969). Taking care of business: The heroin user's life on the street. *The International Journal of the Addictions, 4,* 1-24.

Reinarman, C. (1983). Constraint, autonomy, and state policy: notes toward a theory of controls of consciousness alternation. *Journal of Drug Issues, 13,* 9-30.

Robles, R., Gonzalez, M., Gonzales, A., & Mateos, T. (1990). Social relations and empowerment of sexual partners of IDUs. *Puerto Rico Health Sciences Journal, 9,* 99-104.

Singer, M. (1991). Confronting the AIDS epidemic among IDUs: Does ethnic culture matter? *AIDS Education and Prevention, 3,* 258-283.

Spradley, J. (1979). *Participant observation.* New York: Rinehart & Winston.

Staples, R. (1973). *The black women in America: Sex, marriage, and the family.* Chicago: Nelson Hall.

Staples, R. (1978). The myth of black sexual superiority: A reexamination. *The Black Scholar, 9,* 16-22.

Stephens, R. (1991). *The Street Addict Role.* Albany, NY: State University of New York Press.

Sterk, C. (1996). Fieldwork among prostitutes and drug users during the AIDS era. In C. Smith & W. Kornblum (Eds.), *In the field: Readings on the field research experience* (2nd ed.). New York: Praeger Publishers.

Sterk-Elifson, C. (1993). Outreach among drug users: Ethnography and health education. *Human Organization, 52,* 162-168.

Sterk-Elifson, C. (1995). Drug use patterns among women: The value of qualitative research. In E. Lambert, R. Ashbery, & R. Needle (Eds.), *Using qualitative research in drug and HIV/AIDS research* (NIDA Monograph 157, pp. 65-83). Washington, DC: Government Printing Office.

Tashima, N., Crain, C., O'Reilly, K., & Sterk, C. (1996). The community identification process: A discovery model. *Qualitative Health Research, 2*, 31-45.

Thomas, S., & Quinn, S. (1991). The Tuskegee syphilis study, 1932 to 1972. *American Journal of Public Health, 81*:1498-1505.

Waldorf, D. (1973). *Careers in dope*. Englewood Cliffs, NJ: Prentice Hall.

Waldorf, D., Reinarman, C., & Murphy, S. (1991). *Cocaine changes: The experience of using and quitting*. Philadelphia: Temple University Press.

Weeks, M., Schensul, J., Williams, S., Singer, M., & Grier, M. (1995). AIDS prevention for African-American and Latina women. *AIDS education and prevention, 7*, 251-263.

Wiebel, W. (1990). Identifying and gaining access to hidden populations. In E. Lambert & W. Wiebel (Eds.), *The collection and interpretation of data from hidden populations* (pp. 4-11). Rockville, MD: National Institute Drug Abuse.

Williams, T. (1989). *The cocaine kids*. Reading: Addison Wesley.

Worth, D. (1989). Women at high risk of HIV infection. In D. Ostrow (Ed.) *Behavioral aspects of AIDS*. New York: Plenum.

PART II

ACCESS, RECRUITMENT, AND RETENTION: ADVANCES AND ISSUES

This section focuses on barriers and strategies which may affect researchers' ability to gain access to, recruit, and retain minority persons from the various ethnic/racial groups in drug abuse studies. One significant barrier is the impact of the new informed consent regulations on researchers' efforts to recruit minority persons into drug abuse studies. A second barrier the section treats is the failure by researchers to incorporate into their research designs study samples which will reflect the significant cultural differences that exist within specific ethnic minority groups. Strategies discussed in this section include the appropriate use of advisory boards, indigenous workers, incentives, go-betweens, newsletters, and focus groups in different minority populations. Underlying the discussion on strategies is the need for researchers to treat their study subjects and the communities where they conduct their studies with respect and as equals. Included in this section are papers by Dunlap and Johnson; Nemoto, Huang, and Aoki; Beauvais; Krohn and Thornberry; and Valdez and Kaplan.

Dunlap and Johnson provide a detailed account of how to gain access to and recruit African-American crack dealers and their significant others to become subjects in a research study. The authors discuss the importance of incentives, go-betweens, and respect if researchers are to gain access to African-American crack dealers.

Nemoto, Huang, and Aoki address the importance of cultural values to developing rapport with the various Asian/Pacific Islanders' populations when conducting drug abuse studies in these communities. Nemoto et al. consider how cultural values affect researchers' decisions to use incentives, methods to obtain informed consent agreements from study subjects, the hiring and training of staff, and the development of collaborative relationships between the researchers and communities.

125

Beauvais notes the negative impact that the new federal regulations on active consent have had on efforts to recruit American Indian subjects. He also discusses strategies to involve parents, school officials, and people in the community, such as tribal councils, to recruit American Indian subjects in drug abuse studies.

Krohn and Thornberry focus on strategies associated with the retention of African-American and Puerto Rican youth in drug abuse studies. They explain the effectiveness of newsletters, mail, and other tracking procedures to retain youth in drug abuse research.

Valdez and Kaplan examine the use of gatekeepers to gain access to and recruit male and female Mexican-American gang members as subjects in focus groups in drug abuse research studies. The authors suggest that such focus groups include a wide range of individuals such as active and former gang members, relatives of gang members, community leaders, and community agency contacts.

Gaining Access to Hidden Populations: Strategies for Gaining Cooperation of Drug Sellers/Dealers and Their Families in Ethnographic Research

Eloise Dunlap, PhD
Bruce D. Johnson, PhD

Eloise Dunlap is Project Director, Institute for Special Populations Research, National Development and Research Institutes. Dr. Dunlap is currently Principal Investigator of an ethnographic study that examines violence in drug abusing households. Bruce D. Johnson is Director, Institute for Special Populations Research, NDRI. Dr. Johnson is researching an ethnography of crack distributors/abusers, drug abuse patterns among arrestees and criminals, estimation of hard drug users and operatives, and an analysis of new drug detection technologies.

Address correspondence to: Eloise Dunlap, PhD, 2 World Trade Center, 16th Floor, New York, NY 10048.

The authors wish to acknowledge the many contributions of Ali Manwar, Harry Sanabria, Ansley Hamid, Charles Small, Doris Randolph, Douglas Goldsmith, Terry Furst, Phyllis Curry, and Deborah Murray to this research.

Research for this paper was supported by the National Institute on Drug Abuse (NIDA) (1R01DA05126-08; 1R01DA09056-03) and NIAAA/NIDA Minority Research Supplemental Award, NIDA (1R03DA06413-01). Points of view in this paper are those of the authors, and do not necessarily represent the official position of NIDA, NIAAA, or the National Development and Research Institutes (formerly Narcotic and Drug Research, Inc.).

[Haworth co-indexing entry note]: "Gaining Access to Hidden Populations: Strategies for Gaining Cooperation of Drug Sellers/Dealers and Their Families in Ethnographic Research." Dunlap, Eloise, and Bruce D. Johnson. Co-published simultaneously in *Drugs & Society* (The Haworth Press, Inc.) Vol. 14, No. 1/2, 1999, pp. 127-149; and: *Conducting Drug Abuse Research with Minority Populations: Advances and Issues* (ed: Mario R. De La Rosa, Bernard Segal, and Richard Lopez) The Haworth Press, Inc., 1999, pp. 127-149. Single or multiple copies of this article are available for a fee from The Haworth Document Delivery Service [1-800-342-9678, 9:00 a.m. - 5:00 p.m. (EST). E-mail address: getinfo@haworthpressinc.com].

127

SUMMARY. This article examines strategies for gaining the cooperation of drug sellers and their families in order to conduct ethnographic research. The strategies were developed during an eight year study of drug dealers in New York City. A key element in gaining the ability to talk with and observe drug dealers and their family members was the availability of funds to compensate respondents for interviews and other expenses associated with building and maintaining rapport. Access to more successful crack sellers and dealers rested upon the right contacts. The "right contact" is a critical element.

Locating a trusted "go-between" was adapted from strategies employed by cocaine sellers to arrange transactions involving large quantities of drugs. Such transactions rely upon a trusted associate of a dealer, the "go-between," who performs various roles and assumes risks the dealer wishes to avoid. The role of the go-between became important when ethnographers attempted to reach drug dealers for research purposes.

Favors and trust are central components in the *equation* of access to the dealer and his family. Favors are a part of drug dealers' interaction patterns: everyone owes someone else a favor. Such reciprocity norms exist independently of the amount of drugs involved and outlast any particular transaction. Reputations and favors are related. This framework of favors, trust, and reciprocity provides a basis for the ethnographer to gain an introduction to dealers and sellers. The "go-between" is critical because he/she explains the ethnographer's role to the dealer and helps arrange an initial meeting between the ethnographer and the seller. Once the go-between has provided an initial introduction, the ethnographer marshals the communication skills necessary to convince the dealer to allow further contact and conversations.

This article examines the ritual of initial conversation within its cultural framework. Developing rapport requires showing respect and honesty. Since drug dealers' self-esteem and prestige is generally tied to their drug dealing activities, signs of respect are critical in obtaining repeated appointments and conversations. Issues such as levels of rejection and how to use apparent refusal to the ethnographer's advantage are discussed. Gaining access was broken into two components. One involved permission to engage dealers in in-depth interviews The next involved obtaining permission to directly observe the actual activities of selling. Both of these components were important elements in gaining access and permission to conduct research. Building and maintaining trust and rapport were related to issues of confidentiality and anonymity.

Ill-fated ethnographic strategies, such as relying on street drug users for introductions, were important stepping stones to those strategies that did work. Such strategies revealed the level of interaction between dealer and user. They helped to uncover drug subculture behavior patterns and conduct norms and to tease out the relationship between the dealer and user. Such strategies also revealed hierarchical arrangements and the loyalty within such levels. Those near the top of dealer hierarchies generally are reluctant to introduce their boss (those above them in rank) because of fear of reprisals, a sense of responsibility to the individual boss, or/and a sense of loyalty to the organization. The strategies laid out were experienced in New York and may be adjusted to acquire access to hidden populations in other situations. *[Article copies available for a fee from The Haworth Document Delivery Service: 1-800-342-9678. E-mail address: getinfo@haworthpressinc.com]*

INTRODUCTION

Conducting ethnographic research in inner-cities presents difficulties rarely encountered elsewhere. Gaining access and conducting research in most modern institutions is relatively easy; few dangers to the ethnographer are present, and facilitators are usually easily found. Research among drug sellers/users in inner-cities, however, presents impediments rarely encountered with other study populations. Attempting to walk into a drug-dealing area to do research without proper preparation or introduction could be very dangerous for the ethnographer.[1]

Crack sellers, and especially cocaine dealers (those buying at or near the kilogram level–Johnson, Hamid, & Sanabria, 1991), have numerous reasons for concealing their identity from all but a few of their most trusted associates, denying any involvement in illegal sales of cocaine or crack, and being deeply suspicious of virtually anyone and everyone who may wish to meet them. Remaining "hidden" or "anonymous" to outsiders and "hiding" most of their behaviors from family, friends, and associates are standard operating procedures for most crack sellers and dealers. Any ethnographer or researcher who wishes to study the behaviors and lifestyles of crack sellers/dealers confronts enormous problems in gaining access to key persons immersed in crack/drug selling.

This article discusses the more successful strategies developed during two major ethnographic studies designed to study this elusive and hidden population of crack and cocaine sellers/dealers and households. The main focus is upon the various strategies staff employ when attempting to gain the cooperation of crack sellers/dealers and their families at different levels. Topics covered are: (1) role of incentives, (2) the critical importance of the right "go-between," (3) favors and trust as a central expectation among drug sellers, (4) conveying the ethnographer role via a "go-between," (5) ritual of initial conversation, (6) cultural aspect of developing rapport, (7) research access after the initial conversation; (8) building and maintaining trust and rapport; (9) importance of confidentiality and study purpose in gaining initial access, and (10) ethnographic strategies that did not work well. Over the years, the strategies outlined here have been the most effective in gaining access to inner-city drug sellers and dealers as well as their families. Strategies which did not work well are also provided.

Virtually every text book on qualitative research methods devotes extensive discussion to gaining access to and the cooperation of potential research subjects (see Hughes, 1971; Harris, 1974; Barrett, 1984; Werner & Schoepfle, 1987; Fetterman, 1989). This research builds on that strong tradition. However, few studies delineate the strategies that did not work and why. This paper includes such a discussion to enhance knowledge of gaining access to hidden populations. The strategies that work for staff will be discussed first. This discussion will be followed by a discussion of special problems that can arise and strategies that do not work.

METHODOLOGY

This article compiles experience from two large-scale ethnographic studies.[2] All strategies were used primarily among inner-city minority communities where crack selling became a major career activity (Manwar, Dunlap, & Johnson 1994; Johnson, Williams, Dei, & Sanabria, 1990). Although heroin distributors and marijuana sellers were included, crack/cocaine distributors and users were the focus of these two studies. Their activities were observed and information recorded in field notes. Over 296 crack distributors and 20 households were carefully selected as key informant-subjects, gave informed consent, and participated in in-depth interviews. The "Crack Distribution/Abuse" sample consisted of 63% males and 37% females. African-Americans at 78% were the sample's majority, Hispanic were 16%, and whites, 6%. The "Household Violence" sample consisted of over 54 family members from 20 families. Subjects for both studies were recruited from Harlem, Brooklyn, and the Bronx.

ROLE OF INCENTIVES

A key element and resource available in both research projects is the availability of funds to pay respondents for interviews and other expenses associated with building and maintaining rapport (e.g., food, meals, etc.). Stipends signal subjects that they are perceived to be equals,[3] and the information they provide is important. Stipends and the ethnographers' ability to buy food for families are particularly important for developing rapport with families. Many times, subjects called the ethnographer and asked for food for the family. In such cases, the ethnographer was able to see more of family life. Food also facilitated the ethnographer's access to children of all ages in the family. The children and other family members began to see the ethnographer as a friend and someone who genuinely cared about what happened to the family, especially during times of crisis, such as shortages of food.

Additionally, the ethnographer provided children with coats to wear in the winter; their parents did not have the money to buy such clothing for school. Since the parents are often involved in drug consumption, money received by the parents is not usually used for family necessities. In most cases, money earned by drug selling is spent to purchase drugs; in other cases, individuals are paid in drugs and do not receive money. In all instances, most of the money acquired by parents is not used for household essentials. The minimal funds received from welfare and low-paying employment do not cover the monthly necessities. In many instances, parents' frustration with their inability to provide the bare necessities of family life encourages spending the limited amounts on drugs.

In all instances, field expense money and payments for interviews are critical in the development of rapport: In many poor inner-city communities, friendships are based upon a balance of trust (see Stack, 1974). Friendship is very important; sharing what one has enables these families to exist when monies are insufficient to cover expenses. Friendship helps to fill gaps in income; friends help when something is needed. If the subject is giving information and has opened his/her family life to the ethnographer, there is an expectation that something should be given in return. When an ethnographer develops rapport with individuals as well as families, even when the friendship is in the early stages, some subjects begin to rely quickly upon the ethnographer, expecting advice. Thus the buying of food, purchasing needed articles, attending funerals, and buying flowers for funerals, weddings, and birthdays are important ways to grow more intimate with family members and individual subjects, and to learn more about family life than one ordinarily would discover.

The availability of monetary incentives is very important to all drug sellers. Such funds are critical for creating the "possibility" of approaching high level dealers; but such payments are rarely the only consideration or the most important reason that dealers choose to cooperate.

THE CRITICAL IMPORTANCE OF THE RIGHT "GO-BETWEEN"

Project staff quickly learned that research access to the more successful crack sellers and dealers is effectively closed without the "right" contacts. In fact, successful dealers always limit their contact with "outsiders." The following strategies for gaining research access to crack sellers and dealers are adapted from parallel strategies employed by cocaine sellers to arrange specific transactions–especially those involving more than a thousand dollars (in money or drugs). Most such transactions began with a potential buyer locating a "go-between" who is a trusted associate of a dealer who could supply large quantities of cocaine.

Drug sellers rely heavily on go-betweens to perform a variety of roles and assume risks that the dealer wishes to avoid. Upper-level dealers typically use a variety of persons in various go-between roles. Many dealers hire individuals to perform roles that buffer the seller from the risks of selling. For example, a lieutenant transports and is responsible for drugs and money between the dealer and his sellers. Drug dealers intentionally interact with limited numbers of very trusted people. Dealers' interactions are limited to those known personally and to their workers who are expected to conceal the seller's true identity from outsiders. Ethnographers may imitate such tactics by seeking a go-between to initially approach drug sellers. The role of go-between is extremely important when attempting to reach drug dealers for research purposes. But the specific person must be carefully chosen and advised or trained by the ethnographer. To contact, meet, build rapport with, and interview a dealer, ethnographers need to be "properly introduced" by a "trusted associate" who functions as a go between (Dunlap et al., 1990; Williams et al., 1992). A "trusted associate" is personally known by and has good relations with the potential subject, who is a seller or dealer. Acquaintances such as former school mates, former jail/prison inmates, former sellers, and so on, may be excellent persons to fulfill the role of go-between. Former drug dealing associates and former prison inmates often have good contacts and know many drug dealers. Other people in the drug business, including many drug dealers, know their "reputations." Cross-cutting and outside the drug business are various family members, kin, and old school mates. Such persons may have higher credibility and may be trusted by the dealer to some degree. Several important nuances are involved in finding a trusted associate and having him/her function as a go-between.

FAVORS AND TRUST AS A CENTRAL EXPECTATION AMONG DRUG SELLERS

Because dealers often rely on go-betweens, "favors" are a normal part of their interaction patterns. A key feature of the drug business and an expectation among all in seller roles is that everyone owed someone else a favor. Strong norms of reciprocity exist. People could not survive in sales roles if they did not reciprocate. In the past, Dealer A may have introduced Dealer B to a good supplier, so B now owes a favor to Dealer A. Most dealers owe favors to other dealers and suppliers based upon numerous contacts from many previous transactions. Sellers also owe favors to those who have brought steady customers and/or those who purchase large amounts. Such favors between two persons exist independently of the amounts of drugs or dollars involved in–and long after–the specific transactions are completed.

Persons with several prior years of selling acquire good street "reputations" among a wide network of dealing acquaintances–because they reliably give and receive favors–as the basis for a degree of "trust" that is always relative in the drug business. While nobody is trusted entirely, high-level (kilogram) dealers typically have only a few persons who are trusted in their judgment of other persons and about whom to sell cocaine. A key element among this network of crack sellers and dealers is a recommendation from another trusted associate that a new person is "OK and not a cop," and "will not harm your business" (as would a competitor). The following fieldnotes demonstrate the importance of trust, and how low level sellers like Isabella often "mess up."

Isabella talked about problems with her dealer. She tried to make some extra money by "tapping" the vials of crack, that is, taking a little crack from each vial and making other vials; thus, she had more to sell and could make more money. Her friend was to do the tapping, but her friend smoked the crack, put plaster in the vials, and gave them to Isabella to sell. Customers complained to Isabella's dealer; he checked Isabella's crack and found it was plaster. He was very angry, fired her, and she owed him a large sum of money. She has paid her debt down to $40.

She feels very bad about getting caught; her reputation for trust and dependability has been crushed. This dealer will not let her sell for him anymore because he does not trust her. Among dealers, trust is very important; a person's reputation is like money in a bank. Other dealers quickly learned of Isabella's actions and would not trust her to sell after she lost credibility with her regular dealer. She says it will take her a long time to build back the trust. She cannot blame the dealer for not trusting her; it was her fault for trusting her friend. Isabella's regret over the situation was intense. She repeatedly stated that it would take her a long time to build trust back up but that she would do it. She claimed to be basically a trustworthy person, who does not "mess with nobody's drugs or money."

This framework of favors, trust, and the lack of trust among dealers provides the basis for the ethnographer to gain a proper introduction to dealers. But if not handled properly, finding the right person to function in the role of a go-between is fraught with difficulties. Generally, drug users and persons performing low-level distribution roles use many ways to make money and claim to "know" many sellers–and they do. But such persons often conceal the fact that sellers do not trust them. On the other hand, many persons with "good street reputations" among sellers and dealers are effectively bound by the street rules not to be specific about the dealers they know and who may trust them. The proof of their good reputation could only be established when they arranged a meeting with one or more dealers.

In the world view of crack dealers, every person, until proven otherwise, is assumed to be a cop, an undercover agent, or a potential customer. Crack dealers also have a category for neighbors, persons "seen around" who are neither cops nor customers. But their emic systems have no categories for a researcher. AIDS outreach programs and projects have created street roles that are seen as "siding with" the user and not intending any harm (Williams et al., 1992). But a variety of other roles exist on the street and in the networks of drug distributors, including "high-level dealers" who buy and sell in kilos and distribute eighths, dealers who prepare crack to be sold, street crack sellers, free-lance sellers, employer sellers, lookouts, steerers, and touts (Johnson, Hamid, & Sanabria, 1991; Johnson et al., 1990).

CONVEYING THE ETHNOGRAPHER'S ROLE VIA A GO-BETWEEN

The role of the go-between is a central one in the drug distribution culture. A go-between is expected to assure (and promise) everyone that a new person he introduces is not law enforcement/cop, not a rival who wishes to harm the dealer, and is to negotiate practical "arrangements" for the meeting. All parties expect the go-between to be paid in money or drugs and usually by the person being "introduced" for an audience with the seller.

In adopting such strategies, ethnographers carefully enlisted the potential go-between and persuaded him/her about the importance and reason for making an introduction to a dealer. Often the ethnographer wished to have a complete informed consent discussion with the go-between and answer any questions he/she may raise. The ethnographer effectively attempted to co-opt the person to present the ethnographer's point of view to the seller; but always making sure that it was understood the ethnographer needed to speak for himself face-to-face with the seller/dealer. The go-between rarely revealed the precise identity of the drug dealer or his locale of activity to the ethnographer before the initial meeting. In many cases, however, he would provide information about the ethnographer to the dealer who would eventually agree to a meeting.

The go-between is effective in contacting a potential dealer-subject, providing assurances of personal and business safety, and "encouraging" or "selling" the idea of meeting the ethnographer. With the dealer's assent, the go-between then arranges details of when and where to introduce the ethnographer to the dealer. In the event that an agreement is made, the go-between sets up a time and place that is convenient for the dealer and makes sure that the dealer and ethnographer appear. Generally, the go-between arranges meetings in some public place such as a restaurant, bar, or a club, but which has a private space (a back room, remote booth, or table) where conversation can be undisturbed and out-of-listening range by others. Most times it took several tries before the dealer actually met the ethnographer. A frequent practice is for the go-between to make several appointments before the dealer actually reveals him/herself to the ethnographer. In some instances the dealer may actually be at the meeting place observing and screening the ethnographer before actually deciding whether to meet him.

A "proper introduction" therefore is critical in the drug business. An introduction to a dealer must come from another person of approximately similar rank among former associates, or trusted persons in the dealer's life. "Proper" introductions do not generally come from a lower-status person in the business, even though that person may have worked for the dealer.

The ritual of introduction contains several vital elements. Prior to arranging the first meeting, the go-between convinces the dealer that the ethnographer is "okay," not law enforcement, and not going to harm the dealer. The go-between generally can make no promises that the dealer will cooperate with the ethnographer. An introduction only provides the ethnographer with an opportunity to physically see, meet, speak to, and be heard by the dealer for a few minutes. The ethnographer must use his/her communication skills to convince the dealer to allow further contact and conversations.

RITUAL OF INITIAL CONVERSATION

Usually the go-between participates in the initial conversation. He/she cannot simply introduce the potential respondent/dealer to the ethnographer and leave. Such behavior is grounds for uncertainty, both to the ethnographer as well as the potential respondent. Although the go-between may occasionally participate in the conversation, the focus for the ethnographer is the respondent's replies and questions. Generally, after the potential dealer-subject meets, converses, and feels comfortable with the ethnographer, the go-between likely will not attend future meetings.

Ethnographers have specific outcomes in mind that start with the initial conversation. The overall objective is to develop rapport and trust so that the dealer will eventually open up his/her private world, dealing activities, and family life to the ethnographer. An important first step is to take the mystery out of the ethnographer's role. This involves a discussion about ethnography. Generally, a conversation about oneself helps to ease the respondent's apprehensions and separate the ethnographer from law enforcement.

What Fine (1993) described as the kindly, friendly, and honest ethnographer is a good stance to adopt. Presenting oneself as someone who can be trusted with vital and damaging information is helpful. Staff usually display such virtues as openness and honesty. One important criterion is that the ethnographer should never enter the field with preconceived ideas about any specific behaviors a dealer may practice (e.g., violence) besides the focal activity of interest (e.g., dealing). Since drug dealers can identify insincerity and concealment quite rapidly, ethnographers need to present an honest face. By taking an open and honest stance, the ethnographer exposes ethnography and the individual ethnographer for scrutiny, providing the basis to build rapport.

A key element for a successful initial conversation is to get the potential respondent to talk at some length about any topic of his/her choice. The longer the respondent talks, the better are the chances to build rapport. In general, the ethnographer pays attention to the dealer's language and expressions by listening for key words, word usage, and ideas. Responses are framed within the context the dealer develops by using similar words and expressions and, to some extent, reiterating what the dealer has said.

CULTURAL ASPECT OF DEVELOPING RAPPORT

Development of rapport is accomplished at multiple levels. At each level, an understanding of African-American culture is important. For African-Americans, the highest value is in the relationship between two persons (Nicholas, 1976). Since the relationship is primary, the desire is to keep it intact. This concept of relationship is connected to dealer's ideas and behaviors around respect and disrespect. If the highest value is "relationship," individuals see each other as equal. To treat someone as less than equal reflects a disrespect for the individual. In African-American culture, to treat another as less than equal destroys relationship; such behavior is disrespectful. Although individuals may out rank one another, the expectation is still to be treated equally. Such a value system requires dealing with each person on an individual basis. People have to work to establish and maintain individual one-on-one relationships. Understanding such cultural differences is important when the ethnographer attempts to develop any level of rapport among an African-American population. The first rule, then, is to demonstrate interest in each subject on an individual basis. Subjects must be made to feel that they are seen as equal, respected, and have much to teach the ethnographer. An interest in the individual and his/her life must be demonstrated on an *individual* basis. Dealers place much emphasis upon respect, and adopting this stance will be rewarded by entry into the subject's world.

Showing "Respect" and Successful Research Among Dealers

"Respect" has many elements. Drug dealers are often isolated from the dominant society in inner-city communities. Their limited interactions with the society are through social control and penal institutions. The dealing world also is fraught with danger, schemes, fear of arrest, lack of job opportunities, poor education, and so on. Even though some dealers make a substantial amount of money for awhile, their opportunities and living standards remain linked to the bottom of the American system of stratification. Most dealers find it difficult and next to impossible to move beyond their underclass status. In such circumstances, showing "respect" for them as persons is important in part because the ethnographer is likely to be the only conventional and "straight" person to do so.

Dealers' sense of self-esteem and prestige is generally tied to their activities as drug dealers. In their world, signs of disrespect are cause for some reciprocal action (Dunlap & Johnson, 1996). The ethnographer shows respect by paying close attention to the person's culture, language, expressions, and thinking patterns. Recreating the conversation demonstrates that the listener-ethnographer carefully noticed what was expressed, had some familiarity with their world, and most of all was sensitive to their plight.

Additionally, wanting to hear more about the respondents' views and life also expresses a deep sense of respect and interest in the person. The ethnographer might suggest reversal of usual roles by taking the stance of the student and invite the dealer to assume the role of teacher. The dealer is invited to teach the ethnographer about the dealer's world and way of living. Through such strategies at building initial rapport, respondents likely conclude that the ethnographer is truly an open and honest person and the dealer's views will be presented in a fair manner. In many instances, dealers wanted their story told and to have someone write about their experiences.

To avoid being perceived as an authority figure, the ethnographer locates topics of conversation that might be shared within the dealer's world. In a reasonably inclusive manner, the ethnographer should find ways of being agreeable towards the dealer's position regardless of how ridiculous such ideas might appear by conventional standards. Absolutely nothing the dealer respondent does or says should be called "wrong," "dumb," or "stupid." The ethnographer never expresses negative opinions about anything in the dealer's world unless the dealer says it first. The primary effort during the initial conversation is to achieve concord with the dealer.

RESEARCH ACCESS AFTER THE INITIAL CONVERSATION

Once the ethnographer, the dealer, and go-between complete their introduction and the initial conversation, dealers receive the ethnographer in different ways. There are those who want to tell their story to the ethnographer and to the "outside world." Such desires prompt cooperation from the respondent dealer. Enthusiasm from a dealer subject is good, but too much enthusiasm means that the ethnographer could become consumed by the demands of that person (Werner & Schoepfle, 1987). One dealing family in the "Natural History of Crack Distribution/Abuse" became so comfortable with the ethnographer that they called each time a crisis occurred in the family. Such crises occurred regularly, were highly informative about family processes and tensions, and contributed much to the research process. The ethnographer devoted large amounts of time to the family and their crises. Their enthusiasm about participation in the study gave the ethnographer a chance to observe and record much data about ordinary family life and interpersonal interaction patterns among sellers, prostitutes, and other family members (Dunlap, Williams, & Johnson, 1997).

A cordial reception, on the other hand, can expose the ethnographer to accept much peripheral data just to remain on good terms with the person(s) (Werner & Schoepfle, 1987). Nevertheless, observations and field notes written regarding apparently unrelated topics often provide fertile new areas of investigation; what initially appeared to be "pursuit of the tangential" and serendipity can become linked to the major phenomena of investigation (Johnson & Lipton, 1980).

One common outcome of the initial introduction might be called "benign neglect." The dealer's attitude may range from friendly tolerance to indifference (Werner & Schoepfle, 1987). In some cases, benign neglect might be the best for which the ethnographer can hope. A dealer may sit and listen to the ethnographer but does not give appropriate or detailed responses. In such instances, arranging future appointments will permit necessary time to "gradually break the ice." The ethnographer may encounter rejection (e.g., sellers or dealers decline to cooperate); however, past experience has shown that hostility is rare. Partial or indirect rejection is common.

In the above studies, some dealers have rejected in-depth interviews but have compromised by permitting the ethnographer to interview workers or to remain in a crack spot. Staff often found it difficult to gain full cooperation in ethnographic research of crack dealers and suppliers at their business locations. For example, Isabella sold crack for a dealer from her apartment. She gave many hours of interviews and permitted the ethnographer to observe what happened in her crack house. She explained many behaviors of crack smokers and dealers. Isabella also attempted to introduce the ethnographer to her supplier/dealer who spent much time in the apartment and often had seen the ethnographer. Isabella was able to convince her dealer to have a conversation with the ethnographer. The initial meeting and conversation went successfully, and he promised he would participate in the study. However, he left the ethnographer sitting in the crack house for many hours waiting for him while he associated with his personal friends and, in general, took care of his business.

Thus, the ethnographer had the dealer's verbal consent to participate, but his business activities, girlfriend, and suspicions resulted in avoidance. The ethnographer was able to continue observations at the crack house, and the dealer made no indication to Isabella or others that he disapproved of the study or the ethnographer's presence. But he also remained wary, busy, and reticent about an interview. The major problem was to disengage him from "business" and other persons in his life, especially his girlfriend.

When staff did experience limited rejection by dealers, this was often perceived as due to the "low" reputation of the go-between (like Isabella) who made the introduction. Sometimes initial rejection later became a welcoming situation when another go-between with a good reputation was found and spoke on behalf of the ethnographer. If the ethnographer finds a way to surmount the obstacle of initial rejection, field work in the area can continue. Whether the ethnographer, when introduced to the potential subject/dealer, encounters enthusiasm, benign neglect, or complete rejection, the situation has to be handled with professional sophistication so that rapport may develop.

The case of George, a crack dealer who had several sellers working for him, provides an example of the ethnographer surmounting obstacles. One of George's sellers introduced the ethnographer to George. Not understanding confidentiality issues and unsure whether to trust the ethnographer, George introduced the ethnographer to a female crack seller who was a college graduate in psychology.[4] Building rapport and gaining her trust did not take long. She was outgoing, and she was friendly with many other crack sellers in the neighborhood, though she did not work for or with them. With her subsequent recommendation, George became an active respondent. She also assured other "fellow entrepreneurs" that legitimate research was being conducted and encouraged them to participate. Thus, initial rejection of the ethnographer can be turned into acceptance if the ethnographer can "tough it out" and find new go-betweens.

In other situations, however, the ethnographer may find it more practical to leave one setting and set of potential subjects and seek other dealer-subjects. Another example in which a dealer's initial rejection was overcome came a year later. Marva, an upper level dealer, was approached for participation. Similar to George (Isabella's dealer), Marva was apprehensive at first and declined to become a key subject or be interviewed, but she had no objection to her crew participating in the research. Marva's crew included her daughter and her sister Rita. Rita was recruited as a subject and gave several interviews. Two other persons from Marva's crew were also recruited. Over the course of a year, numerous and lengthy interviews and observations of Marva's and their selling behavior took place. After a year of observing the ethnographer, Marva was assured that no harm or difficulty would occur as a result of an association with the ethnographer. She subsequently agreed to become a key subject in the research and was interviewed on several occasions.

Access to the Dealing Locales

Gaining access to a dealer also involves obtaining permission to directly observe the actual activities associated with selling. As Isabella and Marva demonstrated, the dealer may permit the ethnographer access to workers and dealing locales but may be hesitant to participate in the interview process. In both instances, selling took place inside. Street sellers do not want untrusted people to be present for long periods of time at their distribution site. They temporarily desist from selling activities when suspicious persons enter the block. They permit suspicious persons to enter and pass through, but a person who attempts to strike up a conversation and *not* buy drugs is reason for great suspicion since the individual may be an undercover cop. A critical level of initial access is to gain permission to be present while selling activities are on-going. A second level of access permits the ethnographer to make multiple visits to the same setting. In addition to securing a dealer's individual willingness to participate in the research, the ethnographer also needs to gain permission to make direct observations of selling activity by other(s) the dealer may employ. As Marva and George permitted observations but denied the interview, some sellers denied permission to observe customers and actual transactions but provided extensive interview data (Manwar et al., 1994). Again, the ethnographer's access must not endanger the dealer, the go-between, other street sellers, or the ethnographer. Other participants on the scene also must feel safe (not endangered) by the ethnographer's presence. The seller's "safety zone" must be extended to include the ethnographer (Williams et al., 1992). In specific cases, crack customers may hold respectable jobs, and their identity has to be protected (see Manwar et al., 1994).

Building and Maintaining Trust and Rapport

The first meeting with an individual dealer is a critical first step toward gaining rapport and full acceptance to study and observe dealing activities. If this initial foundation is weak or unstable, the ethnographer needs to spend more time and effort to build a relationship of trust and confidence. When and if a strong foundation is established in the initial meeting(s), the ethnographer begins his/her field research. In subsequent meetings, emphasis is placed upon the dealer-respondent's life and work.[5] The general idea is to introduce non-threatening conversations about dealing that renders the dealer comfortable talking to the ethnographer.

Developing strong rapport means having and showing respect and an interest in the person's beliefs, opinions, experiences, and world views, so that the subject is at ease with the ethnographer's intentions. Acquiring friendships with and developing excellent rapport also entail helping people to do things that they may not know how to accomplish. For example, one crack seller subject, Ross, was interested in playing basketball. But he had been shot several years earlier. He was unable to use the lower part of his body and used a wheelchair to get around. Although he could not use his legs, he was a very active and independent person who desired to participate in sports. He had heard of handicapped teams that played basketball. When he divulged this wish to the ethnographer, she went to a community program in the area and talked with the director about starting a basketball team for men who had been injured and had various physical handicaps. The director was interested in starting such a program, but there was an insufficient number of handicapped people in the area who were interested in participating in sports, and the idea was thwarted. Although no team resulted, Ross believed that the ethnographer had done him a favor, she was sincere, and he could trust her to do what she said would do.

The ethnographer also assisted other potential subjects in inner-city neighborhoods in many ways. Performing such services was an effective way to develop and strengthen rapport with respondents. Information on hospitals, treatment, and detoxification programs was often useful. Staff attended funerals, delivered funeral messages when the pastor did not arrive, visited persons in the hospital, bought food, rented videos, and contributed to helping in times of need in numerous ways. Benevolent concern can lead to friendship, a high degree of trust, and acceptance of the ethnographer's participation in everyday life.

CONFIDENTIALITY AND STUDY PURPOSE IN GAINING ACCESS

The issue of confidentiality and anonymity is especially important for encouraging crack sellers to participate in ethnographic research. Overcoming the well-founded suspicions of crack sellers is critical to research. Concerns about the ethnographer being an undercover agent or about the data being seized for enforcement purposes have to be alleviated before potential dealer-subjects feel free to talk about their dealing activities. After establishing a level of friendship and rapport, staff emphasize the numerous procedures to be followed in protecting the anonymity of individuals and confidentiality of data.

Complete confidentiality is stressed and assured to potential respondents. No personal identifying information about the person, or any persons mentioned, dealing activities nor dealing places can be given to any law enforcement personnel or other government agencies. All information is kept strictly confidential and used for research purposes only. Respondents are informed that the research is protected by a Certificate of Confidentiality. This certificate is taken into the field when doing research and is shown to potential subjects (see details in Williams et al., 1992). Plans by the research project to assure confidentiality (i.e., pseudonyms, code numbers, locked files) are explained carefully. The ethnographer invites the individual to chose a code name for the research that they would like to be known by. One request of the ethnographer is that dealers and subjects use code names for acquaintances, places, and other personally identifying information when talking about their activities. Other methods of concealing the person's identity such as code numbers are discussed and clarified.

The length in time (years) the research will take place, the length of various interviews, and the amount of time the information gathered will be kept on file is covered.

Finally, the subject's right to drop out of the study at any time has the positive effect of encouraging participation. Stressing that persons have the privilege, once they begin, to change their minds if they do not feel comfortable, demonstrates that the subject is not obligated to continue in the study. In short, emphasizing confidentiality, explaining the study, stressing the rights of subjects, steps to assure anonymity, the nature of confidentiality, and freedom to discontinue participation in the study aids in encouraging participation.

Likewise, clarity about the objectives of the study and what it entails, what it seeks to understand, what is expected of the person as a respondent, the kind of information sought, and the outcome or final product of the information collected is discussed with the respondent in detail. In such discussions, the potential subject was given enough information so that he/she could understand what his/her role in the research might be and could ask questions about anything which was not understood. Their questions were answered as clearly and honestly as possible and in language understandable to them. They could then give their fully informed consent and become a willing participant in the study.

ETHNOGRAPHIC STRATEGIES THAT DID NOT WORK WELL

In the crack business, having money to pay respondents for interviews meant that eager subjects were always available (Johnson et al., 1985). Those most eager to volunteer were often the crack users and those least competent as drug sellers. Since the study phenomena was crack selling, persons who routinely sold crack were sought as key subjects. The ethnographer therefore must rapidly learn the various roles and functions performed by participants. Indeed, knowing street roles greatly assisted in the process of initial identification of individuals and activities taking place in drug dealing areas. With such knowledge, the ethnographer more easily identified individuals performing various roles in a "copping" area. Generally, persons willing to communicate with anyone entering a dealing area will be limited to those performing roles of low level distribution and those helping to generate sales. At the beginning of the project "Natural History of Crack Distribution/Abuse," various strategies were utilized to identify crack sellers and dealers. As the project progressed, such strategies were sharpened and refined.

Do Not Expect Crack Users to Help Identify Crack Sellers

One ill-fated strategy was to rely upon crack (or other) drug users to introduce ethnographers to crack sellers or their suppliers. At the inception of the project, when no sellers were known, ethnographers planned to use a variation of the mix and mingle approach (Fetterman, 1989).

Popeye initially appeared friendly and helpful. He talked to ethnographers, walked them through the area, and explained various phenomena. He pointed out crack spots and talked of his experiences selling and using crack. He promised to meet the ethnographers the next day to introduce them to his mother and to act as a go-between. Popeye claimed he knew many dealers and that he could introduce the ethnographers to them.

The next day, however, when ethnographers went to meet him, he was nowhere to be found and persons to whom he introduced the ethnographers on the previous day claimed they did not know Popeye–and further that they had never met the ethnographers. To make matters worse, the police entered the area at the same time that the ethnographers entered the area, making it appear as though the ethnographers were associated with the police.

Popeye turned out to be an ex-crack seller whose deeds had rendered him untrustworthy in the drug distribution business. Usually, long-time crack users like Popeye have ruined or undermined their "reputation" in street life. Even when a street seller or crew boss hired someone like him, they were watched closely and were never trusted with large amounts of drugs to sell. Many could not be trusted with either drugs or money and were so untrustworthy that they worked as "look-outs," "steerers," "touts," or other low level distribution roles (Johnson, Hamid, & Sanabria, 1991).

Popeye survived through serving in the role of "steerer."[6] When ethnographers met him, he was looking for customers. Therefore, crack users and low level distributors generally are not trusted, and have little knowledge of, or access to high-level dealers.

Meeting and Gaining Initial Access
to Crack Users and Lower Level Distributors

Ethnographers could rapidly meet and gain access to crack users and lower level distributors, but converting steerers, touts, lookouts, and like persons into reliable subjects, and especially reliable go-betweens, was most unlikely. Popeye's openness indicated that he had been looking for customers. He was willing to tell his story, what he knew about crack, his experiences, and show us various "copping places" (locales to purchase crack/cocaine). The relationship the ethnographer was trying to acquire with Popeye was undermined by him giving a false address and not returning at the time and to the place agreed upon. Such fleeting relationships were frequently encountered.

Popeye illustrates some of the many difficulties in locating and developing rapport with crack users. The failure to meet with the ethnographer again, and to not keep appointments is a chronic and continuing behavior pattern evidenced by many crack users. Crack users are generally "hustling" and looking for a quick way to make money or gain food, but promises of future cooperation and assistance are often not met. Most live for the moment without making consistent commitments about the future. They do not plan ahead as ordinary persons do. Conducting research among such a population then requires much tolerance and persistence to relocate a potential subject.

After a few encounters with crack users like Popeye, staff learned that more often than not, crack users and low level distributors actually *cannot* facilitate introductions to sellers or dealers. Most sellers and dealers avoid social contact, other than specific sales transactions, with crack users; they distrust them. Most sellers and dealers also avoid the company of the low-level distributors who sometimes work for them or buy drugs from them. While dealers and sellers are known by many purchasers and users, the relationship is limited to a brief exchange of money for drugs. Persons who only buy crack rarely become a "trusted associate" of the seller and so cannot "get to" a dealer on the basis of a personal favor.

The Limitation of Drug Selling Hierarchies
on Low-Level Distributors and Workers

Drug selling hierarchies limited low-level distributors and workers to specific roles and denied them access. Within well-organized cocaine selling organizations (especially those involved in transporting cocaine from Colombia and New York), many persons are "employed" at various times to perform vital roles, but they are systematically not informed about the whole operation of which they are a part.

The story of John, an ex-dealer who was also a "mule," demonstrates this limited access to information, the obstacles researchers encounter when they attempt to enlist upper-level drug dealers as respondents, and the tightly-knit character of drug organizations. Behavior patterns that govern organizations can reach beyond the period of employment to personal relationships between the organization and former employees well after employment ends. John freely talked about various aspects of "organizational distribution," but he flatly refused to introduce ethnographers to the individuals for whom he had worked. He talked about the structure of the dealing organizations by describing certain key roles he had held. His key role was that of "mule."[7] While the amount of drugs transported was substantial, John insisted that he was working at the "lower level." His job was to simply transport the drug. He had no role in the actual agreements, cash transactions, or any other further responsibilities.

The fact that he was unwilling to introduce ethnographers to some of the dealers whom he had known or for whom he had worked is significant. Although not currently employed by these individuals, John was reluctant to contact his former associates and superiors. Several possibilities existed for this reluctance. He may have acted out of fear of possible reprisals, or he may have experienced a continuing sense of responsibility towards these individuals. If the latter were indeed the case, then tightly-knit bonds and understandings would possibly contribute to the cohesiveness and persistence of these organizations through time.

John's perception of himself as a "lower level" employee was also significant for several reasons. First, if arrested in possession of large quantities, "mules" face very long prison terms–usually the maximum sentence for drug sales. Second, his "mule" role entailed a great deal of responsibility since he was accountable for large quantities of drugs and the money these drugs represented. John reported no organizational responsibilities (e.g., supervision of other employees or duty to account for the shipment's cash value) beyond the simple duty of delivering his shipments to some other intermediary. According to John, one criterion differentiating "lower" from "higher" level employees of this organization may be the presence or absence of these organizational responsibilities. Third, John had been sufficiently reliable and able to smuggle drugs past customs and borders to be very valuable to his employers. Fourth, by possessing and transporting one or several kilograms of drugs, John's responsibilities clearly placed him among the upper-level dealing groups. Another reason why John's perception of himself could be significant was that our criteria of what constitutes the "lower" and "higher" ranks of drug selling may differ significantly from that of those who perform various roles in drug distribution organizations.

John had also performed several other key dealing roles (e.g., "captain," "lieutenant," "crew boss," etc.) and had moved through the ranks in a drug distribution organization but never entered the top levels where major "deals" were negotiated. A key expectation of everyone operating at this level was that no one "rats" or "identifies" anyone else in the organization, especially those at levels above them. Everyone was expected to "hide" or "conceal" identities of drug-dealing comrades from everyone else. This expectation also extended into the distant future and included concealing identities from virtually everyone, including ethnographers, so John could not introduce ethnographers to anyone in the organization because it would have violated this rule.

CONCLUSION

Acquiring cooperation from sellers and dealers will always be difficult because of the illegality of their activities and the seriousness of consequences associated with an arrest. Their whole culture is justifiably suspicious that no "straight" is to be trusted. Because of this, many persons will refuse to talk to ethnographers under any circumstances. In other cases, acquiring cooperation has to be readjusted to suit the geographical area of study. Although various adjustments may be necessary, at all times, a trusted go-between is needed. The primary emphasis should be placed upon locating the highest status go-betweens.

The strategies outlined above, therefore, may not work all the time with every crack seller or dealer. Factors such as race/ethnicity, the size of the organization, and the level of suspicion have to be taken into consideration. As evinced by the example of John, in some cases, access to some upper level distribution organizations is impossible. Some dealers are similar; they will not permit themselves to be interviewed, nor will they allow their operation to be studied. Such resistance to outsiders is understood in the framework of the subculture of drug distribution. Using the strategies described in this article, however, success in locating and interviewing many sellers and dealers is possible.

We contend that with a little readjustment, these strategies afford appropriate procedures for ethnographers to reach other hard-to-reach populations. We conjecture, however, that it will be easier to employ these strategies with populations not so stigmatized or as at-risk of serious legal punishments as the crack sellers and suppliers who are the subject of our investigation.

NOTES

1. Williams et al. (1992) delineated several strategies developed to protect the personal safety of ethnographers, research staff, potential subjects, and other persons in the crack selling environment. Following such safety strategies and procedures is directly relevant to, and should be incorporated into, the strategies delineated in this article for gaining "access" for research purpose to crack sellers/dealers and their families. Also please note that names used in examples and excerpts from field notes are pseudonyms.

2. "Natural History of Crack Distribution/Abuse" was an eight-year research effort intended to collect in-depth information on the structure, functioning, and economic aspects of cocaine and crack distribution in New York City. "Violence in Crack User/Seller Households: An Ethnography" was a three year study specifically designed to examine the intergenerational processes and transmission of violence.

3. Refer to section on culture.

4. With Rachel's approval and cooperation, the ethnographer's personal safety was secured in the area (Williams et al., 1992) and much important information about her drug selling career has been subsequently published (Manwar et al., 1994; Dunlap & Johnson, 1995).

5. Showing a keen interest in the dealer's stamina and capacity to survive helped to build rapport by stressing the need for creativity and business management. In subsequent meetings, research emphasis is placed upon the dealer's ability to survive in a dangerous world successfully. This introduces and prepares the dealer for future conversations about his/her activities and what they may encompass.

6. A *tout* is a person who hawks a specific seller's drugs. A *steerer* helps people coming into the neighborhood to purchase drugs; he guides the buyer to purchase drugs. Popeye got customers by touting for the Dominicans in the area. Often the tout or steerer will transport drugs and money between buyers and sellers who never meet.

7. That is, someone in charge of physically transporting drugs from one country to another.

REFERENCES

Barrett, R. A. (1984). *Culture and conduct: An excursion in anthropology.* Belmont, CA: Wadsworth.

DeVita, P. R., & Armstrong, J. D. (1993). *Distant mirrors: America as a foreign culture.* Belmont, CA: Wadsworth.

Dunlap, E., & Johnson, B. D. (1996). Family and human resources in the development of a female crack-seller career: Case study of a hidden population. *Journal of Drug Issues, 26*(1), 175-198.

Dunlap, E., & Johnson, B. D. (1994). A successful crack dealer: Case study of a deviant career. *Deviant Behavior, 15,* 1-25.

Dunlap, E., Johnson, B. D., Sanabria, H., Holliday, E., Lipsey, V., Barnett, M., Hopkins, W., Sobel, I., Randolph, D., & Chin, K. (1990). Studying crack users and their criminal careers: Scientific and artistic aspects of locating hard-to-reach subjects and interviewing them about sensitive topics. *Contemporary Drug Problems, 17*(1), 121-144.

Dunlap, E., Johnson, B. D., Williams, T. (in press). *Drugs and family life in the center city.* Thousands Oaks, CA: Sage Publications.

Fetterman, D. M. (1989). *Ethnography: Step by step* (Vol. 17). London: Sage Publications.

Fine, G. A. (1993). Ten lies of ethnography: Moral dilemmas of field research. *Journal of Contemporary Ethnography, 23,* 267-293.

Harris, M. (1974). *Cows, pigs, wars, and witches: The riddle of culture.* New York: Random House.

Hughes, E. (1971). *The sociological eye.* Chicago: Aldine.

Johnson, B. D., Goldstein, P. J., Preble, E., Schmeidler, J. A., Lipton, D. S., Spunt, B., & Miller, T. (1985). *Taking care of business: The economics of crime by heroin abusers.* Lexington, MA: Lexington Books.

Johnson, B. D., Hamid, A., & Sanabria, H. (1991). Emerging models of crack distribution. In T. Mieczkowski (Ed.), *Drugs and crime: A reader* (pp. 56-78). Boston: Allyn-Bacon.

Johnson, B. D., & Lipton, D. S. (1980). Creative tensions: Issues in utilizing ethnographic research within a single state agency. In G. Beschner, & C. Akins (Eds.), *Ethnography: A research tool for policymakers in the drug and alcohol fields* (pp. 36-45). Rockville, MD: National Institute on Drug Abuse.

Johnson, B. D., Williams, T., Dei, K., & Sanabria, H. (1990). Drug abuse and the inner city: Impact on hard drug users and the community. In M. Tonry, & J. Q. Wilson (Eds.), *Drugs and Crime* (pp. 9-67). Chicago: University of Chicago Press.

Lewis, C., Golub, A., & Johnson, B. D. (1992). Studying crack abusers: Strategies for recruiting the right tail of an ill-defined population. *Journal of Psychoactive Drugs, 24*(3), 323-336.

Manwar, A., Dunlap, E., & Johnson, B. D. (1994). Qualitative data analysis with hypertext: A case study of New York City crack dealers. *Qualitative Sociology, 17*(3), 283-292.

Nichols, E. J. (1976). *Cultural foundations for teaching African-American children.* Paper presented at the World Psychiatric Association and Association of Psychiatrists in Nigeria at the University of Ibadan.

Stack, C. B. (1974). *All our kin: Strategies for survival in the black community.* New York: Harper & Row.

Werner, O., & Schoepfle, G. M. (1987). *Systematic fieldwork: Foundations of ethnography and interviewing.* Newbury Park, CA: Sage.

Williams, T., Dunlap, E., Johnson, B. D., & Hamid, A. (1992). Personal safety in dangerous places. *Journal of Contemporary Ethnography, 21*(3), 343-374.

Strategies for Accessing and Retaining Asian Drug Users in Research Studies

Tooru Nemoto, PhD
Karen Huang, PhD
Bart Aoki, PhD

SUMMARY. Based on a research project that investigates drug use and HIV risk behaviors among Asian drug users in San Francisco, this paper describes barriers and strategies for accessing, recruiting, and retaining Asian drug users. It also presents culturally appropriate and group specific strategies and underlying cultural norms that outreach workers use to build rapport with targeted drug users and community members. The paper describes culturally appropriate strategies for outreach workers and project staff to recruit and retain Asian drug users. These strategies acknowledge diversities within the targeted ethnic groups and offer flexibility to create other strategies specific to targeted Asian drug users. *[Article copies available for a fee from The Haworth Document Delivery Service: 1-800-342-9678. E-mail address: getinfo@haworthpressinc.com]*

Tooru Nemoto is Principal Investigator, Asian American Recovery Services (AARS), and Assistant Research Psychologist, Institute for Health Policy Studies, University of California, San Francisco. Karen Huang is Co-Principal Investigator, AARS. Bart Aoki is Co-Principal Investigator, AARS, and Research Analyst, University-Wide AIDS Research Program, University of California.

This study was supported in part by the National Institute on Drug Abuse (NIDA), grant number R01DA09218. The points of view and opinions expressed in this paper are solely those of the authors and are not those of the NIDA.

[Haworth co-indexing entry note]: "Strategies for Accessing and Retaining Asian Drug Users in Research Studies." Nemoto, Tooru, Karen Huang, and Bart Aoki. Co-published simultaneously in *Drugs & Society* (The Haworth Press, Inc.) Vol. 14, No. 1/2, 1999, pp. 151-165; and: *Conducting Drug Abuse Research with Minority Populations: Advances and Issues* (ed: Mario R. De La Rosa, Bernard Segal, and Richard Lopez) The Haworth Press, Inc., 1999, pp. 151-165. Single or multiple copies of this article are available for a fee from The Haworth Document Delivery Service [1-800-342-9678, 9:00 a.m. - 5:00 p.m. (EST). E-mail address: getinfo@haworthpressinc.com].

151

INTRODUCTION

Very few studies have investigated drug use and HIV-related behaviors among Asian drug users. As a part of research and prevention efforts against drug abuse and HIV/AIDS at the Asian American Recovery Services (AARS) in San Francisco, we have been conducting a study to investigate drug use and HIV risk behaviors among Asians in San Francisco. Participants in the study include self-identified Chinese, Filipino, and Vietnamese drug users, 18 years or older, who are not currently enrolled in a drug treatment program. The study consisted of qualitative interviews followed by structured survey interviews with targeted Asian drug users. The participants in the survey interview are followed-up by our outreach workers for counseling about the results of HIV-antibody, hepatitis B, and syphilis tests. Also, our outreach workers follow-up participants in the targeted communities to provide information and advice for drug treatment programs and HIV/AIDS and other health-related information. Currently, we are completing the study, which has furnished us invaluable experience in accessing, recruiting, and retaining Asian drug users. The study, funded by the National Institute on Drug Abuse (NIDA), has gained much support from other social service agencies, gatekeepers, and members in Asian communities in San Francisco. Based on our experience, we summarize barriers to access, recruit, and retain Asian drug users in the study and present culturally appropriate and group specific strategies for overcoming these barriers.

BARRIERS TO RESEARCH PARTICIPATION
FOR ASIAN DRUG USERS

Cultural issues regarding drug abuse. Cultural factors, which influence accessing, recruiting, and retaining research participants, differ substantially among Asian ethnic groups. Our preliminary data revealed that the types of drugs first used and currently used, the means of taking drugs, and the characteristics of drug users' networks (ethnically or racially homo- or heterogeneous) differ depending on ethnicity and immigrant status (Nemoto et al., 1996). Even within the same ethnic group, cultural factors differ depending on acculturation, socio-economic, immigrant, and refugee status. For example, our outreach workers contacted a few Chinese American drug users at targeted needle exchange sites in San Francisco. However, Chinese immigrant as well as Vietnamese immigrant drug users are rarely seen at the needle exchange sites. Nonetheless, we have found similarities in cognitive, cultural, and socio-environmental factors which influence drug use among Asian drug users. We describe some of these factors below.

Shame. Asian cultures emphasize attending to others, fitting in, and harmonious interdependence with other members in the community (e.g., Markus & Kitayama, 1991), and traditional Asian cultures strongly emphasize family ties, role obligation, and obedience to the elderly. For many Asian individuals, the failure to live up to social role obligations and family expectations results in profound shame (Sue & Morishima, 1982). Even among Asians who use illicit drugs, shame remains a powerful psychological concern. This is because drug abuse, which disrupts the harmonious interdependent relationships among family and community members, is considered an individual failure as well as a family and community failure (AARS, 1996). Individual drug users care very much about what others think and feel if their drug habits are known to them. Based on our preliminary study, more than half of Asian drug users, by indicating the highest number on the 9-point Likert scale, thought that they would feel ashamed of their drug use if their family members found out about their drug habit. In addition, many of them responded that they felt ashamed of their drug habit, being dependent on drugs, and asking for money for drugs.

Viewing drug abuse as a failure or disruption of harmonious relationships brings shame on themselves and their immediate as well as extended family members. One of the most interesting findings of our study is that many Asian drug users live with their family members and hide their drug habit from their family members. They avoid the shame of identification as a failure by hiding their drug use. As long as drug use-related behaviors do not disrupt other family members, or family and community functioning, drug use is ignored or even considered not a problem. However, if family and community functions are seriously disrupted by problems, such as debts or financial difficulties, violence against family members, drug addiction, and criminal activities, the attitudes of the family will suggest a course of action. Family members' perceptions of shame, loss of face, or the expected stigma of the drug users' family in the community will generally determine how to deal with the drug use-related problems (Ja & Aoki, 1993).

When the family members cannot keep the problems within the family, they may seek help within the community; that is, they implicitly admit the family's failure to their community and to the world. Asian families often isolate or insulate drug abusers in order to avoid the potential stigma associated with a family member's drug use and to maintain the family's face or the harmonious relationships with other community members (Ja & Aoki, 1993). Family members may even send drug users to their relatives living far away or in another country. Because of the consequences that may result from a breach of confidence, outreach workers must bear in mind the cultural issues related to drug use in Asian communities and keep participation of drug users in research as confidential as possible. The strategies to overcome these cultural barriers and to maintain confidentiality of research participants are described in a later section.

Lack of familiarity with social services and research. Under-utilization of social services among Asians is well documented (e.g., Bui & Takeuchi, 1992). Barriers to Asians seeking help or using public services include lack of knowledge about health care, legal, and public service systems; lack of English skills; culturally incompetent service providers; cultural ideas about disease; and shame and stigma for seeking help or utilizing public services. For example, based on our outreach experience, most Asian drug users have never been tested for the HIV antibody and do not know about available testing sites or the logistics involved in obtaining a test. A majority of Asian drug users had basic knowledge about AIDS and ways of transmission of HIV, but many perceived themselves to be at low risk for HIV infection; even among injection drug users, there was little or no concern about HIV/AIDS. Almost all participants in our study were tested for HIV antibody, and more than one-third did not return for the post-test counseling. Most of those drug users who did not come back expressed a lack of understanding about the testing to outreach workers. For example, they often stated that they did not know about available treatment programs or that they could not do anything if they discovered they were HIV positive.

In addition to lack of familiarity with public services, most Asians, including Asian drug users, have never enrolled in research projects, nor do they understand research procedures such as recruitment and follow-up. Asian immigrants are particularly unfamiliar with the informed consent process for participation in research. Project staff who share similar cultural, ethnic, economic, and drug use backgrounds with the target groups would help participants understand the objectives and procedures of the project. Interviewers or outreach workers should provide project participants with culturally appropriate and individualized education about the procedures of the study. The strategies for obtaining informed consent and dealing with confidentiality issues in follow-up are described later.

Geographical and physical barriers. Geographical isolation is occasionally a barrier to accessing Asian drug users. Among our study's participants, most Vietnamese drug users live in the Tenderloin district, where violent crimes occur most frequently in San Francisco, and drug and sex trades are visible. Vietnamese drug users' network members can be identified in the Tenderloin by an approach to contact persons, store owners, and other community residents. Many Filipino drug users were recruited through contacts and outreach activities in the South of Market district, where Filipino immigrant drug users hang out. In contrast to Vietnamese and Filipinos, Chinese drug users are hard to locate even in Chinatown, or the other districts in the city where many Chinese or other Asians live. We targeted outreach activities in certain districts where many Chinese and Filipinos live. However, these districts are mostly residential, and we could not locate many drug users through outreach activities at the targeted street corners, bars, playgrounds, and pools in these districts. It is very difficult to access Asian drug users who neither live in their ethnic communities nor appear in the street drug scene; many of our study's participants procure drugs by calling dealers or delivery men.

Asian female drug users are the hardest group to locate and recruit in the targeted Asian community. Asian females who use heavy drugs, such as heroin, cocaine, and crack, often hide from family members and neighbors, and rely on others to perform errands, such as shopping. Many of these female drug users work at massage parlors as commercial sex workers. Typically, the massage parlor owner limits their physical freedom during working hours as well as after work. These women spend their lives indoors providing services, and live with other masseuses in apartments within a few blocks from the parlors. They seem to have little, if any, life outside of the massage parlor. In addition, masseuses are geographically very mobile, frequently changing work places within a city or between large cities. Therefore, they are difficult to locate and retain in a research project.

STRATEGIES FOR OVERCOMING BARRIERS TO RESEARCH PARTICIPATION

Establishing Culturally Appropriate Strategies

Addressing needs. Outreach efforts must focus on the concerns of the target population, not the concerns of the researchers or educators. Successful AIDS education and prevention programs address AIDS in a larger context in relation to drug and alcohol use, STDs and other disease, health promotion and health care, housing, food, employment, and other socioeconomic factors in the targeted communities (Nemoto & Mamo, 1995;

Zimmerman, Janz, & Wren, 1995). Women are more concerned about referrals, encouragement, support, housing, food, and money than about HIV (Rhodes & Holland, 1992). Based on our experience, Asian drug users respond to outreach workers who provided for their immediate needs. This method established rapport and a helping relationship that paved the way for enrollment in the research project and drug treatment programs. Addressing the pressing needs of the targeted Asian drug users was a key mechanism for establishing rapport. This approach to establishing rapport rests on the assumption that targeted respondents will accept what they need from a stranger as long as the offer addresses their needs.

Understanding cultural norms. Establishing rapport with Asian drug users appears to require a somewhat different relationship because of principles that guide the conduct of relationships. In particular, Chinese, Filipino, and Vietnamese cultures all stress kinship rules in helping relationships. Through ritual kinship or informal kinship in which the people are not actual blood relatives, people establish a sense of belonging to a group. It is for the sake of membership in the group that people give and receive help. In our case, we sought to become members in the networks of the target groups before we could offer help, such as information and referrals, and receive help, in the form of interview participation.

In Vietnamese culture, people are closely interconnected in a system of kinship relationships that define the self in terms of roles and responsibilities. Members of a Vietnamese kinship network tend to have a profound sense of interdependence, belonging, and mutual support (Timberlake & Cook, 1984). Everyone in the network has clearly defined roles. Families make decisions as a group; people do not make decisions on their own (Kibria, 1993). The kinship system serves as the bank, the hospital, the social support system. People with material resources give unconditionally to their network of kin. The rich care for the poor; the healthy care for the sick. Those who are "big brothers" help others. This social organization is centuries old. Back in Vietnamese villages, clusters of households were tied together by informal kin-centered networks that acted as mutual aid resources. Households collectively worked in the rice fields and those without land would collectively contract themselves out to do work (Kibria, 1993).

In a similar fashion, Chinese culture stresses interdependence and a group orientation. Relationships are governed by three particular kinship principles: (1) kan chin, (2) yee chi, and (3) ren chin (Wong, 1985). Kan chin is a Chinese term that refers to the emotional component of interdependence. It refers to caring feelings. A person who has kan chin cares about and feels concerned with the welfare of another person. Yee chi refs to a behavioral component of interdependence. It involves treating people with justice, doing things that preserve group harmony, and "doing the right thing" as prescribed by the expectations of the group (Wong, 1992). People with yee chi try to handle things according principles of justice rather than personal need. They put the group's needs ahead of their personal needs. Any indications of selfishness contradicts yee chi and undermines the sense of connection between people in a group. Ren chin refers to a cognitive component of interdependence. It means that one is thoughtful about preserving face for another person. One shows ren chin by trying to avoid doing things that might embarrass the other person. People show ren chin by always working to preserve or enhance the other person's face.

Likewise, Filipino culture emphasizes the need for kapwa or a shared identity among people (Marcelino, 1990). This shared identity refers to a shared sense of one's inner self. It is more than a value for smooth inter-personal relations. It includes a fundamental conviction in the importance of respecting another person's being and of being non-antagonistic. "Paki-kipagkapwa," a concept of the highest humanness, means accepting and dealing with others as equal human beings and with respect and dignity (Marcelino, 1990). A person who does not have kapwa is often considered not fully human. In addition to sharing an identity, Filipino culture also values "pakiramdam," the feeling of sharing another person's inner expe-rience. This concept is similar to the combination of the Chinese concepts of ren chin and yee chi in that it refers to the ability and willingness to consider another person's feeling and to take care to attend to subtle interpersonal cues so as to behave appropriately. This means reading sub-tle non-verbal signals and mentally role playing ambiguous situations in order to avoid causing embarrassment or doing something to cause the other person to lose face.

Establishing ritual kinship with target population. In order to access, recruit, and retain research participants, outreach workers, interviewers, and project staff must be as much a part of the system as possible. They do not have actual kin relations with drug users, but they must become an informal kin member in order to obtain cooperation. Without understand-ing cultural norms, they cannot establish mutually supportive and trusted relationships with Asian drug users. It is particularly helpful for outreach workers to share with targeted Asian drug users the same ethnic and socio-cultural backgrounds. However, because of the ethnic and cultural diversity of Asian drug users, the research project cannot match outreach workers with all targeted ethnic groups. Therefore, the project must provide sensitivity training to all staff who will work with the targeted drug users.

Establishing reciprocal relationships. With an emic approach, Wentowski (1981) studied the cultural dimension of social support exchange among the elderly in southern cities in the U.S.; that is, she was involved in the community and tried to find out the cultural rules of exchange from an insider's perspective. She concluded that independence was the main concern for all elderly in her study and noted that independence means interdependence, that is, a fair share of exchange of materials, behaviors, and psychological support. However, Wentowski's exchange theory cannot fully account for the exchange of support among Asians. Generally, in Asian culture, be it Chinese, Filipino, Vietnamese, or another, people give because someone is member of their group. They do not give because they expect something in return; their giving is not the exchange expressed by, "I'll do this for you if you do that for me." They prefer to avoid transacting business with someone outside of their group. When they choose to give, they do so because, "We're all in this life together, and the right thing to do is to give what we can." Using appropriate cultural norms (e.g., kapwa for Filipinos), our outreach workers make an appeal to prospective participants about the importance of research in the Asian community. Even though drug users in some ethnic groups may be desperate to obtain the incentive money for their participation, they tend to help in referring other drug users if they understand the importance of the research in Asian communities.

Establishing Target Group Specific Strategies

Asian immigrant drug users. Asian immigrants are not familiar with research and are less likely to understand the research project's goals and procedures, such as informed consent. Culturally competent outreach workers or project staff must offer an explanation in their language and not push them to participate in the project. It will take time and extra visits by outreach workers. Immigrants, particularly Chinese and Vietnamese immigrants, are less likely to participate in a research project that requires them to take medical exams or blood tests.

Asian immigrant drug users, when compared to U.S.-born Asian drug users, tend more to use drugs with members of the same ethnic group or other Asians. Therefore, when one member in their drug user's network participates in the research and gives a positive report on the experience to other members, these others will follow. Outreach workers also should encourage immigrant drug users to come to the interview or study site in a group as long as they can participate or be interviewed at the same time or do not mind waiting to be interviewed. Based on our experience, Vietnamese immigrant male crack users are often recruited from a targeted crack house, and they prefer to come to the interview as a group. Since recruitment is unpredictable, staff and interviewers must accommodate a group to the extent possible.

Many Asians, particularly Asian immigrants, are not familiar with the informed consent process of a research project. The informed consent form and the information sheet should be translated into the languages of the target groups. Since project staff may not be able to speak the participant's language, a qualified translator would be better qualified to obtain the informed consent using the translated consent form. A simultaneous translation of staff reading the informed consent in English is not reliable; it often confuses participants both because of ambiguous translation and the ambiguous role of the translator. Interviewers may explain the study's objectives and procedures to a group of prospective participants in either the case where potential participants express difficulties in understanding the informed consent, or when they are recruited as a group. In general, Asians may be hesitant to ask questions about the project and refuse to participate without fully understanding the study objectives and procedures. Therefore, outspoken person's or group leader's questions will help other people to understand the objectives of the project and informed consent process. Outreach workers should contact group leaders if they can be identified in targeted communities. Establishing rapport with group leaders will help to recruit and retain group members in the project.

Strategies for Asian women. Previous research suggests that identifying a woman's most urgent needs and concerns are important for an outreach worker to establish rapport (Hunt et al., 1993). As we explained previously, Asian female drug users are the hardest group to locate and recruit in the targeted Asian community. Most Asian female drug users express shame about their drug use and often hide from family members and neighbors; they may even ask others to perform errands for food and other necessities. Through contact persons or boyfriends, female outreach workers have to gradually establish rapport with Asian female drug users. Without consistent visits to their apartments or contacts by outreach workers, it is extremely hard to recruit them for a research project. In order to recruit and retain Asian female drug users, female outreach workers who have similar cultural and ethnic backgrounds must establish personal relationships with them by addressing their basic needs and concerns. Female outreach workers need to assure them about the confidentiality of the project by talking with contacts and boyfriends about the study.

Many Asian immigrant female drug users work at massage parlors as commercial sex workers. It is absolutely necessary to keep strict confidentiality of their participation with their co-workers and the owners of the massage parlors. As noted previously, masseuses are highly mobile, changing work places within a city or between large cities in the U.S. Therefore, it is difficult to retain or follow-up with them if they leave the city where they were recruited. If massage parlor owners collaborate in the research, close contact with owners or other masseuses at the participants' massage parlors is necessary to follow-up with the masseuse participants.

Injection drug users. According to the drug treatment admission records in San Francisco, very few Asian drug users inject drugs (Nemoto et al., 1996). They tend to use heroin and cocaine by smoking or snorting. Based on our preliminary study, a larger percentage of Filipino drug users, particularly Filipino Americans, than Chinese and Vietnamese drug users, injected heroin (Nemoto et al., 1996). Vietnamese and Chinese drug users mainly use crack and cocaine by smoking or snorting. Injection drug users are often desperate to shoot drugs and tend to be attracted by monetary incentives, such as participant reimbursement or referral fees. Therefore, reasonable participant reimbursement fees are effective to recruit and retain these Asian injection drug users. U.S.-born Asian drug users' networks are racially and ethnically heterogeneous, and they more often use needle exchange and drug treatment programs than Asian immigrant injection drug users. Researchers should consider outreach at these program sites and referrals from drug users in other racial groups.

Homeless. It is very rare to see Asian drug users who sleep on the street or stay in homeless shelters for a long period of time. However, we found several Filipino and Vietnamese drug users who were in and out of single room occupancy hotels (SROs) or homeless shelters, or who were temporarily staying with friends. Outreach activities at these shelters, hotels, or soup kitchens, therefore, are necessary. Our outreach workers contacted Filipino drug users when they were standing in line at a soup kitchen. In order to retain or follow-up with such cases, detailed and accurate location forms are needed to track these participants. We collected the names of their previous five SROs or hotels, or where more appropriate, the addresses and telephone numbers of friends with whom they stayed in the previous year.

Utilizing Culturally Appropriate Incentives

Reimbursement for participation. In addition to appealing to the shared interests of the Asian community, monetary incentives will help to recruit and follow-up with study participants. Participants who spend time to be interviewed or participate in research should be paid for their time. This monetary compensation should be comparable to other studies that have been conducted in targeted communities. Based on our experience, monetary incentives do not work for Chinese drug users, since most of them are not desperate to earn $20 for an hour interview. Most Chinese participated in the study when they felt some obligation to the community or reciprocity to their specific contacts, outreach workers, or interviewers. Chinese participants often suggest that, "I am doing this to help you, not for the money." Instead, Filipino and some Vietnamese drug users who do not have jobs or are in low-income brackets tend to participant in the study for monetary incentives. The monetary incentives for the follow-up interviews should be increased reasonably so participants remember the approximate date of the follow-up interview and feel motivated to call the staff.

Referral fees. Referral fees should be paid to persons who recruit prospective participants or bring enrolled participants in for a follow-up after the completion of the interview. In order to keep good relationships with contact persons, outreach workers or interviewers have to provide the contact persons with physical and emotional support and sometimes provide food. It seems to be not necessary to provide referral fees to these close contact persons. However, the system of referral fees should be explained to the contact persons, leaving it up to the contact person whether or not to ask for the referral fees. Our referral fee is one-fourth of the fee to reimburse an interview. We have found in general that this procedure works to recruit Filipino drug users, but not Vietnamese and Chinese drug users. These latter are recruited mostly by contact persons or through the personal connections of outreach workers.

Incentives other than money. When monetary incentives do not work, research projects may consider enticements such as food, food vouchers, supermarket vouchers, groceries, merchandise, and clothes, which may help to establish rapport with contact persons and other community members. Perhaps as often as twice a year, the project staff should organize parties or events that show appreciation to contact persons and community members. These events also provide an opportunity to inform them about the progress of the project. These occasions also provide project staff an opportunity to obtain information from multiple sources to track participants.

Strategies to Overcome Geographical Obstacles

Geographical differences exist among Asian drug users. In general, recent Asian immigrant drug users tend to live in or to maintain contact with their ethnic communities. On the other hand, many U.S.-born Asian drug users neither live in their ethnic communities nor have contact with ethnic organizations.

Using data from client admission records for the previous five years in a drug treatment program for Asians, our study mapped out the residences, drug use, and demographic characteristics of targeted drug users. Most Asian clients in drug treatment programs are U.S.-born Asians, and their residences are not in ethnic communities but scattered across the city. Outreach activities based on these records, however, proved unsuccessful. Next, we mapped the street drug scenes and needle exchange sites where Asian drug users might appear. We established trust and mutually support-ive relationships with contact persons and extended the number of contact persons in the target groups. We have kept our contact persons well in-formed about the progress of the project. During routine contacts with community members or contact persons, project staff obtain information about possible new recruits and track participants for follow-up. Most Vietnamese participants live in the Tenderloin district in San Francisco. Therefore, following-up with the Vietnamese participants by community outreach is relatively easy, since we can collect information about the targeted persons through our contacts, store owners, and other community residents. However, other groups, particularly Chinese and U.S.-born Asian drug users, are harder to reach, recruit, and follow-up. For recruit-ment of these groups, we have had to more vigorously use referrals and support from contact persons.

Establishing Community Collaboration

At the community level, project staff should contact community mem-bers, such as staff at ethnic community organizations, community health clinics, community leaders, clergy, and ethnic store owners, and inform these community gatekeepers about the objectives of the research project. Project staff should utilize community events, street fairs, and health vans to provide culturally appropriate and sensitive information about the proj-ect, drug abuse, HIV/AIDS, hepatitis, and other diseases. Flyers contain-ing information about the project, drug treatment programs, and HIV/AIDS and other disease should be distributed at events in targeted ethnic communities or street fairs. Of course, the flyers must be written both in English and the languages of the targeted ethnic groups. Visibility of the project at these events and of the project's collaboration with other social service agencies will help project staff to establish rapport with communi-ty gatekeepers and potential research participants.

Project directors must explain the study to staff in community organiza-tions in targeted communities. This groundwork prepares for the later exchange of information with staff in community organizations. If formal referrals are needed, memoranda of understanding should be exchanged with directors of the collaborating organizations. The confidentiality of clients, additional time requirements needed for staff to refer clients, and misunderstandings among supervisors and staff about the referral procedures often inhibit sharing information among community service agencies about clients. Specific meetings among the collaborating organizations will facilitate efficient referral procedures.

Care must be taken to establish a genuine collaboration between researchers and community organizations. It is ideal that research projects are developed and conducted by researchers in ethnic community agencies; it takes time for university researchers to establish supportive relationships with community agencies. Staff in community organizations sometimes perceive university researchers as "hit and run scientists." Researchers will foster the impression that they just use clients for their research if they do not provide feedback or any other benefit to clients or to the community, and do not demonstrate concern for the community after the end of the project.

Because of the recruitment of participants who use illicit drugs, local police departments should be informed. Police officers in special task forces, such as those that target drugs, crime, or prostitution, can lecture staff on safety issues on the street. Staff or outreach workers, however, should never hang out or talk with police officers on the street.

CONCLUSIONS

We described barriers to access, recruitment, and retaining Asian drug users for a research project and culturally appropriate and group specific strategies of overcoming these barriers. Foremost, we must stress the diversity within Asian ethnic groups and Asian culture. Among Asian drug users, the choice of drugs, methods to administer them, network characteristics, and risk and protective factors against drug abuse differ substantially depending on ethnicity, immigrant status, acculturation, gender, age, generation in the U.S., and socio-economic status. Nevertheless, we believe that certain strategies to recruit Chinese, Filipino, and Vietnamese drug users and methods to build rapport with targeted Asian drug users to some extent will work in each of these groups and with other Asian and Pacific Islander drug users. When we recruit and retain Asian drug users for research projects, it is important to keep in mind these culturally common strategies and the applicability of these strategies to the projects' specific target populations. In addition, the geographic uniqueness of our study should be considered. We have conducted our research in San Francisco, a city where one-third of the population is Asian. The strategies or cultural ideas presented in this paper may not be applicable to Asian drug users in other parts of the U.S. In this paper, we did not include Pacific Islanders because our research project focuses on Chinese, Filipino, and Vietnamese drug users. Very few Pacific Islander drug users have been recruited in our study. Future research projects should include Pacific Islanders in addition to other ethnic Asian groups, such as Cambodians, Laotians, Thais, Koreans, Japanese, and Asian Indians. Also, it should be noted that Chinese and Japanese Americans who are assimilated to the U.S. mainstream culture and do not have contact with their ethnic communities or agencies are hard-to-reach populations. Our inclusion criterion for ethnicity is self-identification of the targeted ethnic groups. The study included a number of mixed race individuals who identified themselves as a member of a targeted ethnic group. These Asian drug users of mixed race may need special attention in future research, since the numbers of them are increasing and their psycho-social profiles differ from mono-ethnic Asians. These individuals should not be arbitrarily categorized into one Asian ethnic group. Research studies to document and understand drug use in relation to cognitive, cultural, social, economic, and environmental factors among diverse Asian drug users are needed.

REFERENCES

Asian American Recovery Services (1996). *An Asian outreach intervention model*. Report submitted to SAMHSA's Center for Substance Abuse Treatment.

Bui, K., & Takeuchi, D. T. (1992). Ethnic minority adolescents and the use of community mental health care services. *American Journal of Community Psychology, 20*, 403-417.

Hunt, D. E., Hammett, T., Smith, C., Rhodes, W., et al. (1993). Outreach to sexual partners. In B. S. Brown & G. M. Beschner (Eds.), *Handbook on risk of AIDS: Injection drug users and sexual partners* (pp. 464-482). Westport, CT: Greenwood Press.

Ja, D. Y., & Aoki, B. (1993). Substance abuse treatment: Cultural barriers in the Asian-American community. *Journal of Psychoactive Drugs, 25*, 61-71.

Kibria, N. (1993). *Family tightrope*. Princeton, NJ: Princeton University Press.

Marcelino, E. P. (1990). Towards understanding the psychology of the Filipino. *Diversity and Complexity in Feminist Therapy, 9*, 105-128.

Markus, H. R., & Kitayama, S. (1991). Culture and the self: Implications for cognition, emotion, and motivation. *Psychological Review, 98*, 224-253.

Nemoto, T., Aoki, B., Huang, K., Nguyen, H., Aquino, J., Wong, W., & Muriera, A. (1996). *Drug use and HIV risk behaviors among Asians*. Paper presented at the 8th National AIDS Update Conference in San Francisco.

Nemoto, T., & Mamo, L. (1995). *Evaluating cultural appropriateness of AIDS prevention.* Paper presented at the 5th Biennial Conference on Community Research and Action in Chicago.

Rhodes, T., & Holland, J. (1992). Outreach as a strategy for HIV prevention: Aims and practice. *Health Education Research, 7,* 533-546.

Sue, S., & Morishima, J. K. (1982). *The mental health of Asian-Americans: Contemporary issues in identifying and treating mental problems.* San Francisco: Jossey-Bass.

Timberlake, E. M., & Cook, K. O. (1984). Social work and the Vietnamese refugee. *Social Work, 29,* 108-113.

Wentowski, G. J. (1981). Reciprocity and the coping strategies of older people: Cultural dimensions of network building. *Gerontologist, 21,* 600-609.

Wong, B. (1992). Legal adaptation of the Chinese Americans: From centripetal to centrifugal approaches of conflict management. *Studies in Third World Societies Williamsburg, 48,* 81-87.

Wong, B. (1995). Family, kinship, and ethnic identity of the Chinese in New York City, with comparative remarks on the Chinese in Lima, Peru and Manila, Philippines. *Journal of Comparative Family Studies, 16,* 231-254.

Zimmerman, M. A., Janz, N. K., & Wren, P. A. (1995). Factors influencing the success of AIDS prevention programs. In N. Freudenberg & M. A. Zimmerman (Eds.), *AIDS prevention in the community: Lessons from the first decade* (pp. 149-160). Washington, DC: American Public Association.

Obtaining Consent
and Other Ethical Issues
in the Conduct of Research
in American Indian Communities

Fred Beauvais, PhD

SUMMARY. In order to conduct effective field research, researchers must be cognizant of the social, political, and historical events influencing the communities where the research takes place. American Indian communities have a number of structural characteristics that can become barriers to good research. Researchers can overcome these barriers by understanding and responding to issues of sovereignty, overlapping jurisdictions, scarceness of resources, and a well-founded skepticism about the value of research and the motivations of researchers. An emerging controversy over the form and nature of informed consent to participate in studies also has threatened research in Indian communities. Where signed permission from parents for their child's participation in survey research has been required, the resulting data have been severely compromised. Sever-

Fred Beauvais is Senior Research Scientist, Tri-Ethnic Center for Prevention Research, and an affiliate faculty member, Department of Psychology, Colorado State University.

This paper was supported in part by grants from the National Institute on Drug Abuse of the National Institutes of Health (R01-DA-03371; P50-DA-07074). The opinions expressed in this paper are those of the author and not of the supporting agency.

[Haworth co-indexing entry note]: "Obtaining Consent and Other Ethical Issues in the Conduct of Research in American Indian Communities." Beauvais, Fred. Co-published simultaneously in *Drugs & Society* (The Haworth Press, Inc.) Vol. 14, No. 1/2, 1999, pp. 167-184; and: *Conducting Drug Abuse Research with Minority Populations: Advances and Issues* (ed: Mario R. De La Rosa, Bernard Segal, and Richard Lopez) The Haworth Press, Inc., 1999, pp. 167-184. Single or multiple copies of this article are available for a fee from The Haworth Document Delivery Service [1-800-342-9678, 9:00 a.m. - 5:00 p.m. (EST). E-mail address: getinfo@haworthpressinc.com].

al different attempts to obtain written permission have been attempted, but with little success. *[Article copies available for a fee from The Haworth Document Delivery Service: 1-800-342-9678. E-mail address: getinfo@haworthpressinc.com]*

INTRODUCTION

The term research often brings to mind a number of stereotypes. One of the more common is that of the "mad scientist," a person with a rather wild-eyed, disheveled look who can think of nothing other than the scientific problem at hand. This type of person has no perception of the "big picture" and pursues science with little regard for practical application or the consequences of the research being conducted.

As with most stereotypes, this perception is not entirely unwarranted. With the explosion of knowledge in the physical sciences throughout this century, researchers have been afforded some degree of latitude regarding the impact of the knowledge they generate. However, great debates have also arisen as to whether or not the pursuit of "knowledge for its own sake," without regard for the consequences, is morally justifiable.

By their nature, the social sciences have been more attuned to the social context in which their inquiry takes place. Yet they are not immune to the tendency to gather knowledge without regard for the potential negative impact of both the research process and outcomes. Quite often communities have been the target of a particular research effort, only to have information that was gathered, used, or perceived in such a way that is detrimental to the community or the individuals within it. Unfortunately, this tendency toward exploitation of research participants has been particularly common in research on minority communities (see *American Indian and Alaska Native Mental Health Research,* 1989, for a discussion of an egregious example involving an Alaskan Native community). Oftentimes research has been conducted so it benefits almost exclusively those conducting the research, with very little benefit to the community. In other instances the potential negative impact of the research findings on the community under study are not considered as the results are disseminated.

The Tri-Ethnic Center for Prevention Research (TEC) at Colorado State University has been conducting substance abuse research among American-Indian and Mexican-American communities for the past two decades; the majority of that work consists of surveying young people regarding their history of drug use and eliciting information on other characteristics related to drug use. During that time, we have become aware of the conditions that are required to conduct sensitive, effective, and ethical research with ethnic minority populations. This paper discusses those conditions with a special emphasis on American Indian communities. It addresses an ethical issue of particular concern, that of obtaining consent for participation in survey research of young children and adolescents.

The issue of consent recently has come to the forefront both from the perspective of the tribes with which we work and regulatory agencies which oversee federally funded research efforts. Resolution of the demands of both of these entities is a crucial factor in the process of recruiting and retention of subjects for research projects. Tribes have become very aware of the dangers of exploitative research; however, when the community is well informed of the research and those individuals who participate in the research freely give their consent, the reality and sense of exploitation is substantially reduced, and the research process is greatly enhanced.

INFORMED CONSENT

The National Context

Protection of human subjects in the conduct of research is a topic that has received continuing attention and debate within the research community. Before discussing this issue in relation to research in Indian communities, understanding the current status of the debate at a national level will be helpful. Historically, it was the atrocities committed under the guise of research during World War II that stimulated the modern era of subject protection. The deliberations at the Nuremberg trials resulted in a set of conditions that must be adhered to any time human subjects are involved in a research project. Since that time, these conditions have been further refined (*Belmont Report*, 1978; U.S. Government, 1975) and a set of standards for research have been developed. Several levels of review and oversight for federally funded research projects assure adherence to these standards. There are many aspects to these conditions and standards, but the following elements capsulize the requirements for informing research subjects of the nature of the research and obtaining their agreement to participate.

1. The subject must be fully informed of the nature and intent of the research, including any potential risks.
2. After being informed about the research, the subject must freely agree to participate. Subjects must also understand that they have

the right to terminate their participation at any point during the research without any negative repercussions.

3. The research must involve minimal risk to the subjects. If there are risks, they should be outweighed by the benefit to be gained.

4. If minors (generally defined as under the age of 18) are involved, parents or guardians must give their permission prior to the minor's participation in the research. In this case, the parent or guardian must also be fully informed as to the nature and intent of the research.

While these conditions appear to be straightforward, controversy still surrounds them. Of particular concern is the nature of the consent given. Specifically, does it have to be in writing, or does the act of participation imply consent once the subject is informed of the nature and intent of the research? In addition, do the parents' permission to participate as well as the child's consent have to be in writing? These newly raised questions have created some problems for the conduct of research in minority communities (Dent et al., 1993; Mensch & Kandel, 1988; Severson & Biglan, 1989).

For certain types of research, there is no question that both the subject and the parent or guardian must provide written consent before research can take place. The issue here is the level of possible risk involved. If, for instance, the research involves an intrusive medical procedure such as the testing of an experimental vaccine, there is no question that written consent from the child and written permission from the parent should be obtained. Another example might be an intensive drug abuse rehabilitation program that involves in-patient treatment. Each of these conditions could reasonably involve either physical or psychological risks to the subject and explicit written permission and consent should be obtained from both the patient and parent if the patient is under 18.

When the risks are minimal or non-existent, the need for written permission and consent may not be warranted, particularly if this requirement results in the collection of biased data. For the past 20 years, obtaining written permission to use anonymous drug use surveys, such as those commonly used in TEC research projects, has not been required. As long as all the elements of informed consent described earlier are followed, students in school have been allowed to take these surveys without parental signatures.

Recently, these procedures have been questioned, and some now believe that written parental consent is needed for the collection of any information that is not a part of the regular school curriculum. The requirement for written permission has affected several research projects. Also, some states in the U.S. have passed legislation codifying this requirement. In addition, there have also been recent attempts to pass federal regulations requiring written parental permission for all research projects funded by federal dollars. This shift in human subject consent requirements is occurring in the context of a changing social and legal environment in the U.S. which will be discussed next.

The last several years have witnessed the rise of a social reform movement that is variously configured but usually comes under the rubric of restoring "parental rights" or preserving "family values" (Melton, 1996). While the purported intent of this effort is to reduce social ills through re-establishment of strong family structures, it is clear that it is also a religious/philosophical movement with a far broader agenda. "Parental rights" or "family protection" are code words for a world view that is staunchly fundamentalist-Christian and, at times, unbending in its approach (Jones, n.d.). While there are many parts to this agenda, the one that is of concern here is the attempt to seriously restrict the ability of researchers to gather information from young people regarding attitudes and behaviors that negatively affect their lives. Specifically, this movement is calling for requiring researchers to obtain written parental permission before a child in school can take a survey that contains questions that are not of a strictly academic nature. Surveys that ask about drug use behaviors and attitudes clearly fall under this stricture. As will be shown, this requirement seriously biases the type of information that is collected through certain types of research, including those using drug surveys.

The argument from the "parental rights" perspective states that the deterioration of the nuclear family structure is the root of all problems encountered by youth is the U.S. Furthermore, there is often the imputation that some groups (usually "liberals," "educators," or "researchers") are conspiring to further weaken the family by assuming responsibility for the moral and spiritual development of children (Limber & Wilcox, 1996; Jones, n.d.). Drug education, sex education, AIDS prevention, and the like are believed to be within the purview of the family and should not be assumed by other societal agencies. The administration of drug surveys without written parental permission is seen as the first step in the process of restricting the rights of the parents to properly raise their children.

On the one hand, the "parental rights" argument is compelling and is supported by a great deal of research evidence. The research shows that family does have a powerful impact on the development or prevention of social ills among children. On the other hand, this perspective ignores the reality that many families are not shouldering this responsibility and the lives of many children are adversely affected as a result. The complexities and stresses of modern life and various forms of social inequality make it difficult for every family to operate in a fully functional manner. To simply say to groups under extreme duress to "shape up and do it right" is extremely naive. In an imperfect world, society has the responsibility to assist those who, for various reasons, experience adversity that they lack the resources to counter (Melton, 1996).

Another disturbing aspect that often accompanies the "parental rights" perspective is its anti-intellectual answer to social issues. This perspective states that the answer to social problems is "good moral living" and, thus, there is no need for data that would help define the problems and their solutions; the answers are already known and are contained within the moral or religious framework to which we all should adhere.

These are the pressures that have led to a strong demand that parents provide written permission for the use of drug surveys in their children's schools. The belief is, that with this requirement, many parents would decline to have their child participate in research, thus preserving their right to the moral development of their children and protecting family privacy. However, under the current procedures, parents already have this right; they are informed and can refuse their child's participation. Unfortunately, the major effect of the written permission requirement is to seriously deter the ability to collect reliable research data that can be useful in assisting in drug prevention efforts.

Tri-Ethnic Center Research

During the past 20 years, the Tri-Ethnic Center has routinely administered drug use surveys to Indian youth who are in school. These surveys are anonymous; no identifying information is obtained, and once the survey is completed and turned in, there is no way that anyone can link a child with their responses. In addition to the anonymity of the survey, there are a number of other procedures used to protect the identity of the children. For example, the teachers do not collect the surveys. Rather, a box is passed around and the students randomly place their completed survey into the box. Prior to administering the survey, a notice is sent home to parents informing them of the survey and giving them the opportunity to remove their child from the survey process. The parents can do this by signing the notice and sending it back to the school, calling, or stopping by the school with their request. When this happens, their child is given another assignment during the survey administration. Before the survey is given in the classroom, instructions are read to the students. Included in these instructions is the statement that students can decline to take the survey or decline to answer any individual questions that may make them uncomfortable.

It has been suggested by some that the types of questions asked on the survey may raise anxiety among some students. In the 20 years that TEC has been conducting such surveys, we have never had a reported instance of this discomfort. Indeed, there may be certain types of questions that could provoke anxiety, but we have been careful to avoid such questions. For example, some drug surveys ask students if their parents use drugs or alcohol. Other surveys may ask if the child has ever been abused by a parent. We believe that these types of questions are inappropriate since they may put the student in the position of reporting an illegal behavior within their family and can create anxiety, even if the survey is anonymous. Therefore this type of question is avoided.

Under these circumstances, the risk to any child is negligible, and therefore, we have judged that the need for signed permission from parents is unnecessary. In fact, we have conducted over 50,000 surveys with Indian youth in the past two decades with these procedures and have never encountered a problem. In cases where the risk might be increased, we do insist on parental signatures. For example, in some of our studies, we collect student names since we want to link student responses at two points in time. Even in these instances, precautions are taken to protect the master list which contains the names and it is unlikely that anyone other than our research staff could ever have access to that list. Since there is a slightly elevated chance of identification, we do ask that parents sign a permission slip to allow their child to participate in the survey project, and we obtain the student's signature prior to administering the survey.

Although the procedures described above have been successfully used for over 20 years, our project recently came under pressure to require written permission from parents. We recognized from the beginning that this procedure had the potential to seriously bias the type of information we could collect, so we attempted a number of strategies to maximize the return rate from parents when their written permission was required, including the following.

Strategies

Mail. In several locations, letters were mailed to parents describing the project, and a permission form was enclosed along with a stamped envelope which they could use to return the form to the school. On the form, there were places for parents to sign to either give their permission or withhold it. In order to increase the return rate, three drawings of $100 were held and any parent who returned a form was entered into the drawing. To avoid coercion, parents' names were entered in the drawing just for returning the form irrespective of whether or not they gave permission.

Furthermore, the schools were given $1.00 for each form that was returned to reimburse them for any expenses incurred.

The average return rate with this procedure was about 20%, clearly resulting in a bias that rendered the data unusable. It is likely that the parents who did respond were those more involved in the lives of their children and thus their children would be less likely to be drug involved. These findings, then, would distort the actual level of drug use in the schools by showing lower drug use rates. In two of the locations, parents who did not return the form were queried as to their reason for not returning it. Consistent with what is found in the literature (e.g., Ellickson & Hawes, 1989), the primary reason for not returning the form was of the general nature, "I don't object to the survey; I just didn't get around to sending the form in." This is an important point since it provides a clear indication that most parents did not have a problem with their child participating in the survey. Their lack of written response was not an indication of any desire for "protection of family privacy," it was merely inconvenient for them to respond. We verified this through another project where we sent parents a written permission form and then followed up with a phone call to encourage them to respond. The phone calls indicated that over 94% of the parents said they had no problem with the survey, though only 50% of them sent the form in with a signature. Once again, there was little objection to the survey, only a lack of follow-through on the mailing.

Parent/teacher conferences. At one location the school attempted to obtain signatures at parent/teacher conferences. Unfortunately, conference attendance was exceedingly low, resulting in even lower rates of signatures than with the mail procedure. In general, this approach is not very promising. Even if the return rate could be increased, it is probable that the same bias as found in the mailing procedure would accrue; the parents most involved with their children are those likely to show up at parent/ teacher conferences, resulting in data reflecting lower than actual drug use rates in the school.

Registration. Many Indian schools have a formal registration process at the beginning of each school year. At this time several signatures are required for various school services (e.g., reduced lunch, federal per capita payments). Since these signatures result in significant funds for the school, considerable effort is expended to complete the registration process. If parents do not come in to complete the forms, a school liaison goes to the home to obtain the signatures. In two Indian communities, a permission form for the drug survey was included in the registration packet. Approximately 95% of the parents gave written permission for their children to take the survey. This appears to be a viable method for obtaining permission where an annual registration process is used. The only drawback to this method is that not all schools use this process, and employing a different methodology at different schools might compromise the research design of projects intended to estimate drug use rates across a broad population.

Personal contact. In the past, we have engaged in research projects where we have had to individually contact potential participants and their parents and obtain written permission for participation. This is a variously successful strategy and is totally dependent on the person making the contact. They must have a thorough knowledge of the research project, be able to convey that knowledge accurately, and be familiar with the physical and social context of the reservation. Many Indian families live in remote areas where poor roads and weather make contact difficult. Awareness of these conditions, as well as knowledge of the family systems on the reservation make it more likely that successful contact can be made. This procedure, however, is very costly and not reasonable for large scale survey projects.

In general, it appears that the requirement for written permission from American Indian parents before their child can complete an anonymous drug use survey (or other similar research forms) compromises the quality of the data to the point of making it meaningless. There is ample evidence to demonstrate that this problem is not restricted to research with Indian youth but will hamper data collection with all populations (Ellickson & Hawes, 1989; Kearney, Hopkins, Mauss, & Weisheit, 1983; Severson & Dennis, 1984). If this requirement becomes general practice, our ability to collect meaningful data on behavior patterns of youth will be curtailed. The data have been used for multiple purposes from population surveillance to designing interventions to evaluating program effectiveness. The loss of this type of information will greatly hamper efforts to improve the quality of life for young people. The pressure to implement such a requirement is somewhat puzzling since the youth in our drug survey projects are already well protected: The risks are negligible; youth and parents are both informed of the nature of such projects; and both have the opportunity to decline participation.

Fortunately, and partly as a result of the poor return rate we were getting from parents, our survey project has been cleared to return to the original procedure, whereby parents are informed of the research and can notify the school if they do not want their child to participate. The refusal rate is now less than 5%, which is similar to what we have experienced over the past 20 years.

There is continuing concern that the social and political climate will favor the use of written permission in future research, despite the evidence that this interferes with rational inquiry into the nature and extent of social problems. The only reasonable response to this pressure is to continue to conduct high quality, ethical research that conforms to the standards of informed consent. Further, the results of these studies should be adequately communicated to those who would favor written consent along with the message that this data would be unavailable with the stricter requirements of consent.

ELEMENTS OF SUCCESSFUL RESEARCH IN INDIAN COMMUNITIES

We have found that the procedures for the recruitment and retention of subjects in research projects among American Indians do not differ substantially from those for other populations. For example, the different methods for obtaining consent outlined above would most likely result in the same recruitment rates for other ethnic groups and also for the majority population. Furthermore, the procedures outlined by other authors in this volume would likely be successful in Indian communities. What differ are the historical, political, and social conditions characteristic of Indian reservations. Unless these conditions are recognized and some level of accommodation or negotiation is reached, it will be nearly impossible to gain the cooperation of community members in any research effort.

Context

Conducting good applied research requires a thorough knowledge of the populations that are involved in the research. There are numerous contextual conditions that must be considered both in the design of the research and in the feasibility of conducting it. Research hypotheses that do not take into account the realities and the culture of the population under consideration will only yield uninterpretable results. For example, if the researcher assumes that assertiveness is a positive personal quality and tries to promote that in a community where collectivist values are the norm, the results will be confounded with the values of the cultural system. It is important to remember that even the best designed research is useless if it cannot be effectively carried out. For instance, a project that requires a heavy commitment of personnel from an already resource poor community, will have little chance of success. Many research projects fail because too little effort is expended in the early part of the process in getting acquainted with the community and understanding its history, politics, and culture. The following are some of the contextual issues that we have become cognizant of in our work with American Indian communities (see also Beauvais, 1995; Flemming, 1992; Beauvais & Trimble, 1992; Trimble, 1977). Undoubtedly, a great deal of overlap exists with work in other minority populations.

Tribal sovereignty. Treaty agreements of the last century define the relationship between Indian tribes and the U.S. government. In most instances, the language of these treaties specifies that tribes retain a sovereign status *vis-à-vis* the federal government. As such, tribes differ from states in their relationship to the federal government. While these areas of difference are sometimes vague and complex, tribes maintain that they have much greater authority than states do in regulating their own affairs. Furthermore, in most instances, tribes are not subject to the laws and regulations of the states in which their reservations exist. The recent increase in gambling establishments on many reservations is a good case in point. Most of this activity is occurring on reservations that are located in states that have anti-gambling laws.

When it comes to cultural and family issues, tribes expect and experience greater latitude in specifying regulatory jurisdiction. Thus, tribes feel that the terms and conditions of the conduct of research, including consent procedures, should be under tribal control and often balk at regulations that they believe are inappropriate for their circumstances. On the other hand, there are regulatory requirements that attend the granting of U.S. federal funds for research purposes, regardless of the sovereign status of the grantee. For example, some tribes feel that they have the right to determine what type of informed consent is appropriate for their people; however, the Code of Federal Regulations (U.S. Government, 1975) includes very specific conditions that must be met before subjects can engage in research funded by the U.S. government. Differences between tribal expectations and federal requirements must often be negotiated before federally funded research can take place.

Infrastructure. The educational, social, and health service infrastructures on many reservations are often underdeveloped. Regulations that other systems may be able to handle routinely become difficult to accommodate on the reservation. Many reservations exist in remote areas where the physical infrastructure (e.g., roads and communications) makes ordinary life difficult. Under these circumstances, what may appear to be reasonable demands of research often cannot be met, or are met incompletely. For example, if a project entails families coming to a tribal office for assessment or treatment, there must be a recognition that this may involve considerable inconvenience on the part of the family as it may take hours of travel time. Transportation arrangements and/or reimbursement must be anticipated in the research plan; these expenses may greatly add to the cost of a research project.

Wariness. Relationships between Indian tribes and the U.S. government have often been contentious. Part of the legacy of this is continuing distrust of government regulations. Requiring a signature for research participation, for instance, brings up a host of suspicions about the actual nature and intent of the research. There are untold instances of duplicity in which Indian people have been asked to sign official documents only to find that what they signed was a relinquishment of land or other resources. Additionally, Indian communities have been the target of considerable research in the past and have rarely benefited from that research. There is a sense of exploitation wherein academic researchers have used Indian communities as a source of research data, but the data do not result in amelioration of the many serious problems existing on reservations. As a result, many tribes are in the process of developing research committees that will scrutinize proposed research to insure that it has benefit to the tribe and is neither exploitive of the tribe nor of individual tribal members. It is incumbent upon the researcher to fully inform these committees of the nature of the research and to negotiate a mutually acceptable research plan.

Multiple levels of approval. There is often jurisdictional confusion and multiple layers of bureaucracy involved in affairs on Indian reservations. For instance, if approval were needed for the human subjects protection procedures for a drug survey, the following agencies/offices may be involved at one point or another:

1. School Principal
2. School Superintendent
3. School Board
4. Parent Advisory Board
5. Tribal Council
6. Tribal Education Committee
7. Tribal Health Committee
8. Tribal Drug Abuse Program
9. Tribal Institutional Review Board (IRB) for human subject approval
10. Regional Indian Health Service (IHS) IRB
11. National IHS, IRB
12. The Initial Review Group (IRG) which approves grant related research
13. The IRG of the university or other agencies performing research
14. Federal oversight by the Office of Protection from Research Risks

While it is certainly not typical that all of these groups would be involved, the list illustrates the potential number of conflicting points of view that could occur. It is not unusual for various subsets of this list to have input on the conditions of a particular piece of research, nor is it unusual for the various agencies to desire different outcomes. Adequate time must be allotted to identify and negotiate with the appropriate agencies before research can take place.

Urgent need for data. Often, tribes do not have the luxury of time in their need for data. The social problems encountered on many reservations result in many life-threatening circumstances. For instance, the various negotiations and arrangements that have to be made for extensive consent procedures may preclude the timely collection of needed data. Many tribes feel that the need for supportive data far outweighs the burden imposed by excessive regulation. Of course, this need must be weighed in relationship to the need to use procedures that result in data that are useful in resolving the questions of interest and which are in compliance with regulations.

Parent/school relationships. Many Indian people are very ambivalent about the school systems on the reservation or in nearby border towns. On the one hand, Indian people have a clear recognition that education is vital to the future of tribes and Indian parents are very supportive of their children's efforts to attain the best instruction they can. On the other hand, the institutions of the schools raise some very negative feelings. Early educational efforts by the government were specifically intended to eradicate Indian culture and extremely harsh means were used to accomplish this with Indian children. Later educational efforts consisted of boarding schools where Indian youth were removed from their homes, often forcefully, for months and years at a time. The disciplinary methods of the boarding schools were both physically and mentally severe. This era, which lasted into very recent times, inflicted serious harm on the integrity of Indian families. As a result, there is a strong reservoir of negative feelings toward the schools. Research efforts within the school context are often resisted or ignored. Researchers need to be aware of this and should expect to expend a great deal of time with both the schools and families in building a relationship of trust.

School burden. The more complex regulatory and other research procedures become, the less likely Indian schools are able to comply with the requirements. Indian schools are often right at the margin in terms of finances and personnel, and any project that requires an additional burden is likely not to happen. This clearly is a loss both to research projects and to the schools which have a need for information about various aspects of their students' lives and functioning.

Obtaining Cooperation

The researchers at the Tri-Ethnic Center have worked in Indian communities for over 20 years, receiving excellent cooperation within those communities in the conduct of their research. In analyzing these experiences, there appear to be a number of conditions/approaches that need to be adhered to in the research process. Foremost, the background conditions described above must be recognized and the research needs to be designed with a sensitivity to these circumstances. The following additional strategies have also proven useful. While these are probably approaches that are necessary in all field research, they seem to be particularly relevant in Indian communities.

Adequate description of research. Our work, and that of many others, has entailed research on problems encountered by Indian tribes; thus, there may be some sensitivity in discussing or providing data on these problems. However, when the value of the information to be collected has been accurately and completely explained at both the tribal and individual level, we have encountered very little resistance. Indian people certainly expect the research to be of direct value to them, but we have also found a deep sense of altruism in the communities where we have worked. If the more general value of the work to other Indian tribes, and to non-Indians, is communicated, a high degree of cooperation and collaboration will be achieved.

An early and complete explanation of both the intent of the research and what will be required to conduct it will not only forestall later problems but has been found to be very helpful to the research process. Community members have a better understanding of local circumstances and can provide useful information for how the project can be best carried out.

Confidentiality. The standard of individual confidentiality must be applied when working in Indian communities. Many communities are relatively small, and without proper safeguards, it is easy for personal data to become public. Another important level of confidentiality in Indian research is protection of the community from unwarranted criticism. Indian reservations and communities have been the subject of a great deal of prejudice, having been stigmatized by a focus on the negative aspects of their lives. All too often in the past, research data has entered the public domain in a way that continues and perpetuates negative stereotypes. We have made it an absolute policy that we do not release community or school level data to anyone other than our original collaborators at the local level. If information is requested from the outside, we require written permission from the collaborators before release. Although we work with many individual reservations and regularly publish aggregate data, we do not reveal the identities of the participating schools or reservations in our publications.

In some research projects, when it comes time to publish research results, it is difficult to conceal the identity of the participating communities. This can often create serious problems if the results reflect negatively on the reputation of a community and especially if individuals can be identified. The best resolution of this situation is to have a prior agreement regarding publication wherein community members have the right to review manuscripts prior to publication and can suggest modifications that protect the reputation of the community and its members. This delicate process must balance the rights and needs of the community with the need to disseminate research findings. It has often been found that collaboration with community members in the writing of manuscripts can be extremely valuable. Not only is the community protected, but community members can provide interpretation of results that can enrich the research outcomes.

Reimbursement. Financial and personnel resources are extremely scarce in most Indian communities and participation in research can often be an extra burden. Even costs that might ordinarily seem minor must be recognized and reimbursed. In-kind expenses that normally could be absorbed by schools or service agencies simply are not available in many Indian communities. Research budgets must be structured to take these types of expenses into account. Our recent experience in trying to obtain written consent from parents is a case in point. Sending letters out to parents required nearly an extra one dollar per student for postage (with a stamped return envelope, stationary, and clerical time). In a moderately sized school, this ran into the hundreds of dollars, a sum most of the schools could not afford. We had to adjust our budget to accommodate these costs.

Incentives. When research activities involve a significant amount of personal time on the part of research subjects, it is important to provide compensation for that time as well as for travel expenses they may accrue. The amount of reimbursement needs careful consideration. The amount must be equitable and commensurate with the time involved in the project; however, it should not be excessive. There is sometimes a tendency to provide a larger than normal compensation in recognition of the poverty that exists in many ethnic minority communities. However, given the lack of resources, a larger than normal amount may be considered coercive and interfere with the subjects' freedom of decision on whether or not to participate in a project. In most cases, it is reasonable to provide the same level of incentive that is considered standard for the type of research being conducted in other locations.

Value returned to the community. It has already been mentioned in another context, but the importance of insuring that the research has some payoff for the local community cannot be overemphasized. The research history of most reservations is replete with examples of outsiders collecting data for their own purposes without regard for what is in it for the community.

Technical assistance. Researchers must be cognizant that their services may be requested for assistance in areas that may be related to their research but outside the scope of the formal research plan. This sometimes requires creative ways of financing the assistance, or it may simply be a matter of donating these services. For instance, the schools we work with oftentimes ask for suggestions and help in implementing drug abuse prevention efforts as a follow-up to the data collection. These types of requests are legitimate and must be considered as part of the obligation of the research project.

Longevity. Service providers in any Indian community can point to a long list of outside research and service initiatives that have taken place in their area. The prototype of this is the 3-5 year demonstration project that flourishes for a short period of time but, when the external funding terminates, the project folds, leaving the local people with yet another in a long series of unfulfilled promises. The original problem is rarely resolved through these short-lived efforts, and the community is left to continue to address it with only meager resources. When this happens repeatedly, service providers and others become somewhat jaded and are less than enthusiastic when a new research effort comes along. We have been fortunate to have had extended funding and have maintained continual contact with many Indian communities. This not only cements good working relationships but leaves some assurance that our research procedures will evolve to meet the needs of the local community.

Appropriate clearances. The multiple, and often overlapping, jurisdictions in Indian communities create an interesting challenge for negotiating the needed clearances. No two situations are alike and each requires great sensitivity and patience. A previous section listed the potential sources of official sanction that may be needed for a particular piece of research, but it must also be recognized that there may often be other individuals or groups that must be apprised of and approve of the research. For example, we have often witnessed groups from outside the reservation bring a federally funded project onto the reservation to study a particular problem without an assessment of existing programs that may already be addressing that problem. In most instances, social problems are already being dealt with to some extent by agencies that have operated on the reservation for quite some time. While the effects of their efforts may not be readily apparent, these individuals have worked long and hard, usually with meager resources at their disposal. A new project that does not acknowledge these efforts, and does not incorporate the existing experience and expertise into the project, will likely meet resistance. Projects that forge ahead without a good knowledge of the decision makers and gatekeepers and existing resources are often doomed to failure somewhere.

CONCLUSION

American Indian communities exhibit a number of characteristics that must be recognized and accommodated in the course of research. While these may be seen as barriers to the conduct of good research they represent the realities of life in these often remote areas. There is a growing desire in Indian communities for a true partnership in the conduct of research projects. There is a clear recognition that there are many social issues that need to be resolved but there is also a strong motivation to be in control of the efforts intended to help resolve those problems. The most effective research is that which incorporates local knowledge and expertise but which also recognizes that local resources are often limited.

REFERENCES

American Indian and Alaska Native Mental Health Research, 2 (3, special issue). (1989).

Beauvais, F. Ethnic communities and research: Building a new alliance. In P. Langton (Ed.), *The challenge of participatory research: Preventing alcohol-related problems in ethnic communities* (CSAP Cultural Competence Series #3, pp. 105-128). Rockville, MD: Center for Substance Abuse Prevention.

Beauvais, F., & Trimble, J. (1992). The role of the researcher in evaluating American Indian alcohol and other drug abuse prevention programs. In M. Orlandi & R. Weston, (Eds.), *Cultural competence for evaluators* (DHHS Publ # [ADM] 92-1884, pp.173-203). Rockville, MD: Office of Substance Abuse Prevention.

The Belmont Report: Ethical principals and guidelines for the protection of human subjects of research. (1978). Washington, DC: Department of Health, Education and Welfare.

Dent, C., Galifin, J., Sussman, S. Stacy, A., Burton, D., & Flay, B. (1993). Demographic, psychosocial and behavioral differences in a sample or actively and passively consented adolescents. *Addictive Behaviors, 18*, 51-56.

Ellickson, P., & Hawes, J. (1989). An assessment of active versus passive methods for obtaining parental consent. *Evaluation Review, 13*, 45-55.

Flemming, C. (1992). American Indian and Alaska Natives: Changing societies, past and present. In M. Orlandi, & R. Weston, (Eds.), *Cultural competence for evaluators* (DHHS Publ # [ADM] 92-1884, pp. 147-172). Rockville, MD: Office of Substance Abuse Prevention.

Jones, J. (n.d.). *What's left after the right.* Portland, OR: Washington Consulting Services.

Kearney, K., Hopkins, R., Mauss, A., & Weisheit, R. (1984). Sample bias resulting from a requirement for written parental consent. *Public Opinion Quarterly, 47,* 96-102.

Limber, S., & Wilcox, B. (1996). Application of the U.N. Convention on the Rights of the Child to the United States. *American Psychologist, 51,* 1246-1250.

Melton, G. (1996). The child's right to a family environment. *American Psychologist, 53,* 1234-1238.

Mensch, B., & Kandel, D. (1988). Underreporting of substance use in a longitudinal youth cohort. *Public Opinion Quarterly, 52,* 100-124.

Severson, H., & Biglan, A. (1989). Rationale for the use of passive consent in smoking prevention research: Politics, policy and pragmatics. *Prevention Medicine, 18,* 267-279.

Severson, H., & Dennis, A. (1984). Sampling bias due to consent procedures with adolescents. *Addictive Behaviors, 8,* 433-437.

U.S. Government. Protection of human subjects: Code of federal regulations, 45 CFR 46 (Aug. 8, 1975). *Federal Register, 40.* (Revised March 8, 1983).

Retention of Minority Populations in Panel Studies of Drug Use

Marvin D. Krohn, PhD
Terence P. Thornberry, PhD

SUMMARY. Sample retention is a potentially serious problem in panel studies of drug use that include minority respondents. Minority respondents may be more difficult to retain primarily because their disadvantaged economic status makes tracking and contacting them more difficult. It is suggested that with standard techniques of tracking applied aggressively, high retention rates can be obtained for these respondents. This paper describes strategies that are used in an ongoing panel study of drug use among primarily African American and Puerto Rican respondents and evaluates how effective these strategies have been. Over an eight year period involving ten waves of data collection, 86 percent of the initial 1000 adolescents have

---

Marvin D. Krohn is Professor, Department of Sociology, University at Albany. Terence P. Thornberry is affiliated with the School of Criminal Justice, University at Albany.

Address correspondence to: Marvin D. Krohn, PhD, Department of Sociology, University at Albany, 1400 Washington Avenue, Albany, NY 12222, or to Terence P. Thornberry, PhD, School of Criminal Justice, University at Albany, 135 Western Avenue, Albany, NY 12222.

This research was supported by Grant 5 R01 DA05512-02 from the National Institute on Drug Abuse; Grant 86-JN-CX-0007 (S-3) from the Office of Juvenile Justice and Delinquency Prevention, Office of Justice Programs, U.S. Department of Justice; and Grant SES-8912274 from the National Science Foundation. Points of view or opinions in this document are those of the authors and do not necessarily represent the official positions or policies of the funding agencies.

[Haworth co-indexing entry note]: "Retention of Minority Populations in Panel Studies of Drug Use." Krohn, Marvin D., and Terence P. Thornberry. Co-published simultaneously in *Drugs & Society* (The Haworth Press, Inc.) Vol. 14, No. 1/2, 1999, pp. 185-207; and: *Conducting Drug Abuse Research with Minority Populations: Advances and Issues* (ed: Mario R. De La Rosa, Bernard Segal, and Richard Lopez) The Haworth Press, Inc., 1999, pp. 185-207. Single or multiple copies of this article are available for a fee from The Haworth Document Delivery Service [1-800-342-9678, 9:00 a.m. - 5:00 p.m. (EST). E-mail address: getinfo@haworthpressinc.com].

been retained. Among adolescents, there is little difference in attrition by racial/ethnic status. However, among the parents, Puerto Rican respondents have somewhat lower retention rates than white or African American respondents. Reasons for the attrition of the Puerto Rican parents are discussed. Comparisons of drug use and delinquency at Wave 1 between respondents who remained in the study at Wave 10 and those who did not are not statistically different. Correlations between risk factors and drug use and delinquency computed for those respondents who are retained compared with correlations for the total panel are also not substantially different. The findings suggest that given sufficient resources and aggressive implementation of retention strategies, a high retention rate evidencing no significant selection bias can be obtained. *[Article copies available for a fee from The Haworth Document Delivery Service: 1-800-342-9678. E-mail address: getinfo@haworthpressinc.com]*

INTRODUCTION

Over the past few decades, research has come to rely on prospective panel studies to examine the causes and correlates of drug use (see, for example, Elliott, Huizinga, & Ageton, 1985; Kandel, Davies, Karas, & Yamaguchi, 1986; Newcomb & Bentler, 1988; Thornberry, Lizotte, Krohn, Farnworth, & Jang, 1991). Although panel studies, as compared to cross-sectional ones, offer distinct methodological advantages (Farrington, Ohlin, & Wilson, 1986; Menard, 1991), they also engender a unique set of methodological problems. One of the most important concerns is subject loss or attrition. Even if the initial panel is randomly selected and adequately represents the population from which it is drawn, large and differentially distributed subject loss can bias parameter estimates. Thus, panel studies not only have to select representative samples, they need to *retain* the sample members across time if they are to draw valid inferences.

In recent years, there has also been an increasing recognition of the need to examine the patterns and causes of drug use among disadvantaged and minority populations in the context of panel studies (Brunswick, 1988; De La Rosa, Khalsa, & Rouse, 1990). Some researchers have suggested that respondent attrition may be a particularly serious problem among African American and Hispanic respondents (Aneshensel, Becerra, Fielder, & Schuler, 1989; Kandel, Ravais, & Logan, 1983; Vernon, Roberts, & Lee, 1984). This could be because of higher mobility and potential problems in tracking these respondents, meeting special needs that they may have (i.e., language needs), and engendering sufficient trust to enable them to respond to sensitive questions. While this concern has been voiced, very few studies have actually examined the questions of whether there is differential attrition among African American and Hispanic respondents and, relatedly, whether specific methods to reach and retain these populations are needed.

Because sample retention is a potentially serious problem in any longitudinal study, and may be a particularly severe problem in studies that include minority respondents, it is important to examine the sources of subject loss and to identify techniques for minimizing it, especially for minority respondents. This paper examines this topic in an ongoing panel study of drug use that is composed primarily of African American and Puerto Rican respondents. In particular, we describe the strategies that we have used to locate and interview respondents in the Rochester Youth Development Study. We then examine the level of attrition we have experienced, both for the total panel and within ethnic/racial groups. Finally, we examine whether this subject loss is selective and, based on our experiences, draw some general recommendations about subject retention, especially for minority respondents.

PREVIOUS RESEARCH

We begin with a brief literature review on the issue of subject attrition—defined as leaving a panel for any reason after the initial round of data collection. If respondents who leave panel studies are a representative sample of the entire panel, attrition would not be a serious threat to the validity of inferences drawn from the data. Unfortunately, a number of studies suggest that attrition can be systematically related to respondent characteristics and behaviors.

Most prior research on attrition has focused on the impact that respondent loss has on estimates of the dependent variable. Early studies found attrition rates to be positively correlated with drug use (Hansen, Collins, Malotte, Johnson, & Fielding, 1985; Kandel, 1975; Kandel et al., 1983; Josephson & Rosen, 1978) and with delinquent behavior (Elliott & Voss, 1974; Lefkowitz, Eron, Walder, & Huesmann, 1977; Polk & Ruby, 1978; Polk & Schafer, 1972). On the other hand, studies that have high retention rates report few significant differences in drug use and delinquency between those who remain in the panel and those who leave (Elliott & Huizinga, 1983; Huizinga, Loeber, & Thornberry, 1991; Jessor, Donovan, & Costa, 1991; Loeber, Stouthamer-Loeber, van Kammen, & Farrington, 1991; Newcomb & Bentler, 1988; Thornberry, Bjerregaard, & Miles, 1993).

While prior research on drug use has been sensitive to the relationship between panel attrition and estimates of antisocial behavior, there has been much less attention given to other respondent characteristics that may increase the rate of attrition. A key concern for the present investigation is whether attrition varies by the racial/ethnic status of respondents. Kandel et al. (1983) reported a higher attrition rate for minority respondents than for nonminority respondents. They suggest that the higher attrition rate stems from the fact that these respondents are difficult to track because they are more mobile and less likely to have telephones. The task of tracking respondents with Puerto Rican or Mexican origins is additionally complicated by the fact that they often move back and forth between their place of origin and the United States (Aneshensel et al., 1989; Kandel et al., 1983). The rate of attrition can also be affected by failing to be sensitive to the particular needs of a subpopulation. For example, Aday, Chiu, and Andersen (1980) reported that both language and cultural barriers adversely impacted their ability to retain Hispanic subjects.

Some of the reasons for attrition among minority respondents may be due more to their disadvantaged status than their minority status. A number of studies have indicated that attrition is higher among lower class respondents than it is for middle class and upper class respondents (Cordray & Polk, 1983; Elliott & Voss, 1974; Lauritsen, Sampson, & Laub, 1991). Difficulty in maintaining contact with these respondents is often due to geographical mobility and lack of telephones. In addition, educational achievement and grade point averages are inversely related to attrition (Jessor & Jessor, 1977; Kandel et al., 1983). Because African American and some Hispanic (Puerto Rican and Mexican) populations are disproportionately represented among the economically disadvantaged and less educated, difficulty in retaining them in panel studies may be due to the lifestyle adjustments that are produced by their disadvantaged status.

Although the findings of prior research concerning attrition in panel studies of drug use and delinquency are not uniform, they suggest that attrition is a potentially serious methodological problem. While some studies report low rates of selective subject loss, others indicate that respondents who leave the panel are more deviant than those who remain and that respondents who are less cooperative are more deviant than those who are more cooperative. Also, attrition may be related to minority group status and to poverty and social disadvantage. Based on the admittedly scant literature on attrition for minority respondents, it may be that differential attrition among minority populations is for the most part due to factors related to social disadvantage, such as higher mobility and difficulty in communicating with respondents who do not have telephones. Because of these possible biases, it is important to continue investigating the issue of subject loss and whether it differentially affects minority group respondents in panel studies of drug use. To do so, we first describe strategies used in the Rochester Youth Development Study to locate and interview respondents and explore the level of attrition within racial/ethnic groups to determine if subject loss is selective. We then examine whether the loss of subjects biases the relationships observed between key predictor variables and drug use.

METHODS

The Rochester Youth Development Study is designed to contribute to our understanding of the social and psychological forces that lead to serious drug use, delinquency, and violence. The longitudinal design follows a panel of juveniles from their early teenage years through to their early adult years. To date, we have collected 11 waves of data spanning the ages of 13 through 22.

The subjects and their primary caretakers, in almost all cases their biological mothers, were interviewed at 6 month intervals from the Spring of 1988 until the Spring of 1992. After a 2 year gap in data collection, annual interviews began in 1994. At the end of Wave 11, in the Spring of 1996, we retained 86 percent of the initial 1,000 subjects in the study.

The interviews last about 90 minutes and cover a wide range of topics including social class position, family structure and processes, educational performance, peer relationships, neighborhood characteristics, psychological functioning, social networks, and social support systems. In addition to the interview data, we collect data from the files of official agencies that serve children and youth, including the Rochester public schools, police department, probation department, family court, and social services. Table 1 provides an outline of the overall design of the Rochester Youth Development Study.

Sampling Procedures

The Rochester Youth Development Study oversampled youth at high risk for serious drug use and delinquency since the base rates for these behaviors are relatively low (Elliott, Huizinga, & Menard, 1989; Wolfgang, Thornberry, & Figlio, 1987). To accomplish this, the following strategy was used. First, the target population was limited to seventh and eighth grade students in the public schools of a city–Rochester, New York–that has a diverse population and a relatively high crime rate.[1] Second, a stratified sample was selected from the target population so that: (a) high-risk youth are overrepresented; and (b) the findings can be appropriately weighted to represent the target population.

To oversample high-risk youth, the sample was stratified on two dimensions. First, males were oversampled (75% versus 25%), because they are more likely than females to be chronic offenders and to engage in serious delinquency (Blumstein, Cohen, Roth, & Visher, 1986). Second, students from high crime areas of the city were oversampled on the premise that adolescents residing in high crime rate areas are at greater risk for offending than those in low crime rate areas. To identify high crime areas, each census tract in Rochester was assigned a resident arrest rate reflecting the proportion of the tract's total adult population arrested by the Rochester police in 1986.

There were a total of 4,013 students in the seventh and eighth grades in the Spring of 1988 and of these, 3,372 (84%) were eligible for the sample.[2] All eligible cases were assigned to their census tract of residence at the beginning of sample selection. To generate a final panel of 1,000 students, 1,334 were selected, based on an estimated non-participation rate of approximately 25 percent (Capaldi & Patterson, 1987; Elliott, Ageton, Huizinga, Knowles, & Canter, 1983). The 1,334 cases were selected in the following way: First, in the census tracts with the highest resident arrest rates (approximately the top one-third), all eligible students were asked to participate in the study. Second, students in the remaining census tracts were selected at a rate proportionate to the tract's contribution to the city's resident arrest rate. As a tract's resident arrest rate declined, the proportion of the sample drawn from that tract proportionately declined. Once the number

TABLE 1. Research Design, Rochester Youth Development Study

	Date	Grades	Mean Age
Phase I:			
Wave 1	Spring 1988	7-8	13.5
Wave 2	Fall 1988	8-9	14.0
Wave 3	Spring 1989		14.4
Wave 4	Fall 1989	9-10	14.9
Wave 5	Spring 1990		15.4
Wave 6	Fall 1990	10-11	16.0
Wave 7	Spring 1991		16.4
Wave 8	Fall 1991	11-12	17.0
Wave 9	Spring 1992		17.4
Phase II:			
Wave 10	Fall 1994		20.1
Wave 11	Fall 1995		21.0

of students to be selected from a tract was determined, the student population in the tract was stratified by sex and grade, and students were selected from those strata at random. Based on these procedures, a final panel of 1,000 students and their primary caretakers was selected for study.

Field Procedures

Once the sample was drawn, we contacted the parent (or legal guardian) of each student selected. The purpose and design of the study were described, and the parent was asked to provide informed consent both for their participation and the participation of their child. If the parent agreed to participate, the Wave 1 parent interview was conducted. The children of these parents were then contacted and asked to provide their assent to participate. Wave 1 student interviews were usually conducted at school, but students who could not be interviewed at school, for example, chronic truants, were interviewed at home.

Not all families agreed to participate in the study. The overall refusal rate was 20 percent, and virtually all of that was generated by parent refusals; only four students refused to participate after their parent agreed. Once a parent or student refused to participate, the student was replaced by another student of similar grade, gender, and residence. In this way, minimum distortion was introduced into the final panel; the available data indicate that refusals were not differentially distributed in terms of race/ethnicity, gender, grade in school, or the resident arrest rate of the census tract of residence. These procedures generated a sample that is 68 percent African American, 17 percent Hispanic, and 15 percent white. As virtually all of the Hispanic respondents in the sample are of Puerto Rican descent, we will refer to them as Puerto Ricans in this paper. Males represent 72.9 percent of the sample, and females, 27.1 percent. (See Farnworth, Thornberry, Lizotte, & Krohn, 1990, for a more complete description of the Rochester Youth Development Study sampling plan.)

Retention Strategies

Considerable effort was devoted to maximizing subject retention over the course of the study. First, there was no *a priori* limit to the number of attempted contacts that were made at each wave. As long as the respondent did not refuse to be interviewed, the case was kept open until the end of each data collection period. Second, all subjects who moved from Rochester were followed and, whenever possible, interviewed. Third, even though the sampling frame was generated by the school roster and we conducted adolescent interviews in the Rochester schools whenever possible, adolescents who left the Rochester schools remained in the panel. This includes adolescents who transferred to other schools, dropped out of school, were institutionalized, or, while remaining on the school roster, were chronic truants.

Prior research indicates that retention strategies that are designed for low income, highly mobile populations can be effective when used to retain minority populations if they are implemented aggressively (Capaldi & Patterson, 1987; Gwadz & Rotheram-Borus, 1992; Lucas, Grupp, & Schmitt, 1974; Robles, Flaherty, & Day, 1994; Stouthamer-Loeber & van Kammen, 1995; Thornton, Freedman, & Camburn, 1982). Because of that, with one exception, we did not adopt any strategies specific to a particular minority group to increase retention; we simply implemented a set of basic procedures for all respondents. The one exception was that we translated the interview into Spanish (Puerto Rican dialect) and hired bilingual interviewers who were indigenous to the Rochester community. In some cases, this procedure proved to be essential; in other cases where it was not essential, it served to generate much good will and might have further contributed to the high retention rates we obtained (Rogler, Barreras, & Santana Cooney, 1981).

Tracking Procedures

To maintain high retention, the Rochester study uses a variety of sources to locate respondents who have moved. During each interview, respondents are asked if they plan to move within the next year. If so, we ask for the new address, or at least for the city and state where they plan to move. In some instances, respondents themselves call (using our 800 number) or write our office to give us an updated address and/or phone number. In most cases, however, the Rochester Youth Development Study must rely on less direct methods or sources of information. In order of actual utility, they are: secondary sources, mailings, directory assistance, databases from official agencies, newspaper articles, military sources, credit bureaus, and schools.

1. *Secondary Sources:* Secondary sources, who are nominated by both subject and parent respondents, are relatives or friends who would know the respondent's whereabouts if he or she were to move from their present address. For subjects, we ask for the name, address, and phone number of one of their parents, another relative, and a friend; for parents, we ask for a relative and a friend. This information is combined and entered into a database, which contains the four most recent and complete secondary sources. Secondary sources are contacted by phone, in person, or by mail. If necessary, we can show the person a signed statement from the respon-

dent which gives his or her permission to contact secondary sources in the event that we cannot locate the respondent. Having the subject's signature on the secondary source form has proven particularly helpful in gaining the cooperation of sources who may otherwise be reticent to divulge this information.

As a valuable backup to the current secondary source database, all secondary sources and other relevant information from previous interviews are kept on file. Over time, we have built up a considerable list of secondary sources for each subject; in some cases, names and addresses of up to a dozen different friends and relatives are available. This "historical record" has been invaluable in tracking the most mobile respondents.

2. *Advance Letters and Newsletters:* The Rochester Youth Development Study also uses various mailings (advance letters and newsletters) which help us locate respondents. If mailings are forwarded by the U.S. Postal Service, we ask the respondent to call our toll-free number or return a postage-paid change-of-address card to notify us of their new address. All mailings are labeled, "Address Correction Requested; After 5 Days, Return to Sender," which generates an updated address from the Postal Service, provided that a respondent has filled out a change-of-address card. Typically, however, the Rochester Youth Development Study receives most returned mail with "No such address," "No forwarding order on file," and so on, which initiates a search through the other strategies discussed here. Additional letters are mailed to previous addresses or new ones suggested by secondary sources or from other contacts.

3. *Directory Assistance:* Routinely, the Rochester Youth Development Study calls Directory Assistance for new listings for respondents or for secondary sources. If a respondent's surname is unusual, other people listed in the directory may be contacted. Searches of the Rochester phone directory sometimes lead us to relatives who live on the same street as our respondent. For female respondents, the directory is searched for address and surname to find subjects whose phone listings are in their husbands' names. In addition, we routinely search a CD-ROM National Telephone Directory.

4. *Databases:* The Rochester Youth Development Study also makes use of record searches through the databases of organizations which are likely to serve our respondents. We sometimes locate respondents through contacts at the Department of Social Services for Monroe County, the Rochester Police Department, and the New York State Department of Correctional Services. When searching official records for data about our subjects, we obtain all listed addresses for our files. In addition, state motor vehicles departments are contacted to obtain current address information.

5. *Newspapers:* Another source for locating subjects is the newspaper. On a daily basis, the Rochester *Democrat and Chronicle* is reviewed to see if any respondents are mentioned. The "Courts" section lists the name, age, and address of people appearing in court; study subjects are listed about once a week. There are also columns on military personnel, people attending colleges, marriages, and so forth, that are helpful.

6. *Department of Defense:* We have contacted the Department of Defense to obtain a central locating source for military personnel. Names of subjects who are in the Armed Services are sent to the Personnel Office of the Joint Chiefs of Staff, and they provide current assignments and telephone numbers.

7. *Credit Bureaus:* Credit bureaus, such as Trans Union Credit Corp., are used to obtain updated addresses and telephone numbers.

8. *Central School Records:* Central school records can be searched for a student's home address, phone number, and guardian. We used school resources to locate respondents with great success during the early years of the study. As subjects left high school, this source of information became less useful, but we continue to use it for subjects who have younger siblings of school age. Also, since many Rochester Youth Development Study subjects now have children of their own, school records should again be a useful source for locating respondents as the next generation reaches school age.

Maintaining Cooperation

The Rochester Youth Development Study uses a combination of strategies to maintain subject cooperation:

1. Incentive payments are given to study participants after each interview. These payments increase each year, and subjects are told of these increments in advance.
2. An annual newsletter is mailed to study participants to inform them of project news and results. In addition, packets of findings from the study have been made available to participants, because many of them have requested results over the years. Having a tangible product, in part produced by their own efforts, makes respondents more willing to participate.
3. Participants are reminded of the importance of the study and its potential impact on programs and policy which will affect the youth of tomorrow. Much of this information is contained in the project newsletter and in various letters we send to the respondents.

4. We also remind the respondents that they are unique and cannot be replaced in the study by anyone else. Only they can continue to provide the continuous flow of information on their development that is needed.

RESULTS

Retention Rates

The main issue addressed in this article concerns the success of the techniques described above in retaining subjects in a panel study that has, to date, interviewed subjects 11 times over ten years. Tables 2 and 3 provide the percentage of the total panel that was interviewed in each wave from Wave 2 through Wave 10, the most recent wave completed when this analysis was conducted.

At Wave 10 the overall retention rate for subjects is 86 percent (Table 2). Across adjacent waves the retention rate never drops by more than two percent; this includes Wave 10 after there had been a 2 year gap in data collection. This rate compares quite favorably to other panel studies of drug use and delinquency, especially when it is recalled that we over-

TABLE 2. Subject Retention Rate, Wave 2 to 10 (in Percentages)

	Total Panel (n = 1,000)	African American (n = 680)	Puerto Rican (n = 170)	White (n = 150)	Significant difference (p < .05) between: Puerto Rican and White	Puerto Rican and African American	African American and White
Wave 2	95	95	91	95		x	
Wave 3	93	94	91	93			
Wave 4	93	93	90	96	x		
Wave 5	92	92	91	95			
Wave 6	91	90	91	93			
Wave 7	90	89	89	93			
Wave 8	88	88	84	89			
Wave 9	88	88	87	89			
Wave 10	86	85	83	91	x		

sampled high-risk youth. For example, Cordray and Polk (1983) reviewed 10 interview-based panel studies and reported retention rates ranging from 95 percent to 37 percent with a mean of 66 percent.

Our major focus in this study is on the comparison of retention rates for the three racial/ethnic groups in our study. Table 2 provides these rates and, to test for significant differences across the three groups, we conducted paired t-tests. Of the 27 comparisons, only 3 are statistically significant. Since only 10 percent of the comparisons are significant, they may well be produced by chance. At Wave 2, more African American students are retained than Puerto Rican students; at Wave 4, whites have a higher retention rate than Puerto Ricans; and at Wave 10, we retain a significantly greater percentage of white than Puerto Rican respondents. We will address reasons for these differences for the Puerto Rican respondents after we have presented the retention rates for the parents of our subjects.

Although parent retention rates are still high–83 percent for the total panel at Wave 10–it is evident that it is somewhat more difficult to retain the parents of our subjects than it is to retain our target subjects (Table 3). It is also evident that parents of Puerto Rican adolescents are more difficult to keep in the study than are parents of either African American or white respondents. At Wave 10, parents of 83 percent of the African American adolescents, 78 percent of the Puerto Rican adolescents, and 87

TABLE 3. Parent Retention Rate, Wave 2 to 10 (in Percentages)

| | | | | | Significant difference ($p < .05$) between: | | |
	Total Panel (n = 1,000)	African American (n = 680)	Puerto Rican (n = 170)	White (n = 150)	Puerto Rican and White	Puerto Rican and African American	African American and White
Wave 2	91	93	81	92	x	x	
Wave 3	90	90	85	94	x	x	
Wave 4	87	85	87	92			x
Wave 5	86	85	84	91	x		x
Wave 6	81	81	73	91	x	x	x
Wave 7	79	79	69	89	x	x	x
Wave 8	79	80	73	83	x	x	
Wave 9[a]	--	--	--	--	--	--	--
Wave 10	83	83	78	87	x		

[a]Parents were not interviewed at Wave 9

percent of the white adolescents were interviewed. For every wave except Wave 4, the percentage of Puerto Rican parents that are retained is significantly lower than white parents, and in five of the nine waves the retention rate for Puerto Rican parents is lower than that for African Americans. African Americans are also slightly more difficult to retain than whites, with four of the differences being statistically significant.

The difficulty in retaining Puerto Rican parents is first seen at Wave 2 when we retained 81 percent of them, which is about 10 percent less than the rates for the other two racial/ethnic groups. This initial drop can be explained by two logistical problems. First, it was difficult to hire qualified bilingual interviewers and, second, it took additional time for the interview to be translated into Spanish and for the bilingual interviewers to be trained in both versions of the interview. Because of this, interviews that required bilingual interviewers were fielded later in the wave, thereby decreasing the time we had to locate the families and complete the interviews. In subsequent waves, we were better prepared to deal with these issues, resulting in an increase in retention rates at Waves 3 to 5.

At Wave 6, however, retention rates for Puerto Rican parents drop off significantly, whereas there are small reductions in the retention rates for whites and for African Americans. The reduction in retention rates for Puerto Rican parents is not due to the previous logistical problems with developing and administering bilingual interviews. In exploring possible reasons for the drop in retention, we focused on what was occurring in the lives of our target subjects. At Wave 6, the target subjects were, on average, 16-years-old, and some had already left their parents' homes and were living independently. In earlier waves when we interviewed parents whose children did not live in the home, interviewers reported that parents displayed considerable frustration with the interview because most of the items assumed that the child and parent lived together, or at least had very frequent interaction. Therefore, for the Wave 6 interviews, we decided that if the child had not lived with the parents since the previous interview, the parent would not be interviewed.

Table 4 provides the percentage of subjects who lived independently of their parents or guardians at Waves 5 through 9. Between Waves 5 and 6, there was a substantial increase in the percentage of Puerto Rican subjects who no longer lived in the parental home, from 4.5 percent to 11.7 percent. Although there is also an increase in the number of white (2.1% to 3.6%) and African American (1.9% to 5.5%) subjects living independently, significantly more Puerto Rican subjects do so. This is generally the case from Waves 5 to 9. Hence, a primary reason for the reduction in the retention rates for Puerto Rican parents appears to be due to our decision not to interview the parents of subjects who lived on their own and the higher percentage of Puerto Rican subjects in this category. This also had a spillover effect on tracking Puerto Rican youth and contributes to their slightly lower retention rates.

At Wave 10, we assumed that most target subjects were no longer living at home and the interview was revised accordingly. A renewed effort was made to enlist the cooperation of all parents. This effort was successful as the retention rates for all groups (see Table 3), including Puerto Ricans, rose at Wave 10.

Summary

Retention rates for both our target subjects and their parents remain high through 10 waves of data collection. Retention rates are slightly higher for target subjects (86%) than they are for their parents (83%) which may be due to parents having less involvement in the everyday lives of their children as youth age. The lower retention rate for Puerto Ricans can be accounted for by the fact that more Puerto Rican youth lived independently from the parental home at earlier ages than African American or white youth.

Maintaining high retention rates is critical to panel studies. The Rochester Youth Development Study has been successful at doing so. However, even with these high retention rates, results based on our data could be biased if the characteristics of those individuals who are not retained are distinctly different from those who remain in the study. In the next section, we compare demographic characteristics and self-reported drug use and delinquency rates for these groups.

TABLE 4. Percentage of Subjects Living Independently, by Race/Ethnicity

	African American (n = 680)	Puerto Rican (n = 170)	White (n = 150)	Significant difference (p < .05) between:		
				Puerto Rican and White	Puerto Rican and African American	African American and White
Wave 5	1.9	4.5	2.1			
Wave 6	5.5	11.7	3.6	x	x	
Wave 7	8.6	13.9	6.4	x		
Wave 8	10.4	13.4	6.8			
Wave 9	12.6	18.5	12.0			

Comparison of Retained and Not Retained Subjects

To examine whether there is any selection bias due to attrition, we compare the respondents who were retained in the study with those who were not retained. We compare these groups on gender, social class, and family structure within racial/ethnic categories.

Table 5 presents the demographic characteristics of those retained and those not retained for the total sample and for each of the three racial/ethnic groups. Only small differences in the percentages by gender, social class, and family structure are evident for the total sample and for the various racial/ethnic groups. Indeed, *none* of these differences are statistically significant indicating that the loss of respondents over 10 waves of data collection did not affect the demographic portrait of our respondents.

In any panel study of drug use and delinquency, a key concern is whether the respondents who are lost through attrition may be the ones who are most likely to be involved in the behaviors that are being studied. One way to assess this is to compare the Wave 1 rates of drug use and delinquency of the respondents who are retained in the study at Wave 10 to the Wave 1 rates of those who were not retained. Although measuring deviant behavior at Wave 1 is not ideal because the prevalence of such behavior in the early teenage years is low, it is the only wave for which we have data on all those individuals who left the study sometime after Wave 1. Also, since early onset of deviant behaviors is rather strongly related to later involvement in those behaviors, the Wave 1 measure may be a proxy for more general involvement in deviant careers.

Table 6 provides the prevalence rates of drug use and delinquency at Wave 1 for those who were retained and for those who were not retained at Wave 10. The rates are very similar. For example, 7.7 percent of those retained at Wave 10 self-reported drug use at Wave 1. Of those not retained at Wave 10, 9.7 percent self-reported drug use at Wave 1. Neither this difference in the prevalence rate of Wave 1 drug use, nor any of the other differences in prevalence rates reported in Table 6 are significantly different. This is true even when the panel is divided into racial/ethnic groups. To the extent that Wave 1 drug use and delinquency rates predict the likelihood that youth will continue to engage in these activities, the findings indicate that respondents who left the study are not more likely to engage in deviant behavior than are those who remained in the study at Wave 10.

Another way to evaluate the extent that attrition might affect a study is to see whether estimates of relationships between core variables and rates of deviant behavior are different for the total panel and those who are retained. To do this, we selected four variables that have frequently been included in

TABLE 5. Demographic Characteristics of the Total Panel, Those Retained at Wave 10, and Those Not Retained (in Percentages)

	Total Panel (n = 1,000)	Retained[a] (n = 855)	Not Retained (n = 145)
Gender			
Male			
Total Panel	72.9	72.2	77.2
African American	68.2	66.8	76.5
Puerto Rican	77.1	78.0	72.4
White	89.3	89.0	92.9
Female			
Total Panel	27.1	27.8	22.8
African American	31.8	33.2	23.5
Puerto Rican	22.9	22.0	27.6
White	10.7	11.0	7.1
Social Class			
Lower Class			
Total Panel	42.9	42.8	43.4
African American	43.4	44.1	39.2
Puerto Rican	61.2	59.6	69.0
White	20.0	19.9	21.4
Middle Class			
Total Panel	57.1	57.2	56.6
African American	56.6	55.9	60.8
Puerto Rican	38.8	40.4	31.0
White	80.0	80.1	78.6
Family Structure			
Both Natural Parents			
Total Panel	25.4	26.2	20.7
African American	20.1	21.1	14.7
Puerto Rican	34.7	36.2	27.6
White	38.7	37.5	50.0
Other			
Total Panel	74.6	73.7	79.3
African American	79.9	78.9	85.3
Puerto Rican	65.3	63.8	72.4
White	61.3	62.5	50.0

[a]None of the comparisons between those retained and those not retained are statistically significant at the $p < .05$ level.

studies of the causes of drug use and delinquency–attachment to parents, commitment to school, delinquent beliefs, and peer delinquency–and correlated them with drug use and the general delinquency index at Wave 1 for the total panel and for those remaining in the study at Wave 10. We then examine these same correlations within the three racial/ethnic groups.

The results are reported in Table 7. The correlations of key predictor variables with drug use and with delinquency for the total panel and those retained are very similar suggesting that subject loss has not appreciably affected the conclusions that we would derive from the analysis.

In sum, comparisons of demographic characteristics and of drug use and delinquency rates for respondents who remained in the study with the total sample demonstrated that there is little selection bias in the loss of subjects. Further analysis revealed that correlations among key theoreti-

TABLE 6. Prevalence of Drug Use and Delinquency at Wave 1 for the Total Panel, Those Retained at Wave 10, and Those Not Retained (in Percentages)

	Total Panel (n = 1,000)	Retained[a] (n = 855)	Not Retained (n = 145)
Drug Use			
Total Panel	8.0	7.7	9.7
African American	8.4	7.8	11.8
Puerto Rican	9.4	10.6	3.4
White	4.7	4.4	7.1
General Delinquency			
Total Panel	49.6	48.8	54.5
African American	51.6	50.5	57.9
Puerto Rican	45.9	45.4	48.3
White	44.7	44.9	42.9
Property Crime			
Total Panel	17.7	17.7	17.9
African American	17.1	17.1	16.7
Puerto Rican	24.7	24.8	24.1
White	12.7	12.5	14.3
Violent Crime			
Total Panel	30.6	30.4	31.7
African American	35.1	34.8	37.3
Puerto Rican	22.4	22.7	20.7
White	19.3	19.9	14.3

[a]None of the comparisons between those retained and those not retained are statistically significant at the p < .05 level.

cally relevant variables and drug use and delinquency are not appreciably affected by the loss of subjects in the Rochester study. This is evident within racial/ethnic categories as well.

DISCUSSION

Subject attrition can threaten the validity of the results of any longitudinal, panel study that follows the same subjects over an extended period of time. The difficulty in retaining subjects is increased when those subjects are low-income and highly mobile. Moreover, some researchers (e.g., Aneshensel et al., 1989; Kandel et al., 1983; Vernon et al., 1984) are concerned that racial/ethnic differences may complicate the process be-

TABLE 7. Zero-Order Correlations Between Predictor Variables and Drug Use at Wave 1, and General Delinquency at Wave 1 for the Total Panel, and Those Retained at Wave 10

	Drug Use		General Delinquency	
	Total	Retained	Total	Retained
Attachment to Parent				
Total Panel	−.14*	−.14*	−.16*	−.17*
African American	−.16*	−.15*	−.13*	−.13*
Puerto Rican	−.17*	−.18*	−.32*	−.37*
White	−.00	−.01	−.15	−.16
Commitment to School				
Total Panel	−.12*	−.17*	−.25*	−.25*
African American	−.12*	−.18*	−.22*	−.21*
Puerto Rican	−.17*	−.15	−.30*	−.29*
White	−.12	−.19*	−.39*	−.40*
Delinquent Beliefs				
Total Panel	.16*	.21*	.27*	.29*
African American	.13*	.17*	.26*	.28*
Puerto Rican	.26*	.28*	.25*	.40*
White	.23*	.26*	.25*	.23*
Peer Delinquency				
Total Panel	.20*	.19*	.29*	.30*
African American	.19*	.19*	.30*	.32*
Puerto Rican	.20*	.18	.26*	.28*
White	.29*	.21*	.27*	.24*

*p < .05 (two-tailed).

cause of special issues related to language and other cultural characteristics. Despite this concern, there is, in fact, virtually no empirical evidence to support or refute it. Providing some evidence on this topic, using data from the Rochester Youth Development Study, was the central concern of this paper.

An important feature of the Rochester Youth Development Study is the oversampling of subjects from high crime neighborhoods. By doing so, a sample of low-income, predominately minority group youth was obtained. Following this group for 10 waves of data collection over a nine year period was a daunting task. In this article, we have outlined the procedures that we found particularly effective in tracking and in maintaining the cooperation of our subjects. We have also provided data which suggest that we have been successful in retaining a high proportion of the panel and that the subject loss we have experienced has not biased the sample or the conclusions that one would derive from the results.

In conclusion, a few general suggestions and comments can be offered concerning longitudinal studies, especially those with low-income, minority populations. Any undertaking of this kind must be well-funded. Without the generous support of agencies like the National Institute on Drug Abuse and the Office of Juvenile Justice and Delinquency Prevention, it would have been impossible to track and elicit the cooperation of our subjects. In prior analyses of our data (Thornberry et al., 1993), we found that the most difficult and expensive respondents to track were also the most interesting for a study of drug use and delinquency. It is, therefore, essential that longitudinal studies make every effort to retain difficult subjects and be given the resources to do so.

To successfully execute this type of study, the field staff must be fully committed to maintaining high retention rates. We are very fortunate to have a field director, Mr. William Miles, who has relentlessly pursued this mission. Our success can largely be attributed to his determination and that of his staff.

Overall, we do not think that it is inherently more difficult to obtain cooperation or to track African American or Hispanic subjects. Rigorously applying standard tracking procedures–incentive payments, use of secondary sources, treating respondents honestly and courteously at all times, and so forth–to all respondents seems to be the most effective strategy. In our case, doing so yields satisfactory, and relatively uniform, retention rates, especially for the target respondents. Recall that at Wave 10, we retained 83 percent of the Puerto Rican, 85 percent of the African American, and 91 percent of the white respondents. Moreover, our field staff reports that the strategies for tracking and locating respondents were uniformly effective across the three racial/ethnic groups. In particular, an accurate, current list of secondary sources is the single most effective strategy for maintaining subject participation for all respondents.

That is not to say that there are no unique issues for different racial or ethnic groups. We did have some difficulty with the logistics of conducting the initial rounds of bilingual interviews that increased attrition in the early waves. We also noted that Hispanic youth left the parental home earlier than white or African American youth, resulting in somewhat higher attrition among Hispanic parents. We do not know if this tendency is specific to our population or is a general phenomenon. If Hispanic youth do leave the parental home earlier than other youth, then provisions need to be made for this in the study design. More generally, whenever a segment of the sample has special interview needs, the design of the project must place those needs high on its priority of concerns if high retention for that group is to be achieved. Moreover, if that group represents a relatively low proportion of the total sample, a decision on the relative costs and rewards of investing resources into acquiring those interviews must also be made. In our case, having a sufficient number of Hispanics in our sample was very important and, therefore, we chose to invest the necessary resources.

Our experience with conducting a large scale panel study with a disadvantaged, minority sample has demonstrated that with the necessary resources and commitment, high retention rates can be maintained, and any bias in results due to attrition is minimized. While such an undertaking constitutes a major commitment of time and money, the benefits of longitudinal panel studies make the effort worthwhile.

NOTES

1. In 1986, the city of Rochester had an index crime rate of 9,351 per 100,000 inhabitants, considerably above the national rate (5,480), that of New York State (5,768), and even that of New York City (8,847). In terms of violent crimes, Rochester's rate (1,301 per 100,000) was higher than the state's (956) and somewhat lower than New York City's (1,995). A similar pattern is seen for murder rates per 100,000: Rochester's was 16, New York State's was 11, and New York City's was 22 (Flanagan & Jamieson, 1988). Clearly Rochester is a city with a substantial level of serious and violent crime.

2. Students were ineligible if they moved out of the Rochester school district before Wave 1 data collection began, if neither English nor Spanish was spoken in the home, if a sibling was already in the sample pool, or if they were older than the expected age for eighth graders given the Rochester schools' admission policy.

REFERENCES

Aday, L., Chiu, G. Y., & Andersen, R. (1980). Methodological issues in health care surveys of the Spanish heritage population. *American Journal of Public Health, 70*, 367-374.

Aneshensel, C. S., Becerra, R. M., Fielder, E. P., & Schuler, R. H. (1989). Participation of Mexican American female adolescents in a longitudinal panel survey. *Public Opinion Quarterly, 53*, 548-562.

Blumstein, A., Cohen, J., Roth, J. A., & Visher, C. A. (1986). *Criminal careers and "career criminals."* Washington, DC: National Academy Press.

Brunswick, A. (1988). Young black males and substance use. In J. T. Gibbs (Ed.), *Young, black and male in America: An endangered species* (pp. 166-187). Dover, MA: Auburn House.

Capaldi, D., & Patterson, G. R. (1987). An approach to the problem of recruitment and retention rates for longitudinal research. *Behavioral Assessment, 9*, 169-177.

Cordray, S., & Polk, K. (1983). The implications of respondent loss in panel studies of deviant behavior. *Journal of Research in Crime and Delinquency, 20*, 214-242.

De La Rosa, M. R., Khalsa, J. H., & Rouse, B. A. (1990). Hispanics and illicit drug use: A review of recent findings. *International Journal of the Addictions, 25*, 665-691.

Elliott, D. S., Ageton, S. S., Huizinga, D. H., Knowles, B. A., & Canter, R. J. (1983). *The prevalence and incidence of delinquent behavior, 1976-1980.* (National Youth Survey Report No. 26). Boulder, CO: University of Colorado at Boulder, Behavioral Research Institute.

Elliott, D. S., & Huizinga, D. H. (1983). Social class and delinquent behavior in a national youth panel, 1976-1980. *Criminology, 21*, 149-177.

Elliott, D. S., Huizinga, D. H., & Ageton, S. S. (1985). *Explaining delinquency and drug use.* Beverly Hills, CA: Sage.

Elliott, D. S., Huizinga, D. H., & Menard, S. (1989). *Multiple problem youth: Delinquency, substance use, and mental health problems.* New York: Springer-Verlag.

Elliott, D. S., & Voss, H. L. (1974). *Delinquency and dropout.* Lexington, MA: D.C. Heath and Company.

Farnworth, M., Thornberry, T. P., Lizotte, A. J., & Krohn, M. D. (1990). *Sampling design and implementation.* (Technical Report #1). Albany, NY: University at Albany, Rochester Youth Development Study.

Farrington, D. P., Ohlin, L. E., & Wilson, J. Q. (1986). *Understanding and controlling crime: Toward a new research strategy.* New York: Springer-Verlag.

Flanagan, T. J., & Jamieson, K. M. (Eds.). (1988). *Sourcebook of criminal justice statistics-1987.* U.S. Department of Justice, Bureau of Justice Statistics. Washington, DC: U.S. Government Printing Office.

Gwadz, M., & Rotheram-Borus, M. J. (1992). Tracking high-risk adolescents longitudinally. *AIDS Education and Prevention, Fall (Supplement)*, 69-82.

Hansen, W. B., Collins, L. M., Malotte, C. K., Johnson, C. A., & Fielding, J. E.

(1985). Attrition in prevention research. *Journal of Behavioral Medicine, 8,* 261-275.

Huizinga, D. H., Loeber, R., & Thornberry, T. P. (Eds.). (1991). *Urban delinquency and substance abuse: Technical report.* Washington, DC: U.S. Department of Justice, Office of Juvenile Justice and Delinquency Prevention.

Jessor, R., Donovan, J. E., & Costa, F. M. (1991). *Beyond adolescence: Problem behavior and young adult development.* New York: Cambridge University Press.

Jessor, R., & Jessor, S. L. (1977). *Problem behavior and psychosocial development: A longitudinal study of youth.* New York: Academic Press.

Josephson, E., & Rosen, M. (1978). Panel loss in a high school drug study. In D. B. Kandel (Ed.), *Longitudinal research on drug use: Empirical findings and methodological issues.* Washington, DC: Hemisphere-Wiley.

Kandel, D. B. (1975). Reaching the hard to reach: Illicit drug use among high school absentees. *Addictive Diseases, 1,* 465-480.

Kandel, D., Davies, M., Karas, D., & Yamaguchi, K. (1986). The consequences in young adulthood of adolescent drug involvement. *Archives of General Psychiatry, 43,* 746-754.

Kandel, D., Raveis, V., & Logan, J. (1983). Sex differences in the characteristics of members lost to a longitudinal model: A speculative research note. *Public Opinion Quarterly, 47,* 567-575.

Lauritsen, R., Sampson, R., & Laub, J. (1991). The link between offending and victimization among adolescents. *Criminology, 29,* 265-291.

Lefkowitz, M. M., Eron, L. D., Walder, L. O., & Huesmann, L. R. (1977). *Growing up to be violent.* New York: Pergamon Press.

Loeber, R., Stouthamer-Loeber, M., van Kammen, W., & Farrington, D. P. (1991). Initiation, escalation and desistance in juvenile offending and their correlates. *Journal of Criminal Law and Criminology, 82,* 36-82.

Lucas, W. L., Grupp, S. E., & Schmitt, R. L. (1974). Longitudinal research and marijuana smoking. *Criminology, 12,* 315-327.

Menard, S. 1991. *Longitudinal research.* Newbury Park, CA: Sage Publications.

Newcomb, M. D., & Bentler, P. M. (1988). *Consequences of adolescent drug use: Impact on the lives of young adults.* Newbury Park, CA: Sage Publications.

Polk, K., & Ruby, C. H. (1978, August). *Respondent loss in the longitudinal study of deviant behavior.* Paper presented at the International Symposium on Selected Criminological Topics, Stockholm, Sweden.

Polk, K., & Schafer, W. (Eds.) (1972). *Schools and delinquency.* Englewood Cliffs, NJ: Prentice Hall.

Robles, N., Flaherty, D. G., & Day, N. L. (1994). Retention of resistant subjects in longitudinal studies: Description and procedures. *American Journal of Drug and Alcohol Abuse, 20,* 87-100.

Rogler, L. H., Barreras, O., & Santana Cooney, R. (1981). Coping with distrust in a study of intergenerational Puerto Rican families in New York City. *Hispanic Journal of Behavioral Sciences, 3,* 1-17.

Stouthamer-Loeber, M., & van Kammen, W. (1995). *Data collection and management: A practical guide.* Thousand Oaks, CA: Sage Publications.

Thornberry, T. P., Bjerregaard, B., & Miles, W. (1993). The consequences of respondent attrition in panel studies: A simulation based on the Rochester Youth Development Study. *Journal of Quantitative Criminology, 9,* 127-158.

Thornberry, T. P., Lizotte, A. J., Krohn, M. D., Farnworth, M., & Jang, S. J. (1991). Testing interactional theory: An examination of reciprocal causal relationships among family, school and delinquency. *Journal of Criminal Law and Criminology, 82,* 3-25.

Thornton, A., Freedman, D. S., & Camburn, D. (1982). Obtaining respondent cooperation in family panel studies. *Sociological Methods & Research, 11,* 33-51.

Vernon, S. W., Roberts, R. E., & Lee, E. S. (1984). Ethnic status and participation in longitudinal health surveys. *American Journal of Epidemiology, 119,* 99-113.

Wolfgang, M. E., Thornberry, T. P., & Figlio, R. M. (1987). *From boy to man, from delinquency to crime.* Chicago: University of Chicago Press.

Reducing Selection Bias
in the Use of Focus Groups
to Investigate Hidden Populations:
The Case
of Mexican-American Gang Members
from South Texas

Avelardo Valdez, PhD
Charles D. Kaplan, PhD

SUMMARY. This paper examines the problem of selection bias in the recruitment of focus group participants. Selection bias is a methodological concern because it hinders the generalizability, representativeness, and comparability of focus group findings. Data for this paper was based on 24 focus groups conducted as part of a study on Mexican-American gangs. Discussed are specific strategies that minimize bias in the selection process among hidden populations. These include acquiring extensive information on gangs, avoiding institutional references, maintaining high visibility, making social contact,

---

Avelardo Valdez is Director, Hispanic Research Center, The University of Texas at San Antonio. Charles D. Kaplan is affiliated with the Department of Psychiatry, Maastricht University, The Netherlands.

This research was supported by the National Institute on Drug Abuse grant R01 DA0864-02 to the Hispanic Research Center, The University of Texas at San Antonio.

[Haworth co-indexing entry note]: "Reducing Selection Bias in the Use of Focus Groups to Investigate Hidden Populations: The Case of Mexican-American Gang Members from South Texas." Valdez, Avelardo, and Charles D. Kaplan. Co-published simultaneously in *Drugs & Society* (The Haworth Press, Inc.) Vol. 14, No. 1/2, 1999, pp. 209-224; and: *Conducting Drug Abuse Research with Minority Populations: Advances and Issues* (ed: Mario R. De La Rosa, Bernard Segal, and Richard Lopez) The Haworth Press, Inc., 1999, pp. 209-224. Single or multiple copies of this article are available for a fee from The Haworth Document Delivery Service [1-800-342-9678, 9:00 a.m. - 5:00 p.m. (EST). E-mail address: getinfo@haworthpressinc.com].

using community gatekeepers, and gender differences in accessing. The strategies recommended rely on traditional field work methods that involve immersion into the social world of the participants. *[Article copies available for a fee from The Haworth Document Delivery Service: 1-800-342-9678. E-mail address: getinfo@haworthpressinc.com]*

INTRODUCTION

The focus group has received attention for some time as a tool in applied research to obtain qualitative data (Krueger, 1988; Stewart & Shamdasani, 1990). In the fields of drug abuse, violence, and HIV/AIDS, the focus group has become a popular methodology for investigating the hidden populations where these problems are present.[1] This paper provides a methodological treatise on a number of issues which have arisen in reference to reducing selection bias in the use of focus groups for the study of hidden populations. This treatise is based upon a study that has employed focus groups among Mexican-American gang members in South Texas. Gang members qualify as a hidden population because their behavior is highly stigmatized and they tend to avoid revealing their social world to outsiders. This status makes them difficult to identify and recruit into social science studies. The challenge for social scientists is to develop sampling strategies that engage these hidden populations into methodological frameworks that can assess study results for internal and external validity. Five topics related to the selection bias among Mexican-American gang members that emerged in the course of our focus group research will be discussed in this treatise. These topics include: acquiring extensive information on gangs, avoiding institutional references, maintaining high visibility, making social contact, using gatekeepers and gender differences in accessing.

Focus group methods involve the systematic formation of groups that range from 4 to 12 members with reasonably homogeneous characteristics. The focus group is organized for the purpose of obtaining qualitative data on a wide assortment of information, including answers for specific research questions, generating descriptive information, developing and elaborating hypotheses, and producing theoretical insights. This differs from delphic and brainstorming groups which are also commonly used in research. The focus group is led by a group facilitator who stimulates an informal, but structured, discussion encouraging participants to express themselves in their own words. The topics for discussion are carefully selected and sequenced and are designed to provide maximum focused information from the point of view of the participants selected for their special experience that is of research interest.

The focus groups in the study of Mexican-American gang members served six purposes. One purpose was to gain information on drug-related violence among gang members and youth peer groups. A second purpose was to learn about the organizational structure, goals, and activities of gangs and peer groups. The third purpose was to explore the existence of adult criminal and drug-based groups. A fourth purpose was to gather information that will help develop the rosters of gang members and other non-gang youth in order to provide a sampling frame for the selection of a representative sample to administer an interview instrument (Yin, Valdez, Kaplan, & Mata, 1996). The fifth purpose was to obtain information on the institutional completeness of the neighborhood.[2] The sixth purpose was to identify what questions to ask and how to ask them in the structured interview instrument.

A total of 24 focus groups were conducted; these groups were comprised of: (1) male gang members, (2) female gang members, (3) male and female gang members, (4) other youth (male and female) involved in drug-related violence but who are not gang members, (5) youth not involved in drug use and violence, (6) adults involved in violence and the drug culture, (7) parents (single-headed or intact families) of gang and non-gang members, and (8) law enforcement and corrections personnel.

The recruitment of focus group participants was conducted by persons indigenous to the local community who functioned as "community researchers." The selection of the community researchers is important in gaining and sustaining access to gangs and non-gang members. These individuals were either ex-gang members and/or former drug abusers who were indigenous to the research sites. The actual focus groups were lead by one of the principal investigators with the assistance of the community researchers.

STRATEGIES FOR REDUCING SELECTION BIAS

Selection bias of focus group participants, as with other field research methods, is always a matter of concern. This universal concern has well been articulated by Berk (1983):

> The potential for sample selection bias exists whenever one is working with a nonrandom subset of the population. While our application was necessarily limited to selection problems within a survey framework, other data forms are hardly immune. . . . Much like specification error and measurement error, the potential for bias is virtually universal. (p. 396)

Selection bias in focus groups, like surveys, affects the validity and generalizability of study results. It also affects internal validity, a problem that is generally overlooked by researchers. Selection bias is especially apparent in social science investigations of hidden populations.

The bias to recruit the most accessible members frequently occurs in studies of hidden populations; this concern is one of utmost importance in studies of gang members. Most studies do not take into consideration in their selection procedures the diversity of gang member status (e.g., leaders, original gangsters, and core and fringe members) and gang organization types (e.g., criminal gangs, territorial/barrio gangs, school gangs, and others). Reasons for this failure are numerous and include inappropriate field work, lack of familiarity with the population, and the social class bias of the researchers (Hagedorn, 1996). The end result is that participants who are recruited into the study may not represent the target population.

After a thorough review of the literature and from consultations with experts before entering the field, we became highly sensitized to this threat. Therefore, we invested much of our attention on specifying gang member status and gang organizational type in the recruitment of participants in our focus groups. In addition, we developed a set of standard operating procedures to safeguard the selection procedure. These procedures emerged in the course of our fieldwork and were implemented "on the spot" in order to consistently improve the quality of the selection process. As will be discussed below, these selection process procedures provided us with both a partial listing of the principle sources of bias we encountered in our fieldwork as well as specific methods for controlling these in practice.

Acquiring Extensive Information on Gang Structure, Types of Memberships, and Range of Activities

We had not had prior contact with the majority of the gangs and gang members, but we did have extensive knowledge of the population from our community membership and prior field studies of injecting drug users. The focus groups were a means to acquire initial baseline information on this population and to learn more about the gang from the member's perspective. Therefore, we saw a need to be certain that individuals selected for the focus groups were not selected based on simple convenience, that is, because of their availability or their uniqueness. Participants in the focus group had to be homogeneous as gang members, but diverse enough to represent subtle variations within the gang population based upon our prior knowledge.

In order to assure that the project's existing stock of knowledge was sufficient enough to help control selection bias, the researchers had to broaden their base of prior knowledge by learning as much as they could about types of members, cliques, and ranges of gang activities. The more that we learned about gang structure, the more we also learned about the gaps in our prior knowledge. Through this gradual social learning process, we were able to reduce the unconscious systematic sampling bias that has remained largely uncontrolled for in many of the previous gang studies. For instance, we came to appreciate how easy it is for researchers to recruit their initial contacts into focus groups without asking themselves how these contacts fit into the existing gang structure. This action often results in the inclusion in the focus group of a specific segment, set, or clique within the gang that is socially closer to the researcher at the expense of the exclusion of others. Therefore, there is often an unknown built-in bias in focus group participants that results from recruiting mainly from the pool of initial contacts.

Gaining an early comprehensive understanding of gang structure is difficult, especially within a short period of time; however, it is worth the effort. This preparatory work provides essential insights into the various types of memberships and their individual roles in the gang. The structure of the gang is often dependent on the gang's primary activities. For example, if a gang is highly involved in drug dealing, their gang structure is going to be more complex than if it is a barrio/territorial gang. This knowledge is essential to assure that the focus group recruits will represent the range of gang types as well as the distinct types of gang members. The comments of one community researcher illustrated this point:

> I am having trouble getting into that gang because they're moving a lot of stuff (drugs). They do not want to cooperate with us. They have more to lose than the other gangs. A lot of these guys have ties with older guys in the neighborhood.

The community researchers began to make inroads with this gang only after months of intensive field work. Eventually, we found that it was impossible to bring them into a focus group. As a result of this type of extensive field research, we not only knew whom the focus groups included, but also whom they excluded and why some specific kinds of gangs and gang members were not represented in the sample. This knowledge allowed us to describe the limitations of our sample in more precise terms.

Avoiding Institutional Referrals

Researchers should avoid referrals from institutional representatives such as school officials, social service agents, and criminal justice officials. Institutionally based studies tend to be less systematic, lack precise knowledge of inclusion and exclusion characteristics necessary for systematic study, and have other serious limitations. Individuals identified by these sources often represent only a certain segment of the targeted population. For example, a methadone clinic may only refer heroin users who are currently in treatment.

One of the most important safeguards against selection bias in our study was to avoid acquiring gang members' names from police, schools, public housing officials, and other institutions. There is a strong possibility that individuals identified by these sources may not have ever been gang members or may no longer be affiliated with gang activity. Because data is often not available to verify an individual's gang membership, and there is no knowledge of the context of their selection, inclusion of these persons in the focus group likely will bias the study findings. Many of the focus group's participants may not be gang members, but rather, "wannabes," or other types of gang member "look-a-likes."

To illustrate this concern with one concrete example, the city police department's special gang unit had developed an extensive dossier on San Antonio gangs over a 4-year period. This included identification of gangs, territory, names of members, gang structure and affiliations, tags, and hand signs. The problem with this dossier is that it tended to overestimate the number of members in specific gangs. In particular, the city police estimated that 126 individuals belonged to the Bad Boys, a notorious Mexican-American gang. This figure was almost twice the estimate our community researchers developed through their field work.

Several reasons emerged in the course of our fieldwork to account for this difference. According to several sources, the procedures for registering a person in the police's gang dossier allowed for identification simply by being seen in the company of gang members. This "registration by association" may have occurred at a school, recreational center, playground, in a stopped vehicle, or any other numerous places where young people hang out together. It should be noted that this kind of association was made for the convenience of the police. It had little to do with the process of "differential association" described in the literature where deviant groups differentiate themselves from the general population through their own behavioral codes and subculture (Sutherland & Cressey, 1978). In contrast to the police fieldwork, our sampling tried to systematically incorporate and *verstehen* these processes of differential association in order to register true gang members from inside the immediacy of their own social worlds (Ferrell, 1997). Ferrell defined *verstehen* as:

> (A) process of subjective interpretation on the part of the social
> researcher, a degree of sympathetic understanding between research-
> er and subjects of study, whereby the researcher comes in part to
> share in the situated meanings and experiences of those under scruti-
> ny. (p. 10)

In ecologically dense inner-city communities where gangs are numerous, it is difficult for young persons to avoid contact with hardcore gang
members. There is not an obvious segregation of activities in these neighborhoods. One of the community researchers described the following after
observing a school scene:

> As we were told, we approached the large group of students who
> were boarding the buses. There were kids all over, interacting with
> each other. The teachers were there trying to get everyone on the
> buses. From this mass of kids emerged Monica our contact with
> several other girls. When she saw us, she waved the other girls off.

Monica is a member of a girl's gang who hangs out primarily in the
downtown area. Given the operating procedures, the police gang unit
could have identified all of the girls who were with Monica that afternoon
as gang members when this was not the social fact. This example illustrates an essential point that often is obscured in the methodology of gang
research: Contact with the gang is not the same thing as gang membership.
Guilt by association is not a legal argument, and it should also not be an
argument for inclusion in a sample or case register.

Another procedural factor that influences the overestimation of the
police's gang dossier is that there is no system of updating. In the gang
member rosters we received from the police, we found that many of the
individuals identified as Bad Boys gang members actually had not had any
contact with the police for over three years. Many of these inactive gang
members were no longer active, having matured out of the gang, been
incarcerated, or left the "hood" for various reasons, including joining the
military. Along with registration by association, failure to update is likely
to explain why the police gang unit's estimates of gang members tend to
be so much higher than those of our community researchers.

In conclusion, while avoiding institutional referrals is a good practice
and a fieldwork ideal, in specific situations, a mechanical avoidance will
be counterproductive. If the researcher has few contacts with the target
group, or certain institutions have exceptionally good relationships such
that they are truly part of the community, institutional referrals can be
useful. In our own situation, we remained open to the possibility that given

individuals can play multiple roles in the community and can either speak officially with their institutional hats on or unofficially as bona fide community members. In these cases, we tried to approach them outside of their institutional roles. Therefore, we would recommend not to automatically exclude such individuals as resource persons in the recruiting of focus group members.

Maintaining High Visibility

A veteran gang social worker offered one of our community researchers clear advice regarding gaining entree to gangs, "Maintain a high visibility among them." This advice proved to be very important in safeguarding against selection bias. Researchers attempting to make contact and build rapport with highly exclusive and hidden populations such as gangs cannot sit behind their desk and expect to get a representative sample. The mere introduction by a gatekeeper or other person trusted by gang members is often not enough to control selection bias. The researchers must personally prove themselves to be interested and engaged with the gang members as something more than their scientific and academic objects. They must work diligently to gain the confidence of the population through the high visibility of simply "being there" and then reinforcing this presence by displaying that they are sincere and can be trusted.

As an example, our community research staff was attempting to recruit to a focus group session members of one of the most active and violent gangs in the city. A local community agency had successfully negotiated a truce for this gang, whose turf covered a particular housing project and surrounding environs and several other gangs. As part of the truce, the agency organized a basketball league in which some of the gangs participated. These games were held twice a week during the evenings. The center was considered a neutral area relatively free of gang conflict.

With the permission of the agency, a community researcher started working the basketball games as a scorer and referee. After several weeks, the community researcher became a familiar face to the gang members. A point was reached where gang members felt comfortable with the researcher's presence. The researcher stated, "It took a while before those guys accepted me. They had to make sure that I wasn't an undercover cop or police informer." Subsequently, the agency occasionally invited the researcher to other scheduled meetings with the gang members such as the gang war council meetings. At the war council, issues related to the truce were discussed. Once this stage of the access process was accomplished, the researcher was able to go onto the next step of recruiting for the focus group.

Making Social Contact

As necessary as establishing visibility is, it is not sufficient to safeguard against selection bias. The researchers must establish social contact with gang members, in some manner, becoming a part of their social networks. After several weeks of high visibility in the field, the gang members whom we were targeting, suspiciously approached our community researcher and asked what he was doing. The researcher was able to briefly describe the project and the aim of the focus groups. Subsequently, he was able to approach gang members on the streets, thereby bridging the gap between the community center agency and the gang network. The researcher had built up enough trust with these youth that he could then approach and contact them on their turf and terms. This enabled the establishment of a relationship with the gang members outside of the community agency. As one researcher stated:

> Once they knew me, I could go and talk to them at their own hang-outs. Like this one gang was always at this corner building in the projects. When I spotted them there, I could now get out of my car and go rap to them. They wouldn't all scatter, think I was a cop or narc.

Other contacts with gang members were made more directly. For example, one of the focus groups was conducted with a gang called "Los Homies." Our researcher's first contact with this gang was through a young man who was approached while waiting for a bus at one of the bus stops near the courts (public housing projects). After explaining the project and giving him his card, the young man admitted to the researcher that he belonged to Los Homies. A few days later, the researcher received a call from this person. We suspect that this might have been to check if the project was associated with the police. The researcher was asked to meet with him again and other members of the gang. After two or three such meetings, the gang was relatively comfortable with the researcher and began to trust him and the project.

These types of contacts usually lead to more social interaction between researcher and members of the gangs. The increase in the frequency of face-to-face social contacts increases the imbeddedness of the project within the social network of the gangs. Increased frequency of interaction also involves an increase in the personal emotional ties between the project team members and the gang members. This results in an emerging sense of mutual commitment to the objectives of the study and with that, a sense of shared ownership. This sense will not only lead to making the hidden population more accessible for research, but will provide natural validity checks of gang member status of selected persons and of gang organizational type as the study subjects gradually are transformed to study participants.

Using Community Gatekeepers

The role of gatekeeper has been extensively discussed in literature on fieldwork methods. It is well established that identifying the proper gatekeeper is essential in gaining entree into the world of hidden populations. The gatekeepers selected often are those that are most convenient for the researcher. This is particularly the case among gang members since gaining access to street gangs is so difficult.

Our study employed a multi-site design (San Antonio and Laredo) which enabled us to compare the role of gatekeepers in two distinct but related community settings. The recruitment of focus group participants was progressing more rapidly in Laredo than in San Antonio. Initially, we attributed the success of the recruitment to the hard work of the Laredo staff. However, we learned that most of the focus groups in Laredo were recruited primarily through personal and agency contacts. This selectivity of focus group participants biased information that was generated from these sessions. Once aware of this problem, our initial satisfaction with the efficiency of the recruitment in Laredo gave way to a serious concern with attempts to modify the recruitment process.

Using gatekeepers in this manner often ignores the implications of such convenience selectivity (Hagedorn, 1996; Moore, 1978; Whyte, 1943). As mentioned above, the gatekeepers may be providing access to only a segment of the gang or another hidden population. If used extensively, this process may jeopardize the reliability of the information generated from the focus groups unless the role and limitations of each gatekeeper are transparent to the research process. Hagedorn (1996) discusses this extensively in his critique of theory and methods in gang field research.

In the 24 focus groups conducted in our study, approximately 75 percent were initiated by a gatekeeper. The reliability of using a high percentage of gatekeepers can be increased by assuring that they come from diverse positions in the social structure of the community. Thus, gatekeepers in our study included:

1. Gang members,
2. Parents of gang members,
3. Relatives of gang members (e.g., aunt, uncle),
4. Personal contacts of community researchers,

5. Previous clients of community researchers, and
6. Community agency contacts.

Gang members have proven to be the best gatekeepers in gaining access to this population. Using this kind of individual will provide direct access to the gang without "go betweens," such as friends, parents, and social agencies. As previously discussed, however, making these contacts is a lengthy process which may not be practical for focus groups in every instance. In San Antonio, one of our focus groups was initiated by a direct street contact with a member. This contact was with the second head of a gang. Most gangs in San Antonio have a leadership structure consisting of two or three ranked leaders (i.e., first head, second head, and third head). When a rapport and trust was established, he invited the researcher to meet with several of the other gang members. The following account illustrates what happened during the first meeting with the leader:

> We met at the San Juan Projects. There were about seven members from the gang there. Most were cooperative, asking about the study and so forth. One of the guys named Pingo was giving me a hard time. Pingo was a shooter in the gang. Pingo had been in TYC and was suspicious. We had to convince him; plead with him. This went on four separate times, before two of the other guys finally got him to agree to participate in the focus groups.

This focus group, initiated by the gang member gatekeeper, turned out to be one of the best sessions we conducted. Pingo brought the first head to the session. If we had not taken the time and made the effort to convince Pingo, we would have excluded one of the most violent members of the gang.

Parents and relatives of gang members also played important gatekeeper roles in this study. Lupe was a parent of two teenage girls who were once active in gangs. When she heard about the study from a co-worker at a battered women's shelter, she contacted the office. She volunteered to recruit several of her daughter's friends who belonged to a gang called "Puras Rucas." After getting the phone number of one of the heads, she managed to coordinate a meeting. They agreed to meet at a downtown convenience store. When the researcher asked how he would recognize them, she replied that they would be wearing their colors. The first obstacle was to convince them that he was not a cop or associated in any way with law enforcement. After the third meeting, both heads of the gang agreed to participate in the focus group session. Interestingly, this was the only gender mixed gang focus group which we conducted. It consisted of two female heads, one other female, and two males.

Community agencies were another source of gatekeepers for a particular segment of this population. In some cases, agencies can be very effective in gaining entree, particularly if the agency has established good rapport and trust with gang members. One such agency located on the West Side of San Antonio has been working with gangs for years. During the last couple of years, the agency has managed to negotiate a truce among some of the most violent gangs in the city. Outreach workers with this agency functioned as gatekeepers for several of the gangs that were involved in the focus groups.

On the other hand, if an agency has a bad reputation with gang members, using them as gatekeepers can be ineffective (see Delgado in this publication). In San Antonio, there were several agencies that claimed to work with gangs, but who had bad relations with the gangs. One of these was an agency associated with the public housing authority who was primarily responsible for monitoring gang activities of its residents. If any members of families were caught in illegal gang activities, the family could be evicted. This policy was reinforced with recent federal legislation. Being referred to gang members by persons associated with this office would create serious barriers to gang members that resulted from their animosity towards the agency. Unfortunately, we were not always aware of the reputation of the agencies with gang members; at times, this lack of awareness may have hindered our access to this population.

The personal contacts of the community researchers also functioned as effective gatekeepers. All of our researchers were indigenous to the local community and had extensive personal and familial networks from which to draw gatekeepers. Some of these community researchers worked in social agencies prior to working on the project. They were able to identify gang members and adult clients who provided access to this population. One problem with relying on the personal contacts of the researchers is the tendency to become overly dependent on these sources. This often deters them from developing other contacts. Additionally, the personal contacts may only provide access to persons that are within their own limited social networks. This sort of gatekeeper bias can be attributed to the city's small population and the familiarity of residents with one another (i.e., everybody knows everyone else). Our experience suggests that demographic differences can significantly influence the role of gatekeepers in focus group selection and data quality. The process of using gatekeepers should be carefully monitored for demographic differences.

Gender Differences in Accessing

In this study, we initially proposed that the sample of gang members should include a ratio of two females to seven males in both cities. The two to seven ratio was based on preliminary findings on the participation of females in gangs and drug-related violence. Eventually, forty-three percent of the total focus group participants were female. A major finding from the focus groups was that females were integrated into gang life differently than males. Distinct types of women associated with gangs were identified:

1. girlfriends (wives, common-laws, sweethearts),
2. good girls (sisters, relatives, neighbors, childhood friends, etc.),
3. relatives (sisters, cousins), and
4. hood rats (party girls, sluts, bad girls).

Conclusions drawn from these focus groups, which the preliminary fieldwork supported, were that the number of independent female gangs were not as numerous as anticipated and that most females associated with gangs in both San Antonio and Laredo were not formally incorporated and/or organized into gangs. Young females' involvement in the local gang and other drug scenes appears related to their male partners and to their fluid social networks.

Reflecting a different social position and organization, the methods for recruiting female gang members for the focus groups proved to be slightly different than for males. Often entree to female participants was through boyfriends, family members, and male gang members. A community researcher described how he recruited the female members of the BA Queens, the female counterparts of the BA Kings, one of the largest and most active male gangs in Laredo:

> Hercules, the leader of the BA Kings, gave us the name and address of Gabby who was head of the BA Queens. The first two times we went to the house her mother thought we were narcs, and we were there to pick-up the daughter. Only after the third time did the mother and brother, after overhearing us speak in slang, did she talk to us.

After explaining the purpose of the focus groups, the mother arranged for the staff to meet with Gabby who assisted in organizing the focus group with the BA Queens. In this situation, a male gang member, brother, and mother provided entree to this female gang.

Other female gang members were recruited through more institutionalized contacts, such as service centers and schools. One female group consisted of the "Las Locas" gang, who hung out in the San Antonio downtown area. They described themselves as primarily a "party and fighting gang." They were recruited through a counselor at a drug treatment center who had one of the leaders of the girls as a client. The counselor, an acquaintance of one of the researchers, spoke to the leader of the gang about the focus group. She subsequently agreed to participate along with seven other members. The other members who participated were selected by the community researchers and the leader. Another all female focus group consisted of delinquent non-gang members with arrest histories. These girls were selected from an alternative high school program.

DISCUSSION AND CONCLUSION

The paper has presented some specific strategies for controlling and reducing sources of selection bias that may emerge in implementing focus group research designs among hidden populations such as gang members. These strategies address aspects of the selection process, including proper use of gatekeepers, avoiding institutional bias, making social contact, acquisition of extensive information, and adapting field work methods to gender differences. Underlying these strategies is a fundamental appreciation of the value of the available stock of community "common sense" knowledge and the importance of *verstehen*.

These strategies may be tempered by the researcher's prior knowledge of the population, resources, time limitations, and other situational factors. For instance, focus groups are often used in drug research to gain new insights into new or emerging drug use patterns. In this case, the focus group's limited objective and urgency calls for a rapid response that may trade off control for convenience. These types of research projects are usually funded for short periods of time and prevent extensive field work. An example of this type of research is a study on Rohypnol in Mexico City which was conducted over a short-time period (Ortiz, Galvan, Rodriguez, Soriano, & Unikel, 1996). This type of urgency may force the researchers to use or modify different strategies than those suggested here.

Despite the use of the strategies suggested here and by other researchers (Van Gelder & Kaplan, 1992) there are some intrinsic limitations to the focus group that elude the reduction of bias. The strategies recommended here rely on traditional field work methods that involve immersion into the social world of the participants by community researchers. The use of community researchers provides an access to hidden populations not normally available to professional academics. However, they are quite likely to lack the social distance to make selection decisions in an objective, systematic, and open way. This problem may be overcome somewhat by regular meetings between professionals and community researchers, but it still remains a persistent limitation of this methodology.

Another limitation of the focus group among hidden populations is the lack of a collateral group to verify the quality of those selected to participate in the group. There are usually no independent persons to check the selection of the focus group participants. In the rare case where other research groups are working with the same population at the same time, there is no way of telling on the face of it if the subjects chosen are the best ones to represent the hidden population. Since there is no sampling frame and collateral reference group, there is no hard standard to assess the characteristics of the selected focus group members for representativness and authenticity.

The strategies we presented in this paper were developed in the particular social context presented by Mexican-American working class life. Their accuracy will undoubtedly have to be adapted to the different contexts in which other ethnic group gang members act. Future research will have to determine whether these strategies provide a basis of formal methodological theory that fits the varying realities of other ethnic groups. For example, the characteristics of Mexican-American communities, with the central role of the extended family, affect the way gatekeepers are used and gender differences are treated. Nevertheless, we would defend our position by saying that the processes we describe must be entertained if selection bias is to be reduced. For example, gender differences in the black community will not be the same as in the Mexican-American community, but these differences will have to be recognized if representative samples of male and female gang members are to be recruited.

While there is consensus that the potential for selection bias exists in all social research methods, the problem of selection bias is even more acute and threatening in studies of hidden populations within minority communities. The challenge for social science is to limit these biases in order to maximize the generalizability, representativeness, and comparability of findings. This paper described an attempt to minimize selection bias when using focus group methods. However, even when implementing these strategies and taking into consideration the precautions suggested here, there will continue to be a certain level of bias in the selection process. It is then advisable to clearly state the intrinsic limitations of the specific design in question so that the conclusions drawn can be weighed accordingly.

NOTES

1. Hidden population refers to "a very small subpopulation or a subpopulation of individuals who are unwilling to disclose themselves" because of their involvement in socially sensitive, undesirable, or even taboo activities. Such hidden populations include heroin addicts, cocaine users, and street gangs (Frank & Snijders, 1994).

2. "Institutional completeness" refers to resiliency of community institutions such as family, ethnic businesses, church, and schools. We theorize in our study that the weakening of these institutions leads to the disappearance of indigenous social control mechanisms such as multigenerational linked peer groups.

REFERENCES

Berk, R. A. (1983). An Introduction to sample selection bias in sociological data. *American Sociological Review, 48(June)* 386-398.

Ferrell, J. (1997). Criminological *verstehen*: Inside the immediacy of crime. *Justice Quarterly, 14(1)*, 3-23.

Frank, O., & Snijders, T. (1994). Estimating the size of hidden populations using snowball sampling. *Journal of Official Statistics, 10(1)*, 53-67.

Hagedorn, J. M. (1996). The emperor's new clothes. *Free Inquiry in Creative Sociology, 24(2)*, 111-122.

Krueger, R. A. (1988). *Focus groups: A practical guide for applied research.* Newbury, CA: Sage.

Moore, J. W. (1978). *Homeboys: Gangs, drugs, and prisons in the barrios of Los Angeles.* Philadelphia, PA: Temple University Press.

Ortiz, A., Galvan, J., Rodriguez, E., Soriano, A., & Unikel, C. (1996). *Rohypnol use in Mexico City.* Community Epidemiology Work Group International Report.

Stewart, D. W., & Shamdasani, P. M. (1990). *Focus groups: Theory and practice.* Newbury Park, CA: Sage.

Sutherland, E. H., & Cressey, D. R. (1978). *Criminology* (10th ed.). New York, NY: Lippincott.

Van Gelder, P. J., & Kaplan, C. D. (1992). The finishing moment: Temporal and spatial features of sexual interactions between streetwalkers and car clients. *Human Organization, 51(3)*, 253-263.

Whyte, W. F. (1943). *Street corner society.* Chicago, IL: University of Chicago Press.

Yin, Z., Valdez, A., Mata, A. G., & Kaplan, C. D. (1996). Developing a field-intensive methodology for generating a randomized sample for gang research. *Free Inquiry in Creative Sociology, 24(2)*, 195-204.

TRAINING AND DEVELOPMENT
OF MINORITY AND NON-MINORITY
ABUSE RESEARCHERS
AND RESEARCH TEAMS:
ADVANCES AND ISSUES

This section focuses on the training of minority and non-minority drug abuse researchers to conduct research in minority populations. One common theme within this section is the training of researchers to be sensitive to the cultural values of the minority population which they are studying. A second common theme is the need to develop guidelines to build and effectively manage drug abuse research teams that effectively gain access to minority populations. Included in this section are papers by Alegría and Vera, and Grills and Rowe.

Alegría and Vera's paper focuses on the training of effective drug abuse minority and non-minority researchers to conduct research with Puerto Rican populations. The authors consider the advantages and disadvantages of being a minority researcher who heads a research project in a minority community. Alegría and Vera provide recommendations on critical issues which researchers should address in the development of effective research teams to conduct drug abuse research studies with Puerto Rican populations. Grills and Rowe discuss various strategies which are effective in the formulation and regular management of research teams that conduct drug abuse research in African-American communities. They present information on the importance of developing a value orientation which is respectful and congruent with the values of the African-American community a study investigates.

225

Building Effective Research Teams When Conducting Drug Prevention Research with Minority Populations

Margarita Alegría, PhD
Mildred Vera, PhD

SUMMARY. This article offers guidelines on how to structure effective research teams for drug abuse research with minority populations. Highlighted are several advantages and disadvantages of being a minority researcher who heads a project in a minority community. Contributions to understanding the social, political, and economic context of minority populations are discussed from the point of view of minority researchers. The paper argues that cultural differences color both the product and process of the research endeavor. It reviews the special considerations related to the organizational structure, culture, and climate pertinent to a minority researcher. This article presents recommendations that others may find useful in

Margarita Alegría is Associate Professor, Health Services Research, and Director, Center of Evaluation and Sociomedical Research, and Mildred Vera is Associate Professor, Graduate School of Public Health, both at the Medical Sciences Campus, University of Puerto Rico.

Address correspondence to: Margarita Alegría, School of Public Health, Medical Sciences Campus, University of Puerto Rico, P.O. Box 365067, San Juan, PR 00936-5067 (E-mail: M_ALEGRIA@RCMACA.UPR.CLU.EDU).

This work was funded by Grant No. 1 R01 DA09438 from the Division of Epidemiology and Prevention Research, National Institute on Drug Abuse.

[Haworth co-indexing entry note]: "Building Effective Research Teams When Conducting Drug Prevention Research with Minority Populations." Alegría, Margarita, and Mildred Vera. Co-published simultaneously in *Drugs & Society* (The Haworth Press, Inc.) Vol. 14, No. 1/2, 1999, pp. 227-245; and: *Conducting Drug Abuse Research with Minority Populations: Advances and Issues* (ed: Mario R. De La Rosa, Bernard Segal, and Richard Lopez) The Haworth Press, Inc., 1999, pp. 227-245. Single or multiple copies of this article are available for a fee from The Haworth Document Delivery Service [1-800-342-9678, 9:00 a.m. - 5:00 p.m. (EST). E-mail address: getinfo@haworthpressinc.com].

building teams for drug abuse research with minority populations. *[Article copies available for a fee from The Haworth Document Delivery Service: 1-800-342-9678. E-mail address: getinfo@haworthpressinc.com]*

INTRODUCTION

As one enters the competitive arena of a research career, the absence of a blueprint on team building can become a barrier to success. The aim of this paper is to provide some general guidelines on structuring effective research teams when conducting drug abuse research with minority populations. These guidelines are designed to include four general topics: (1) the advantages and disadvantages of being a minority researcher heading a project in a minority community; (2) the barriers encountered with funding agencies; (3) the relevant elements of an effective research team; and (4) recommendations for building effective research teams. This work seeks to encourage other minority investigators in the hope that many more will join our ranks.

ADVANTAGES AND DISADVANTAGES OF BEING A MINORITY RESEARCHER HEADING A PROJECT IN A MINORITY COMMUNITY

Understanding the history, experiences, troubles, and other cultural elements of the study population is one of the significant advantages of minority researchers. Minority researchers in minority communities share the group's cultural inheritance of feelings, values, ideas, behaviors and interactions (Gertz, 1973). They have been subjected to the social transformations, social conflicts, power relationships, and migrations that are part of life experiences and histories at a collective level (Good, 1994). The minority researcher profits from a first hand experience of the life in the community. Through participation in the process of local community interaction, he/she learns local worlds of interpersonal experience that help organize perception, emotion, and cognition (Ware & Kleinman, 1992). These shared worlds of interpersonal experience help the researcher to understand how an event is constructed and the actions taken to deal with that event. An example of such is the description presented by Singer (1993) of the interaction of a young monolingual Spanish-speaking mother who took her 8-month-old baby to the emergency room of a Hartford hospital. The English-speaking physicians and nurses who treated the infant saw the mother as "hysterical" and "overreactive" in her behavior. The mother felt she was treated "harshly" and in a "cold manner." This unproductive interaction in two hospitals culminated in the infant's death due to dehydration. The tragedy of this child became an event that transformed health care from a personal to a collective policy issue for the Puerto Rican community in Hartford. It concretely addressed the frustration of the Puerto Rican community that health professionals misunderstood their needs.

Explanations for behaviors can involve circumstances which may not be readily apparent to an outsider. For example, drug use may be seen as an illness or resulting from a wider spectrum of interpersonal networks and community dynamics necessary to cope with difficulties (Pedigo, 1983). In surveying Hispanic drug using women, drug use was frequently described as the vehicle that neutralized their anger, frequent episodes of domestic violence, and everyday frustrations of life in poverty. Hypotheses of what drives drug behaviors can be voiced from the cultural and social-political context, expressing an empathy for the problems, burdens, and difficulties faced by minority populations. Such an understanding will help enrich the conceptual orientation and provide for an increased awareness of relevant processes under study.

Minority researchers also have the advantage of including constructs relevant and appropriate to characterize the dynamics surrounding the problem under study. Gary and Berry (1985) raise the importance of racial consciousness and religious involvement in substance use in the Black communities. Schinke, Moncher, Palleja, and Zayas (1988) discuss the function of informal networks, acculturation, and psychological stress in understanding and preventing substance use among Hispanic adolescents. Nyamathi (1991) chronicles the role of somatic complaints in drug recovery among homeless minority women. Other contributions range from stressing the importance of poverty, prejudice, and lack of economic opportunities on American Indian reservations (Oetting, Edwards, & Beauvais, 1988) to the relevance of taking into consideration differences in physiological responses to medication of Asians and the implications these differences may have for treatment and rehabilitation (Leung & Sakata, 1990).

Minority researchers also have advantages in the development of culturally relevant instrumentation. Understanding and measuring behaviors can only occur if unbiased measures can be used in drug abuse research. For example, Ramirez (1967) developed a Family Attitude Scale that assessed values thought to be relatively more important to Hispanics than to Anglo-Americans by those personally familiar with both cultures. Similarly, these authors were asked to pilot test the Spanish version of a lifestyle scale with a poor Hispanic population in the U.S. Items assessing use of seat-belts and consumption of a low cholesterol diet were seen as offensive given the target population's lack of cars and scarce food resources. There is evidence that sharing the language, idiomatic expressions, and life experiences of minority communities is central in assessment (Marcos, Urcuyo, Kesselman, & Alpert, 1973; Marcos, Alpert, Urcuyo, & Kesselman, 1973).

Minority researchers share an awareness of the relationship between culture and specific behaviors and beliefs. For example, the acceptance of auditory hallucinations as a common experience for Hispanic populations could be seen as psychotic symptoms for someone alien to these experiences (Escobar, Randolph, & Hill, 1986). Expectations of family embeddedness or cohesion in both Asian and Hispanic communities may be characterized as abnormal dependency or harmful overcrowding by an outsider. Yet both are normal behaviors within these communities. Good and Good (1986) emphasized how understanding a process such as illness or drug use across cultures is actually a sorting out of what is culturally normal and abnormal. To deal with this "normative uncertainty," the researcher needs to comprehend both the cultural and social reality that serves as context for the problem under study. An example of this recently occurred in a Massachusetts hospital when a depressed Spanish speaking mother undergoing mental health treatment went to view her newborn baby in the nursery. An English speaking psychiatrist who knew Spanish heard the mother refer to her baby as "mamacita," that is, "little mother." He assumed the woman was having a psychotic episode, where the woman was regressing and ascribing the mother's role to the baby, and reported the event. Family members who spoke English alerted the hospital staff of the meaning of "mamacita" as an affectionate term also used with babies.

Symptoms reflect both the illness as well as the cultural process of what is "a case" in psychiatric epidemiology (Guarnaccia, Guevara-Ramos, González, Canino, & Bud, 1992; Lukoff, Lu, & Turner, 1992). Therefore, understanding the cultural and racial differences in behaviors (Neighbors, Jackson, Campbell, & Williams, 1989) as well as the idioms of distress (Norton & Manson, 1996) is essential for developing instruments that can tap into problem entities of culturally diverse populations. In addition, testing instruments for cultural equivalency requires the evaluation of five dimensions: content, semantic, technical, criterion, and conceptual (Canino & Bravo, 1994). In order to provide accurate assessment, expert and local knowledge of the population under study is essential.

Another advantage of a minority researcher heading a project in a minority community includes being able to decode and take into account the sensitivities and responses of the community to local organizations and treatment modalities in order to generate useful recommendations. Aron, Alger, and González (1974) narrate the importance of adopting Chicano-oriented treatment concepts and values in the process of developing a drug-free therapeutic program. They describe the role of integrating Chicano drug users who have become rehabilitated through their therapeutic program into the Chicano community as a way to discourage use of drugs by other Chicano youth. Brown, Joe, and Thompson's results (1985) show how minority status had particular relevance for treatment retention and for type of discharge in drug-free outpatient programs. Leung and Sakata (1990) found that drug and alcohol rehabilitation programs that used confrontational approaches were inappropriate with Asian Americans. Beauvais and LaBoueff (1985) illustrate how ineffective and inappropriate intervention programs addressing substance abuse are partly the result of the failure of intervention programs to understand the cultural, social, and economic realities of American Indian life. They suggest chronic unemployment, economic depression, and political conflict are part of the abuse problem in American Indian communities that need to be addressed in searching for solutions to drug abuse.

Minority researchers who lead a drug abuse research project in a minority community can also readily discern issues that influence sample selection, research design, and interpretation of results. The understanding of the drug social context allowed a team of researchers to conduct observations at drug copping areas to estimate the number of drug transactions by "servi-car" in urban sites (Alegría et al., 1994). This information helped determine whether this exclusion criteria would bias the sample estimates. Similar circumstances were faced by Norton and Manson (1996) in specifying the recruitment criteria for purposes of sampling American Indian Vietnam Veterans. Tribal enrollment, a common way to identify American Indian and Alaskan Native people, varies widely from tribe to tribe. Based on their knowledge of tribal enrollment, and using residence in the community and military service in Vietnam, they established eligibility for inclusion in their study. In another example, Moncher, Holden, and Trimble's integration (1990) into communities of Native American youth allowed them to move accurately and identify youth at high risk for substance abuse.

The opportunity to mentor ethnic-minority researchers is an additional benefit to a minority investigator who heads a drug project. The benefits available in this relationship to young researchers include: (1) a role model who has had the success of being awarded research funds; (2) access to a research community which includes information about investigators who can provide relevant instrumentation, methodological, or analytical consultation; (3) development of skills to navigate the maze of funding agencies; and (4) identification of topics of interest and their complementary literature in the field.

Furthermore, another advantage to minority investigators who head a research project is the opportunity to serve communities. Their work may discredit erroneous stereotypes, focus research on the needs of minority communities, or pose relevant policy issues. Snowden, Muñoz, and Kelly (1979) emphasize the importance of presenting research results in a simple and meaningful way that can be used to address the problems of minority communities (Norton & Manson, 1996). Chavez (1993) stresses the moral responsibility of using research data to serve social change within minority communities. He suggests that discriminatory or inequitable practices within the school system for Mexican American and Puerto Rican students may only serve to pull them out of the system. He offers caution about the role that research results may have in stereotyping minorities and maintaining the status quo in traditional American institutions.

Concerns about studies conducted by non-minority researchers also have been voiced; apprehensions about these studies have included assessments that they lacked relevance and did not respond to the needs of the studied minority communities (Debro & Conley, 1993). Cognizance of the socio-cultural context allows the minority researcher to focus the study on the needs of minority communities. Amaro (1994) described the paucity of drug research aimed at understanding the structural and community-level factors that foster severe drug abuse in Hispanic communities. She identified how, with few exceptions, most studies have focused on psychological factors rather than economic forces which may play a more powerful role in commencing drug-related activities in the poor inner-city communities where many minorities live.

Researchers have observed that enlisting field staff members sensitive to a study's targeted minority group leads to higher recruitment and retention rates (Miranda, Azocar, Organista, Muñoz, & Lieberman, 1996) and greater access to the community (Pettiway, 1993; Debro & Conley, 1993). For example, Pettiway (1993) stressed the importance of having outreach workers who have knowledge of the history of the neighborhood, the "right" speech and appearance, and a well-established reputation in the community. Similarly, Joe (1993) showed how fieldworkers' ability to engage three Hispanic gangs in research resulted from their ties to the neighborhoods. Debro and Conley (1993) suggested that gaining access to some African American populations requires that investigators of different racial or ethnic background have strong connections or be pseudo-members of the community by having lived there for a significant time. However, other researchers report that matching interviewers and African American participants on the basis of ethnicity did not have much of an impact in the research process (Thompson, Neighbors, Munday, & Jackson, 1996).

There are, however, disadvantages associated with being a minority researcher leading a project in a minority community. Study populations may display unrealistic expectations about what the project can do for them. A persistent difficulty in conducting research is the lack of services offered as part of the research enterprise. Research allows minority investigators to become attentive listeners, yet passive helpmates. It is hard to give ear to the multitude of barriers drug users face within service delivery agencies and not feel impotent. As Pettiway (1993) observed:

> It is hard to look into the eyes of countless African-American faces that seem to be without any hope of a better life and to realize that, for many, their common experience is all they expect life to be–hopelessness. (p. 273)

Another disadvantage to being a minority researcher lies in the frustration that results from the expectation that research data will be a catalytic agent for policy or service change. Often it is not. Alegría et al. (1991), based on their research data, suggested the need to advertise the location and service offerings of mental health and drug facilities as a strategy to promote access to care. The commissioner of the relevant government agency emphatically agreed.

Nonetheless, he admitted that the implementation of this recommendation was not feasible due to the limited supply of services for new clients.

There are also advantages and disadvantages in becoming a token minority researcher for various funding agencies. There is a scarcity of minority researchers; for this reason, minority researchers receive invitations to participate in national committees, offers of a multitude of career enhancement opportunities, and the chance to interact with a network of recognized researchers. The disadvantages lie in addressing excessive demands to participate in conferences, workshops, and grant review committees. The need to represent minority issues, and at the same time to comply with the duties of work, places excessive burdens on these investigators. Whether these opportunities lend themselves to nurture and enhance the careers of minority investigators or actually disturb their career trajectories is an area in need of investigation.

BARRIERS ENCOUNTERED WITH FUNDING AGENCIES

There seems to be an underrepresentation of minorities in drug abuse research. While minorities represented 25.1% of the U.S. population in 1992, 6.5% of NIDA's research project grants that year examined minority populations. And, in spite of some effort by agencies, there appears to be a limited presence of minorities in top administrative positions in the research institutes and in peer review committees (Mata & Alegría, 1993). The impact of the underrepresentation of minority scientists in funding opportunities, in the content and design of requests for applications, and in the actual policies for recruitment and promotion of minority staff, remains unknown.

Even if these issues have no impact on minority representation in research, applications for minority drug abuse studies may still be in a disadvantaged position when reviewed. Research of minority populations may have unclear payoffs. Projects usually lack instruments adapted and validated for the target minority population (Norton & Manson, 1996). This lack requires testing the validity and reliability of translated instruments (Ribera et al., 1996; Bravo, Woodbury-Fariña, & Canino, 1993), and increased time and budget costs over similar studies in Anglo populations.

Applications for minority drug abuse issues are also at a disadvantage because the investigator cannot rely on transporting conceptual frameworks developed for mainstream populations. Attention to issues of acculturative stress (Vega, Zimmerman, Warheit, Apospori, & Gil, 1993), migration (Rogler, 1994), and discrimination (Snowden, 1993) may need to be incorporated. Issues relative to the external validity of the results may also be raised by the internal peer review group that evaluates the application and by reviewers of professional publications. Questions concerning the generalizability of the findings to other populations could influence the assessment of the scientific merit of the application. For example, reviewers may contend that drug treatment services for Native Americans are extremely dissimilar to the rest of the U.S. As such, outcome data may not be replicable outside the study population.

An additional barrier encountered with funding sources has to do with the few peer review committees with members attuned to the problems that minority researchers confront. A persistent difficulty faced by minority scientists regards the scarce supply of certain experts crucial in the research endeavor. This can be a consequence of the few professionals with a solid track record on certain topics, such as random effects modeling and the cost-effectiveness of substance abuse treatment, in the geographical area of the minority scientist or the non-competitive salaries available to recruit such a professional.

BUILDING EFFECTIVE RESEARCH TEAMS

The minority investigator, when building a research team, brings his/her cultural background to the structure, culture, and climate of the organization. Characteristics such as support and fairness, democratic values, and receptiveness to diversity are all strongly influenced by culture (Davis & Rassol, 1995). Cultural differences in values, such as "power distance," "uncertainty avoidance," "individualism," and "masculinity," also emerge in the work environment (Jackson, 1995). Power distance defines the degree to which inequalities among people are seen as normal, ranging from low power distance (equal relations being highly valued) to high power distance (inequalities being accepted as normal). Uncertainty avoidance represents a predilection for structured situations such as work rules and regulations (high uncertainty avoidance) versus a choice for unstructured situations where one is comfortable with ambiguity (low uncertainty avoidance). The tendency to act as individuals rather than as part of a social group (collectiveness) is the value of individualism. Masculinity corresponds to possessing values that uphold masculine traits, such as assertiveness and competition, rather than valuing feminine traits, such as personal relationships and caring for others. These values represent different cultures (Jackson, 1995), not the conventional value orientations of North American organizational theory: free will, individualism, and low context. It could be expected that minority researchers, given their history and socialization, favor values such as low power distance, low uncertainly avoidance, collectivism, and femininity in their research teams. Whether such is the case has not been the focus of organizational cross-cultural research (Jackson, 1993).

However, culture's impact on organizational behavior and interpersonal relations in the work environment takes place at such a deep level that workers fail to become conscious of its influence and extent (Triandis, 1983). Sekaran (1983) has stated that one serious obstacle of cross-cultural research is its failure to operationalize the concept of culture within the organizational context:

> Culture has an impact on organizations because cultural norms, values and roles are embedded in the way that organizations develop, organizational structures emerge, and informal and formal patterns of behavior occur. (p. 67)

How may this be significant to the research endeavor? Graham and Gronhaug (1989) suggested that the social system of scientists and the context of scientific activity confines the production of knowledge. Or as Merton (1968) suggested: "Social organizations of intellectual activity are significantly related to the character of the knowledge which develops under its auspices . . ." (p. 53a). This emphasizes the need to be sensitive to how one brings his or her cultural baggage to the day-to-day functioning of the research organization. Culture transpires in how one imposes cultural assumptions to understand behavior, in how one constructs models in the social sciences, and in decision-making and interaction within the organization (Hofstede, 1980). For the minority researcher to become sufficiently aware that ethnocentrism can trap the investigator into a false aura of wisdom, he/she needs exposure to different contexts, models of behavior, and values. The minority researcher who leads a research team survives by being open to different value systems, willing to listen and responsive to changing contexts. Moreover, acceptance of dissimilar value systems can help integrate the team into different socio-cultural networks conducting research.

In building an effective research team, three elements are crucial: the organizational structure, the culture, and the climate. Structure is the orderly aspects of relationships among members of the organization (Scott, 1992). This dimension encompasses centralization of decision making, levels of authority, and formalization of policies and procedures. Centralization of decision making refers to the perceived input that staff have relative to administrative decisions, while levels of authority corresponds to the extent to which staff reports to supervisors (Daft, 1995). Formalization of policies and procedures refers to the extent to which such policies and procedures are formal and explicit. The second element, organizational culture, can be defined as the behavioral norms and values specific to organizational policies, procedures, preferred outcomes, and other normative elements within an organizational frame of reference (Cooke & Rousseau, 1988). According to Morris and Bloom (1995), organizational culture is highly related to staff morale and organizational commitment by its members. Organizational climate, the third element, represents the shared perceptions of the social context of the organization that include perceptions about staff interaction, management support and fairness, as well as program attitudes and practices (Richers & Schneider, 1990).

In studying the ingredients of organizations characterized by effective outcomes, Glisson (1992) states:

. . . (T)he structure technology research has confirmed that less routine and more complex core technologies require organizational structures that are less hierarchical, more flexible and that more routine and less complex technologies require structures that are more hierarchical and less flexible. (p. 184)

Because research in minority communities involves less routine and a more complex endeavor, the organizational structure of the research team should be: less hierarchical, with wide participation and decision-making power by all personnel involved; more flexible, allowing for diversification of roles and responsibilities as well as for the opportunity to learn a variety of skills; less formal, that is, with little procedural specifications so that the lines of authority are diffuse; and less centralized, with everyday decisions made by those in charge of field procedures, training of personnel, or data analysis.

A decentralized, flexible, and informal organizational structure has major disadvantages. For one, it requires constant team communication to update tasks and expectations as well as to monitor progress. It demands a democratic system of decision-making which may not be effective in crisis situations. Consulting the team and scheduling meetings under pressing deadlines can wrack nerves. To delegate responsibility and decision-making authority, resourceful staff members who take initiative, are creative, and sense that their competencies are needed. Furthermore, such organizational structure requires frequent staff meetings to discuss views, tasks, and frustrations. Also, having a less hierarchical structure sustained by a system of wider participation translates into acceptance of how others do the job, whether or not there is agreement. But there is evidence that active participation and shared interests are critical to the maintenance of group productivity and a healthy degree of cohesion.

A second central element in forming an effective research team is the organizational culture that drives the work contingencies in the job scenario. This process usually has a high degree of uncertainty in both implementation and outcome. Furthermore, it is hard to characterize since it involves a set of expectations held by the individual as to what the organization will provide in return for his/her contributions to the organization. Van Fleet and Peterson (1994) capture these transactions through the psychological contract. It establishes the necessity for a comparable exchange of effort, skill, ability, time, loyalty, and competence on the part of the worker, for equitable monetary incentives, job security, benefits, career promotion opportunities, and status pledged on the part of the organization. If both the individual and the organization perceive the psychological contract to be fair, they will be satisfied with the relationship and will continue with it.

As part of this psychological contract, the following is recommended. Be reasonable regarding monetary incentives. Community involvement for research in minority communities requires an enormous amount of contact with people as well as increased efforts by field staff. Much of this effort is not readily ascertainable, which in itself can lead to burn out. Receiving appropriate monetary compensation and management support gives recognition to these arduous tasks. Staggering amounts of time, effort, and energy are invested in complying with the complexities of research activities. That is why the organizational culture which values scientific achievement should also value personal achievement. This can be evidenced by demonstrating interest in non-job related successes. As a consequence, staff should be compensated with flexibility in time schedules in order to advance their education or their careers. Another mechanism of reward is to provide the resources and opportunities to initiate their own research interests, incorporating them as part of the study.

Commitment to the project and emphasis on quality and performance goals (Shortell et al., 1995) should also be stressed as part of the organizational culture. Usually, the commitment is achieved by the involvement of staff in decision-making and by a psychological contract that rewards loyalty, effort, and initiative. Recognition of quality standards in the process of research can be accomplished by modeling excellence in the everyday activities of the organization.

Such an approach carries inherent difficulties. It requires negotiating higher salaries and more benefits for employees whom the university bureaucracy only wants to evaluate on the basis of academic credentials. As a consequence, frequent conversations with personnel directors are necessary to explain the multiplicity of tasks and activities surrounding field work. Another problem in offering flexibility with staff schedules has to do with the constant monitoring of the whereabouts of personnel and the need for cumbersome arrangements to schedule meetings.

Another element crucial in building an effective research team is the organizational climate. The organizational climate is reflected in the output (Glisson, 1994); therefore, serious attention must be paid to it. Research proposals written under undue stress, conflict, or turmoil usually fail to be successful. A nurturing organizational climate focuses on the person, not only on his/her work. This means going the extra mile and requires sensitivity and responsiveness to the needs of staff members, not only to their performance at work. Frequent expressions of appreciation for tasks performed must be weaved into the opportunities for organizational interaction. Chances to voice dissatisfaction and displeasure with job demands must be available to staff. This organizational climate also encourages research by holding high standards for tasks achieved and by positive attitudes in conducting research. It provides supportive environmental conditions, such as adequate space, attractive and functional surroundings, and safety. It furnishes resources, such as equipment, research assistants, administrative and clerical support, and access to references, that facilitate the research endeavor. It promotes acceptance of responsibilities by staff members, where all perform their tasks without the need to be told.

RECOMMENDATIONS FOR BUILDING EFFECTIVE RESEARCH TEAMS WHEN CONDUCTING DRUG ABUSE RESEARCH WITH MINORITY POPULATIONS

The following are several recommendations for building effective drug abuse research teams:

- When recruiting staff, require willingness to work with non-conventional study populations.
- Use as criteria for staff selection the social skills and initiative of the individual, not only his/her professional or academic experience.
- Hold periodic staff meetings to share the process, not the procedures, of the research.
- Avoid hidden agendas and encourage staff to voice their concerns, plans, or petitions.
- Rotate the positions of authority, so everyone experiences how difficult responsibility is.
- Be fair and caring; this is what team members appreciate most.
- Always try to maintain a sense of humor, even under critical conditions, like when a proposal is due, and the computer freezes at 5:00 A.M.
- Provide a space for team members to share positive and negative experiences of their work environment.
- Be generous in sharing resources, such as equipment, consultants, and the P.I.'s time.
- Have an in-house crisis hotline, through e-mail or phone, for moments of desperation.
- Avoid and discourage gossip by staff members.
- Share references, articles, or materials with colleagues.
- Be willing to learn from the staff; do not hear only the words, but try to understand the implications of their stories.

- Allow members' areas of interest to be included in the research agenda.
- Promote team spirit by consulting and including everyone in important decisions.
- Remember that team members have a life beyond work demands; the investigator may need them, but so do their families.
- Understand that tasks usually require more than the time and human resources available; be reasonable in choosing what can be done today and what can be postponed for tomorrow.
- Give recognition for each member's contribution to the research.
- Promote an environment that shows respect and tolerance for alternative views. Debates are allowed, but disrespect is not.
- Try to make staff meetings stimulating, with a rich interplay of ideas, even at the cost of not following the agenda.
- Include consultants as collaborators, particularly in those areas where there is no expertise on the team.

CONCLUSION

Some investigators may flourish in a sole-practice; very few do. A competitive research endeavor usually demands a healthy degree of multi-disciplinary collaboration. Teams are much more than collaboration. They are temporary alliances brought about by research opportunities. Yet forming a team is no small feat given the time demands that routinely surround it. But maintaining a team is where the greatest trial lies. It is with team spirit and support that stressful events can be overcome, successes and frustrations shared. This is what makes teams such an attractive feature of work.

Given the privatization of health care, welfare reform, general assistance budget cuts, and new immigration policies, these are times of monumental system changes. Minority issues will surface, bringing both opportunities and challenges for research in minority communities. What our role will be within this research arena, and how our communities can best be served by the research enterprise might be our greatest tasks. In these changing times, minority researchers will be invited to collaborate with researchers who wish to understand the dynamics and issues of these communities. It is our responsibility to assert a leadership role in showing how the expert advice rests within the communities and their service providers, not in academic scholars. Our role can only be as links to the communities.

Finally, three caveats are in order: First, this is a collection of ideas and suggestions based on the investigators' day-to-day experience, not an all inclusive guide to how others have structured effective research teams. Second, forming an effective research team stems from what is conceptualized as "effective." This paper proposes that effective teams are those successful in obtaining research funds, that deal with conflict, and provide a nurturing environment that allows for growth and challenge among its members. Third, these guidelines reflect not only the minority status of the investigators but also mirror issues of gender, age, socioeconomic status, and location that color perceptions of emerging issues. It is in this spirit that these guidelines are presented. The recommendations voiced here spring from having caring mentors who modeled investigators as leaders who could provide new ideas and opportunities for team members at all levels of the organization.

REFERENCES

Alegría, M., Robles, R., Freeman, D. H., Vera, M., Jiménez, A. L., Ríos, C., & Ríos, R. (1991). Patterns of mental health utilization among island Puerto Rican poor. *American Journal of Public Health, 81*(7), 875-879.

Alegría, M., Vera, M., Freeman, D. H., Robles R., Santos, M., & Rivera, C. (1994). HIV infection, risk behaviors, and depressive symptoms among Puerto Rican sex workers. *American Journal of Public Health, 84*(12), 2000-2002.

Amaro, H. (1994). Hispanic research in NIDA's portfolio: Setting future research priorities. National Institute on Drug Abuse, *Policy report: AIDS and drug abuse research and technology transfer in Hispanic communities, Hispanic AIDS and substance abuse initiative of the Human Interaction Research Institute* (pp. 5-23). Rockville, MD: National Institute on Drug Abuse.

Aron, W. S., Alger, N., & González, R. T. (1974). Chicanoizing the therapeutic community. *Journal of Psychedelic Drugs, 6*(3), 321-327.

Beauvais, F., & LaBoueff, S. (1985). Drug and alcohol abuse intervention in American Indian communities. *International Journal of the Addictions, 20*, 139-171.

Bravo, M., Woodbury-Fariña, M., & Canino, G. (1993). The Spanish translation and cultural adaptation of the Diagnostic Interview Schedule for Children (DISC 2.1) in Puerto Rico. *Cul Med Psychiatry, 17*(3), 329-344.

Brown, B. S., Joe, G. W., & Thompson, P. (1985). Minority group status and treatment retention. *International Journal of the Addictions, 20*(2), 319-335.

Canino, G., & Bravo, M. (1994). The adaptation and testing of diagnostic and outcome measures for cross-cultural research. *Intern Review Psychiatry, 6*, 281-286.

Chavez, E. L. (1993). Hispanic dropouts and drug use: A review of the literature and methodological considerations. In M. R. De La Rosa, & J. L. Recio (Eds.), *Drug Abuse among minority youth: Advances in research and methodology* (NIDA Monograph 130, NIH Publication No. 93-3479, pp. 224-233). Washington, DC: Government Printing Office.

Cooke, R. A., & Rousseau, D. M. (1988). Behavioral norms and expectations: A quantitative approach to the assessment of organizational culture. *Group and Organization Studies, 13*, 245-273.

Daft, R. L. (1995) *Organization theory and design* (5th ed.). St. Paul, MN: West Publishing.

Davis, H. J., & Rasool, S. A. (1995). Values research and managerial behavior: Implications for devising culturally consistent managerial styles. In T. Jackson (Ed.), *Cross-cultural management* (pp. 38-49). Oxford, England: Butterworth Heinemann.

Debro, J., & Conley, D. J. (1993). School and community politics: Issues, concerns, and implications when conducting research in African-American communities. In M. R. De La Rosa, & J. L. Recio (Eds.), *Drug Abuse among minority youth: Advances in research and methodology* (NIDA Monograph 130, NIH Publication No. 93-3479, pp. 298-307). Washington, DC: Government Printing Office.

Escobar, J. I., Randolph E. T., & Hill, M. (1986). Symptoms of schizophrenia in Hispanic and Anglo veterans. *Culture, Medicine, and Psychiatry, 10,* 259-276.

Gary, L., & Berry, G. (1985). Predicting attitudes toward substance use in the Black community: Implications for prevention. *Community Mental Health Journal, 21,* 42-51.

Geertz, C. (1973). *The interpretation of cultures.* New York: Basic Books.

Glisson, C. (1992). Structure and Technology in Human Service Organizations. In Y. Hasenfeld (Ed.), *Human services as complex organizations* (pp. 184-202). Newbury Park, CA: Sage.

Good, B. J. (1994). *Medicine, rationality and experience: An anthropological perspective.* Cambridge: Cambridge University Press.

Good, B. J., & Good, M. J. D. (1986). The cultural context of diagnosis and therapy: A view from medical anthropology. In M. R. Miranda, & H. H. Kitarro (Eds.), *Mental health research and practice in minority communities: Development of culturally sensitive training programs* (pp. 1-27). Washington, DC: National Institute of Mental Health.

Guarnaccia, P. J., Guevara-Ramos, L. M., González, G., Canino, G. J., & Bud, H. (1992). Cross-cultural aspects of psychotic symptoms in Puerto Rico. *Research in Community and Mental Health, 7,* 99-110.

Graham, J. L., & Gronhaug, K. (1989). Ned Hall didn't get a haircut: Or why we haven't learned much about international marketing in the last 25 years. *Journal of Higher Education, 60*(2), 152-157.

Hofstede, G. (1980). *Culture consequences: International differences in work-related values.* Houston, TX: Gulf.

Jackson, T. (1993). *Organizational behavior in international management.* Oxford, England: Butterworth-Heinemann.

Jackson, T. (1995). Methodology. In T. Jackson (Ed.), *Cross-cultural management* (pp 1-7). Oxford, England: Butterworth-Heinemann.

Joe, K. A. (1993). Getting into the gang: Methodological issues in studying ethnic gangs. In M. R. De La Rosa & J. L. Recio (Eds.), *Drug Abuse among minority youth: Advances in research and methodology* (NIDA Monograph 130, NIH Publication No. 93-3479, pp. 234-257). Washington, DC: Government Printing Office.

Leung, P., & Sakata, R. (1990). Drug and alcohol rehabilitation counseling with Asian Americans. *Journal of Applied Rehabilitation Counseling, 21*(3), 49-51.

Lukoff, D., Lu, F., & Turner, R. (1992). Toward a more culturally sensitive DSM-IV: Psychoreligious and psychospiritual problems. *Journal of Nervous and Mental Disease, 180*, 673-682.

Marcos, L. R., Urcuyo, L., Kesselman, M., & Alpert, M. (1973). The language barrier in evaluating Spanish-American patients. *Archives of General Psychiatry, 29*, 655-659.

Marcos, L. R., Alpert, M., Urcuyo, L., & Kesselman, M. (1973). The effect of interview language on the evaluation of psychopathology in Spanish-American schizophrenic patients. *American Journal of Psychiatry, 130*, 549-553.

Mata, A. G., & Alegría, M. (1993). *Strategies for increasing Hispanic researchers and building a research agenda.* Paper presented at the Hispanic Policy Workshop, AIDS and Drug Abuse Research and Technology Transfer in Hispanic Communities, The Hispanic Research and Technology Transfer Work Group, Bethesda, MD.

Merton, R. K. (1968). *Social theory and social structure.* New York: Free Press.

Miranda, J., Azocar, F., Organista, K. C., Muñoz, R., & Lieberman A. (1996). Recruiting and retaining low-income Latinos in psychotherapy research. *Journal of Consulting and Clinical Psychology, 64*, 868-874.

Moncher, M., Holden, G. M., & Trimblem, J. (1990). Substance abuse among Native-American youth. *Journal of Consulting and Clinical Psychology, 58*, 400-415.

Morris, A., & Bloom, J. R. (1995, September). *Predictors of staff morale and commitment in community mental health centers preparing to undergo capitation of Medicaid financing.* Poster presentation at the NIMH Conference on Mental Health Services Research, Bethesda, MD.

Reichers, A. E., & Schneider, B. (1990). Climate and culture: an evolution of constructs. In B. Schneider (Ed.), *Organizational climate and culture* (pp. 5-39). San Francisco: Jossey-Bass Publishers.

Shortell, S. M., O'Brian, J. L., Carman, J. L., Foster, R. W, Hughes, E. F. X., Boerstler, H., & O'Connor, E. J. (1995). Assessing the impact of continuous quality improvement/total quality management: Concept versus implementation. *Health Services Research, 30*(2), 377-401.

Snowden, L. R. (1993). Emerging trends in organizing and financing human services: Unexamined consequences for ethnic minority populations. *American Journal of Community Psychology, 21*(1), 113.

Snowden, L. R., Muñoz, R. F., Kelly, J. G. (1979). The process of implementing community-based research. In *Social and Psychological Research in Community Settings* (pp. 14-29). San Francisco: Jossey-Bass Publishers.

National Institute on Drug Abuse. (1993, January). *Minority-related extramural research grants, fiscal year 1992.* Bethesda, MD.

Neighbors, H. W., Jackson, J. S., Campbell, L., & Williams, D. (1989). The influence of racial factors on psychiatric diagnosis: A review and suggestions for research. *Community Mental Health Journal, 25*, 301-311.

Norton, I. M., & Manson, S. M. (1996). Research in American Indian and Alaska Native Communities: Navigating the Cultural Universe of Values and Process. *Journal of Consulting and Clinical Psychology, 64*, 856-860.

Nyamathi, A. (1991). Relationship of resources to emotional distress, somatic complaints, and high-risk behavior in drug recovery among homeless minority women. *Research in Nursing and Health, 14*, 269-277.

Oetting, E., Edward, R., & Beauvais, F. (1988). Drugs and Native-American Youth. *Drugs & Society, 3*, 1-34.

Pedigom, J. (1983). Finding the "meaning" of Native American substance abuse: Implications for community prevention. *Personnel and Guidance Journal, 61*, 273-277.

Pettiway, L. E. (1993). Identifying, gaining access to, and collecting data on African-American drug addicts. In M. R. De La Rosa & J. L. Recio (Eds.), *Drug Abuse among minority youth: Advances in research and methodology* (NIDA Monograph 130, NIH Publication No. 93-3479, pp. 258-279). Washington, DC: Government Printing Office.

Ramírez, M. (1967). Identification with Mexican family values and authoritarianism in Mexican-Americans. *Journal of Social Psychology, 73*, 3-11.

Ribera, J. C., Canino, G. J., Rubio-Stipec, M., Bravo, M., Bird, H. R., Freeman, D., Shrout P., Bauermeister, J., Alegría, M., Woodbury, M., Huertas, S., & Guevara, L. M. (1996). The Diagnostic Interview Schedule for Children (DISC 2.1) in Spanish: reliability in a Hispanic Population. *J Chil Psychol Psychiatry, 37*(2), 195-204.

Rogler, L. H. (1994). International migrations: A framework for directing research. *American Psychologist, 49*, 701-708.

Schinke, S. P., Moncher, M. S., Palleja, J., & Zayas, L. H. (1988). Hispanic youth, substance abuse, and stress: Implications for prevention research. *International Journal of the Addictions, 23*, 809-826.

Scott, W. R. (1992). *Organizations: Rational, natural, and open systems* (3rd ed.). Englewood Cliffs, NJ: Prentice Hall.

Sekaran, V. (1983). Methodological and theoretical issues and advances in cross-cultural research. *Journal of International Business Studies, 14*(2), 61-73.

Singer, M. (1993). Knowledge for use: Anthropology and community-centered substance abuse research. *Social Science Medicine, 37*, 15-25.

Thompson, E. E., Neighbors, H. W., Munday, C., & Jackson J. S. (1996). Recruitment and Retention of African American Patients for Clinical Research: An Exploration of Response Rates in an Urban Psychiatric Hospital. *Journal of Consulting and Clinical Psychology, 64*, 861-867.

Triandis, H. C. (1983). Dimensions of cultural variations as parameters of organizational theories. *International Studies of Management and Organization, 12*(4), 139-169.

Van Fleet, D. D., & Peterson, T. O. (1994). *Contemporary management*. Boston: Houghton Mifflin Company.

Vega, W. A., Zimmerman, R. S., Warheit, G. J., Apospori, E., & Gil, A. G. (1993). Risk factors for early adolescent drug use in four ethnic and racial groups. *American Journal of Public Health*, *83*, 185-189.

Ware, N. C., & Kleinman, A. (1992). Culture and somatic experience: The social course of illness in neurasthenia and chronic fatigue syndrome. *Psychosomatic Medicine*, *54*, 546-560.

Constructing and Managing Culturally Competent Research Teams for Community-Based Investigations

Cheryl N. Grills, PhD
Daryl M. Rowe, PhD

SUMMARY. Pragmatic methodological issues are presented to enhance the effectiveness of research teams operating within ethnic-cultural communities. Operating from an African-centered conceptual framework, recommendations are presented regarding: (1) the importance of clarifying the cultural value orientation that directs the research; (2) team-building issues that impact the construction and maintenance of research groups; (3) strategies for increasing awareness and understanding of the ethnic-cultural community being investigated; and (4) methods to establish mechanisms within the team to support individual and group needs. Immersing research teams in the culture of ethnic-cultural groups can enhance the planning, design, and implementation of various research projects and improve the quality of data obtained. The paper argues that such a perspective can lead to the discovery of more authentic voices within historically

---

Cheryl N. Grills is Associate Professor of Psychology and Alcohol and Drug Studies, Loyola Marymount University. Daryl M. Rowe is Associate Professor of Psychology, Graduate School of Education and Psychology, Pepperdine University.

Address correspondence to: Cheryl N. Grills, Psychology Department, Loyola Marymount University, 7900 Loyola Boulevard, Los Angeles, CA 90045.

The preparation of this article was supported by contracts received by Dr. Grills from several community-based agencies within the Los Angeles metropolitan area.

[Haworth co-indexing entry note]: "Constructing and Managing Culturally Competent Research Teams for Community-Based Investigations." Grills, Cheryl N., and Daryl M. Rowe. Co-published simultaneously in *Drugs & Society* (The Haworth Press, Inc.) Vol. 14, No. 1/2, 1999, pp. 247-268; and: *Conducting Drug Abuse Research with Minority Populations: Advances and Issues* (ed: Mario R. De La Rosa, Bernard Segal, and Richard Lopez) The Haworth Press, Inc., 1999, pp. 247-268. Single or multiple copies of this article are available for a fee from The Haworth Document Delivery Service [1-800-342-9678, 9:00 a.m. - 5:00 p.m. (EST). E-mail address: getinfo@haworthpressinc.com].

247

oppressed ethnic-cultural communities. *[Article copies available for a fee from The Haworth Document Delivery Service: 1-800-342-9678. E-mail address: getinfo@haworthpressinc.com]*

INTRODUCTION

There has been long-standing concern among social scientists regarding the viability and/or limitations of traditional research strategies for determining scientific knowledge with diverse cultural groups (Hughes & DuMont, 1993; Betancourt & Lopez, 1993). Sasao and Sue (1993) suggested two broad domains within which problems often occur. The first reflects pragmatic methodological issues–gaining community access, increasing subject compliance, minimizing measurement bias, and obtaining representative samples. The second domain involves conceptual methodological issues or "interrelated meta-methodological assumptions" (p. 707)–how ethnic-cultural communities are defined, the applicability of cross-cultural methods and theories to research strategies, and the ecological stability of ethnic-cultural communities. While the pragmatic issues address strategies to conduct research within ethnic-cultural communities, the conceptual issues impact both how those communities are defined (Sasao & Sue, 1993) and the psychological sense of community (Sarason, 1974; Hill, 1996).

This article presents various pragmatic strategies found to be effective in the formulation and ongoing management of culturally-competent research teams. These strategies can improve the quality of research done in and about ethnic-cultural communities. Information will be presented on: (1) the importance of developing a value orientation within the team which is respectful of and congruent with the particular community being investigated; (2) constructing and maintaining research teams; (3) strategies for fostering more community familiarity among the team; and (4) supporting the research team over the course of the project. Fundamental to these efforts has been the identification of specific resources and talents *within* the community and incorporating them into all critical phases of the research-project formulation, population and problem definition, concept and measurement development, research design and methodology, and the interpretation of results (Hughes, Seidman, & Williams, 1993). By doing so, the quality and utility of data gathered can be maximized in each study. Inherent in the discussion regarding pragmatic strategies are community parameters, and the meta-methodological assumptions involved in defining community. The reader is referred to Sasao and Sue (1993) for a fuller discussion regarding how ethnic-cultural communities are defined and constructed.

Between 1991 and 1996, the first author conducted a series of studies with the African American, Hispanic, Asian/Pacific Islander, and gay and lesbian youth communities of Los Angeles. Although the particular research objectives, samples, and methodology are important points of discussion for each project, this article seeks to describe strategies to implement and manage studies, strategies that will aid the development and management of effective research teams. The teams constructed for these projects became indispensable to the implementation and successful completion of over 15 alcohol, tobacco, and other-drug surveys. These were quasi-experimental and experimental studies conducted in a 5-year time frame involving over 6,600 participants. Although a majority of the studies were conducted within the African American community, similar strategies were successfully employed in studies among Asian/Pacific Island Americans, gay and lesbian youth, and the Hispanic communities. In each study, through the dynamic interaction of the team and community, we learned more effective ways to approach research in historically oppressed communities-of-color. Table 1 provides an overview of the range of investigations, basic topics, purposes, and sample sizes associated with these projects.

VALUE ORIENTATION IN COMMUNITY BASED RESEARCH

No research is exempt from assumptions and value orientations. Making these explicit in the development of the team and the various research strategies provided clarity to the project's work. For example, behavior was assumed to be the result of a dynamic interaction between person and environment (Walsh-Bowers, 1993). Research questions and hypotheses reflected this perspective. The cultural values of the community were the values of the project, and this was explicitly stated.

It is important that each project operate from a clear cultural value orientation. Community psychology, which has served as the psychological discipline for promoting community-based research, has long advocated the centrality of locating research within the value systems or orientations of various communities (Rappaport, 1977). This position was recently re-stated by Weinstein (1994) as a need for "reconceptualization of our knowledge base as well as of how we gain understanding . . . concerning human behavior within context" (p. 815). Similarly, Hughes et al. (1993) identified two cultural elements that significantly impact community-based research: (1) Culture influences *what* researchers consider worthy of examination and the interpretation of empirical observations; and (2) cultural variations influence *how* participants/subjects respond to

TABLE 1. Community Based Studies Conducted Between 1991-1996

Survey Name	Topic	Purpose	Surveys Completed
Resident Survey	Needs assessment of African American and Hispanic South LA residents	To assess the extent to which residents of South LA perceive ATOD issues to be a problem in their community	1,125
Alcohol Availability Survey	Retail outlet nuisance problems in the African American community	To document extent of nuisance problems associated with liquor stores	385
East/West Neighborhood Survey	African American East and West South LA neighborhoods' perceptions of community	To obtain community perceptions of critical issues affecting their daily lives	202
Assessment of Tobacco Sales to Minors	Illegal tobacco sales to African American and Hispanic minors	To determine the extent of tobacco sales to minors and related concerns	30
Billboard Advertising Survey	Tobacco and alcohol billboard ads in African American and Hispanic neighborhoods	To compare billboard advertising in two LA council districts	237
Earthquake Survey	Northridge earthquake impact in the African American community	To assess the emotional, social, and structural impact of the earthquake on South LA residents	1,751
Agency Director's Survey	Agency Director's perception of the ATOD problem in South LA	To compare agency directors' perceptions of the ATOD problem with the perceptions of the residents of South Los Angeles and the agency line staff	15
Line Staff Survey	Agency line staff's perceptions of the ATOD problems in South LA	To compare agency line staff's perceptions of the ATOD problem with the perceptions of South LA residents and agency directors	38
Environmental Impact Outcome Study	Impact of alcohol availability in the African American community	To assess the extent to which availability influences perceptions of a variety of community problems	906
Housing Development Survey	ATOD and community problems in African American and Hispanic housing developments	To assess impact of community based prevention on ATOD and related community problems	388
East West ATOD Outcome Survey	ATOD problems in the Asian Pacific Island American Los Angeles community	To assess the impact of community based prevention on ATOD and related community problems	920
Gay and Lesbian Youth Survey	ATOD problems in the gay and lesbian youth community in Hollywood	To assess ATOD and related community problems, attitudes and behaviors of gay and lesbian youth	202
UCLA Treatment Engagement Study	Drug abuse treatment for African American substance abusers	To test a culturally congruent model of treatment engagement with African American substance Abusers	550

task demands or assessment tools, interpret research settings, and compre-hend the constructs and behaviors in the research context. Failure to ad-dress these issues can lead to myopic and self-serving conceptualizations of research questions: a distortion of the experiences, beliefs or behaviors of a group; and data that has limited utility for ameliorating the concerns of a particular group (Seidman, 1978).

The studies outlined in Table 1 operated from the values inherent in community psychology and an African-centered perspective. Community psychology's viewpoint and its associated values (i.e., recognition of the inherent cultural bias of research; an ecological orientation; commitment to social innovation; empowerment; and respect for cultural diversity; see Kelly, 1990) are consistent with an African-centered value orientation. The blend of these two perspectives contributed to the successful develop-ment and completion of several studies conducted within the African American community. Three African-centered values, in particular, informed our research: (1) *interdependence*–respecting the community by including it as a functioning collaborator in the research enterprise; (2) *order*–recognizing the cultural biases inherent in western empiricism and in the world view of the constructed research team; and (3) *subjective interpretation*–recogniz-ing and attending to the environmental context of the phenomenon under investigation, such that the meaning applied to the behavior is integrally tied to the contextual setting in which that behavior occurs (Rowe & Grills, 1993).

Community interdependence or collaboration increases the likelihood that the research questions are valid; that the data to be collected has integrity, approximates reality, and is accurate; and that the attempt to access the beliefs, practices, and issues germane to the community in-volved is successful (Hughes et al., 1993). As Vega (1992) suggested, "Increasingly groups and communities are refusing to accept at face value research activity which does not speak to their interests or fails to articu-late an appreciation of specific cultural nuance" (p. 389).

What and how a subject is investigated is *not* simply a result of the "objective" scientific enterprise (Hughes et al., 1993). Community order instructs us that research on various cultural-ethnic groups should be con-ducted with the understanding that researchers are as prone to cultural bias as other members of society. Researchers conceptualize the research ques-tions, define the populations to be investigated, determine both the design and methods of the study, and carry out the interpretation and summation of findings. Whatever the researcher decides to investigate influences the research findings. Furthermore, the imposition of particular types of re-search/intervention strategies reflects social values and a cultural orientation. Care must be taken to limit or at least define the biases inherent in these processes.

Ethnocentric biases inhibit the development of a knowledge base for understanding diverse cultural communities (Hughes et al., 1993). Teper (1977) and others have found the following tendencies to be characteristic of biased research: (1) equating the dominant culture's values with an idealized norm and perceiving other cultural values as deviant or dysfunctional rather than different; (2) focusing on negative attributions and pathological behaviors in studies that ultimately reinforce stereotypes; (3) conceptualizing issues in "either-or" polarizing terms; (4) avoiding causality and focusing on symptoms; and (5) giving more credibility to rational, absolute, concrete, or "objective" factors to the neglect of affective, intuitive, relative and subjective factors.

Social values and cultural orientations should be made explicit within the team and exposed to critical examination and discussion. These discussions should be held against the backdrop of the social values and cultural orientation of the communities that will participate in the study. If these biases are not recognized and taken into consideration from the beginning of the study's design to the final dissemination of results, the research may be guilty of fundamental errors and faulty attributions of causality, meaning, and theory. Said differently, the research may violate the community's sense of order and purpose. This is particularly true of research on or in historically oppressed communities-of-color.

An active, participatory research team reflective of the cultural and psychosocial reality of a given target population can help projects avoid or diminish the pitfalls of cultural bias maintained by the researcher and his/her western empirical tradition. In a discussion of Wicker and Sommer's (1993) model of resident researchers, Lykes (1993) suggests that *"being in* and *doing research within* the community in which one lives"* (p. 489) is central to conceptualizing a resident research process. In resident research, the community is integral to the project–the principal investigator and his/her research team is both of and in the community. Thus, the application of scientific scrutiny, based on the presumption of objectivity, is complex and requires consistent examination.

Finally, the research team must operate from the premise that behavior is best understood as an interaction between the person and their environment. Subjective interpretation reflects the intuitive and emotive appreciation of cultural or contextual symbols instead of a reliance solely on "objective measurement" (Weinstein, 1994). Even if intrapsychic variables are the focus of investigation, the team cannot disregard contextual factors and their influence on project implementation or data collection.

Community conditions, sociopolitical factors, the "personality" or characteristics of the respondent's community setting, and experiences of social phenomena such as racism and discrimination have explanatory power that is often overlooked or misunderstood. Failure to consider these aspects decontextualizes the behaviors of community members and can lead to the imposition of inadequate conceptualizations regarding the etiology or course of the phenomena under investigation (i.e., a community being blamed for deteriorating conditions). More substantive attention to these factors is warranted and a research team that is sensitive to, knowledgeable of, and conversant with these settings, contexts, and realities becomes a crucial asset to the research enterprise. Indeed, Fine's (1992) typology of perspectives for conducting research from a feminist point of view is illustrative. She delineates three standpoints: (1) the ventriloquist, who simply advances her theoretical position and interprets the responses of her subjects in ways which support this position; (2) aggregated voices, such that multiple subjects' viewpoints are expressed, but never viewpoints that contradict the researcher's perspective; and (3) the activist, who advocates on behalf of her community participants, by standing with, rather than apart from, them. This activist standpoint best captures the idea of subjective interpretation and appreciation of the cultural context of various communities.

A few examples from the studies in Table 1 may help to illustrate the above points. In the UCLA Treatment Engagement Study, considerable attention was given to the confluence of politics, history, and economics as a conceptual framework for understanding addiction in African American communities in South Los Angeles. Thus, the meaning was extended to understand addiction, not merely as an individual affliction, but also as a social control mechanism that has served to maintain Euro-American hegemony (Rowe & Grills, 1993). The team utilized this conceptualization in recruiting, tracking, and locating participants; establishing rapport with participants; eliciting information; engaging participants in a collaborative alliance; and in the interpretation of findings. In the assessment of the effects of the Northridge Earthquake in South Los Angeles, an understanding of the historic disregard of South Los Angeles by city administrators contributed to the study's design. Ultimately, the data from this study was used to educate policy makers and garner resources for this predominantly African American and Hispanic community.

In the Community Coalition's public nuisance abatement studies, a broader historical, political and economic perspective on urban African American and Hispanic communities contributed to the design and implementation of a series of neighborhood studies documenting the environmental impact of alcohol availability. Again, this data provided critical support for community efforts to regain control over their environments. These were environments ridden with alcohol and drug problems *not* due to community apathy or lax standards regarding consumption, but to an over concentration of liquor stores and drug trafficking establishments.

Finally, in the Teen Tobacco Awareness Project (TTAP), a social-political view led to the design and implementation of a study of the illegal sale of tobacco to African American and Hispanic minors. Inspired by the political consciousness of African American and Hispanic youth in South Los Angeles, an analysis of contextual issues applied to tobacco marketing and sales generated the research questions, contributed to the study's methodology, and contributed to the interpretation and utilization of findings. African American and Hispanic youth immediately utilized the findings in a community empowerment campaign directed at policy makers and advertisers. Youth in this community did not accept the primacy of the host theory in etiological explanations of tobacco use by minors. Instead they sought to document the role of availability and utilized this data to not only educate policy makers and merchants but to bring about greater enforcement of public policy and advertising standards regarding tobacco sales to this population.

In each example, the values of the research team complimented those of the community. This facilitated a fuller appreciation of factors affecting the communities and phenomena under investigation. Working interdependently, appreciating the community's sense of order, and utilizing their subjective interpretations were invaluable to the research efforts.

Cultural principles that reflect the cultural heritage and diversity of the research team are an integral part of the team environment and outlook. For example, Hispanic and African American principles of respeto; dignidad; cortesia; delicadeza; collective work and responsibility; character and transformation; spirituality; purpose; and cooperation explicitly and implicitly guide the team's sense of obligation to the project, the community, and to each other. These, and other related cultural principles that direct social order and prescribe human behavior within African American and Hispanic cultural contexts, are employed to guide and direct the functioning and day-to-day management of the research team.

ELEMENTS OF CONSTRUCTING AND MAINTAINING AN EFFECTIVE RESEARCH TEAM

Although teamwork is recognized as an important attribute within the business, social service, and scientific arenas, with the exception of those in business, many professionals are unfamiliar with the factors associated with forming, building, monitoring, nurturing, and sustaining effective teams (Briggs, 1997). Understanding team building is particularly important within scientific endeavors. The scientific enterprise most often occurs within the context of research teams, teams which must be managed (Payne, 1990). To sustain innovativeness, we must learn how to manage teams effectively and understand how different contexts and different research or development goals demand diverse management strategies. For example, the UNESCO study illustrated this in their examination of correlates of effective research teams. Based on 1,222 academic and industrial organization research groups in six countries (Andrews, 1979a), two important findings emerged. First, team performance is multidimensional. Second, performance criteria apply differentially to different kinds of research.

The UNESCO study found that research team performance is directly related to resources, leadership, group size, communication, motivation, and diversity. While having sufficient resources to employ good people in reasonable research facilities was important, the study found no added value associated with "more" resources and "better" facilities. Leadership in the form of leader productivity, good planning, and creating a climate that encourages members of the team to be innovative and productive was central to effective teams. Leadership accounted for 51% of the variance in the UNESCO study's examination of the relationship between leadership and group performance. Similarly, Stolte-Heiskanen (1979) noted that human resources were more critical than other types of resources in research team effectiveness. Of these human resources, the contacts of the team and the competence of the team leader were the most important objective resources. When it came to group size, maximal benefits were derived when groups were no larger than seven. If larger than seven, group cohesion and leadership involvement must be high; group members must be involved in the management of the group and the range of the projects must be limited (Stankiewicz, 1979).

Several important features of communication were delineated in these studies; among these were issues associated with group size, internal verses external communication, and quality of communication. Group size was found to be directly related to communication; for example, in larger groups, intragroup communication may be negatively affected. Internal communications are more important than external communications. This internal communication should reflect good scientific and technical exchanges as well as good interpersonal communication. Furthermore, quality of communication directly affects motivation (Andrews, 1979b). Measures of motivation used in the UNESCO study included subjective reports of dedication, voluntary overtime, and interest in the work itself. Motivation accounted for between 10% and 20% of the variance in group performance (Andrews, 1979).

Finally, over 70 measures of diversity were examined in the UNESCO study. Analyses suggested there were six relevant diversity-related clusters: diversity in projects, interdisciplinary orientation, specialties, funding resources, research and development activities, and professional functions, which enhanced team performance.

Our experience establishing and sustaining multiple research teams is consistent with the findings of the UNESCO study with one exception. In addition to the contribution of resources, leadership, group size, communication, motivation and diversity to team effectiveness, we believe conscious promotion, articulation, and subscription to cultural values in the operation of the team enhanced team performance, communication, motivation, and commitment. Within the context of this cultural ethos, several factors contributed significantly to team performance and productivity. They included: (1) building a shared vision; (2) establishing a team culture; (3) minimizing individuality while simultaneously affirming and celebrating individuated talent, skill, and contribution; (4) encouraging and stimulating ongoing learning, skills development, and expanded consciousness among team members; (5) providing emotional and practical support to members of the team; and (6) the diversity of team member activity. Elements external to team dynamics that were germane to the construction and maintenance of our culturally based research teams were: (1) familiarity and knowledge of the community (which enhanced team commitment and purpose), and (2) community input and involvement (which enhanced the integrity of the project and internal and external communication). Each of these elements contributed to the effective operation of research activities within African American and other ethnic communities. They are summarized in Table 2.

Our conclusions are supported by the findings of Pinto and Prescott (1987) who examined the "critical success factors" associated with the four stages of a project's life (conceptual, planning, execution, termination). Pinto and Prescott (1987) studied projects from a cross-section of industries. They hypothesized that different phases of a project would succeed or fail according to the presence or absence of "critical success factors." Having a clearly stated mission was important to success throughout the life-span of a project. The involvement of the client (i.e., an organization, a community) was important throughout the different stages of the project. Technical skills and expertise were most crucial only during the execution and termination phases of the project. Finally, particularly important in the execution stage are specific managerial skills related to trouble-shooting and scheduling/planning.

Familiarity

Often, in conducting research in historically oppressed communities-of-color, community residents are the real scholars in residence (Lykes, 1993). They regularly demonstrate great expertise and insight into community dynamics, human relations, and socio-environmental systems. The above clearly illustrates an essential factor in successful community-based research; get to know the community or assess the psychological sense of community associated with the project's target population. Yet, to become familiar with a community requires that the parameters of a community be sufficiently delineated.

The seminal work of McMillan and Chavis (1986) suggested that psychological sense of community consisted of four elements: membership, influence, integration and fulfillment of needs, and shared emotional connection. McMillan (1996) has extended these original principles and re-

TABLE 2. Elements of Constructing and Maintaining the Research Team

Familiarity
Knowledge of the community Identifying the leaders and sources of knowledge within the community Research project becomes familiar to the community
Community Involvement
Obtaining community input Recruiting the community's involvement Conduct pilot tests to obtain community input on procedures and instrumentation
Team Skill Building
Training of team members Ongoing supervision
Supporting the Research Team
Building team spirit Recognize and appreciate efforts and contributions of team members Regular team debriefings and periodic project updates Develop support mechanisms for the team Integrating the team into the broader community Making the research data directly applicable to the community

fined them as: *spirit,* the integral sense of belonging emergent out of the reciprocal forces of emotional safety and obligatory ties to others; *trust,* the development of an authority structure which orders expectations regarding roles, rules, and responsibilities among members; *trade,* the development of an intricate system of mutual aid and benefit which is both self- and other-rewarding; and *art,* evolving a common symbol system which recognizes and represents the group's values. Thus, psychological sense of community refers to the sense of place, its people, their interrelationships, their shared caring for one another, and their sense of belonging embedded in specific contextual realities, for example, geographical settings, and social, political, historical, and economic frameworks (Lorion & Newbrough, 1996).

Taking the time to determine *how* the community views an issue, how they will examine it, how they may seek to prevent it, and how they intend to resolve it, is critical for developing insight into the established patterns of a particular community. This requires a multi-disciplinary approach that attempts to understand what exists in terms of the social service network, community resources, and the community's prior experiences with research. This familiarity must be reciprocal: Not only must the researcher get to know the community, but the community must become familiar with the researcher, the intentions of the research, and the research team (Wicker & Sommer, 1993).

There are several successful methods that can be used to recruit and engage community members to work alongside the research team. First, research team members should be recruited from the various communities in which access is desired. This process can significantly increase the: (1) project's credibility; (2) reliability and validity of the study design and implementation; and (3) ability to access the target population. It may also be helpful in addressing the various levels of cultural complexity for ethnic-cultural groups (Sasao & Sue, 1993). Secondly, an investment of time is required to identify key community leaders and organizations in which reciprocal relationships, grounded in mutual trust and respect, can be developed. These relationships become critical in several ways: (1) The researcher becomes known to the community as she or he begins to develop a feeling for, or understanding of, the community–its needs, history, and aspirations; (2) this understanding can significantly improve the quality of the project's conceptualization, methodology, design, and implementation; and (3) the established connections with community leaders, stakeholders, power brokers, and constituent members of the community can be useful in sampling a broader cross-section of the community (Hughes et al., 1993). Finally, it is important to select research team members who have a long-term commitment to the communities under investigation. Such a commitment can facilitate the development of co-constructed, experiential knowledge essential for comprehensive data interpretation (Lykes, 1993).

Thus, taking the time to establish these linkages gives the developing research team the capacity to understand the dynamic social relationships in the target population's neighborhood, city, or cultural group. It also allows the researcher to operate, not from outside of the community, but from within.

Community Involvement

A central premise of this model is the assumption that the research team can operate most effectively if it is an integral part of the community. In this position, the team has the ability to insure the integrity of meaning, symbols, and procedures in the research endeavor. Thus, the team will often work in partnership with the community and contribute to all phases of the project's development.

How this integration translates into the overall research process is a crucial aspect of culturally congruent research strategies. For example, an important component of the Treatment Engagement Study was to raise consciousness about substance abuse among African American substance abusers. To insure that participants received an equal dosage of exposure to this part of the intervention, the issues considered to be instrumental to consciousness raising were delivered via the medium of a 19 minute video addressing social, historical, cultural, and psychological factors associated with addiction within the African American community (see Rowe & Grills, 1993, for a fuller discussion of the assumptions that guided the development of the engagement video). While the primary investigators were knowledgeable about these issues and were grounded in an Africentric world view, the video was subjected to a number of pilot tests with a cross section of members of the community (i.e., clients in recovery, treatment providers, community activists, youth, and with prospective and existing members of the research team). These pilot participants were members of the community's naturally existing system of self-help support groups, service providers, residents, leaders, and clients. Their feedback resulted in valuable refinements in the video.

Live footage segments of the video included members of the target community discussing relevant consciousness raising issues. Subsequent revisions were then subjected to further scrutiny of meaning in additional pilots with African American substance abusers living in the communities from which our sample would be recruited and with service providers.

This feedback led to the final version of the video that was used in the project. While time intensive, this collaborative process increased the integrity of the procedure and convergence of meaning among and between researcher, research team, and the target population.

In the Coalition study, community input was obtained and used in the design of needs assessment instruments, in the methods associated with data collection, and with the interpretation and presentation of findings. A similar process was employed in the East/West Community Partnership project in the Asian/Pacific Island community. Community residents assisted in the design of the instrument, were trained in the administration of the protocol, and went door to door with the research team to collect data. They also contributed to the process of data interpretation. Out of this community involvement, new and future team members were identified and valuable ideas incorporated into the project.

In these community-based studies, community members become an essential component (in both a paid and volunteer capacity) to the research team. As a collaborative research model, target populations are not considered "subjects" of an "objective analysis." Rather, consistent with Lewinian social science, attention is given to the relationship between "experimenter and subject" (Walsh-Bowers, 1993). What emerges in the research praxis is a relational research model oriented toward social action.

Team Skill Building

As Briggs (1997) noted, a team is a "group of individuals who are committed to a shared purpose, to each other, and to working together to achieve common goals" (p. xxi). Within our culturally grounded research groups, the team is a collective alliance which supersedes the primacy of individuality. Individual skills and talents are harnessed to form a creative force that brings about innovative results, effective problem solving abilities, and members' commitment to each other. The responsibility with which the team is charged acts as a beacon for shared vision and direction. It informs and shapes the behavior and development of the team. This operational definition subsumes within it a set of beliefs, values, skills, and expectations. Specifically, the beliefs and values are captured in the guiding principles of the Kusudi Saba (Rowe & Grills, 1993) that implicitly ground the research projects. The skills require collective and personal consciousness, self-determination, a sense of self-efficacy, the willingness to engage in open and honest exchange, and good communication skills. The expectations include personal commitment, integrity, and the application of a strong work ethic.

The seven guiding principles in the Kusudi Saba are consistent with Briggs' (1997) three C's to guide team formulation and management. Briggs argues that commitment, collaboration, and communication must work together synergistically for teams to flourish and develop. Encompassing and extending Briggs' schema, team development and management are guided by the culturally-based *seven C's* of the Kusudi Saba: consciousness, creed, commitment, collectivity, competence, conduct, and caring. An eighth value, "celebration," has been added in recent years to this model (Nobles, 1996). Celebration highlights the importance of community acknowledgment and affirmation of efforts to the well-being of the community.

Generally, team skill building includes attention to establishing a cohesive group and routinely attending to the group development through the enhancement of personal and technical skills. Teams must be empowered by contributing to its continuous learning and by recognizing and rewarding the team (Briggs, 1997). Our team approach is consistent with Briggs' concepts, Bertalanffy's (1968) general systems theory, and corporate approaches (Price Waterhouse Change Integration Team, 1996) in which employees are encouraged to share the vision and goals of the corporation or group. Among other things, what can result is achieved learning, improvement, and mastery by each individual in the team (Woodward, 1994); the opportunity for independent creative thought; and enhanced commitment to the process through the sense of ownership.

Team skill building activities included (1) group discussions about the project's objectives and individual member's perspectives on the issues involved; (2) group process meetings with the entire team to reflect upon the evolution of the working team and to resolve any conflicts; (3) discussions about the values driving the project and personal reactions to these values; (4) social gatherings to reduce interpersonal distance and increase cohesion; (5) team rituals that routinized daily check-in and debriefing meetings; (6) investment in continuous learning and self-development through in-service trainings and team attendance at conferences and community events; and (7) recognition and rewards for team members through celebrations, awards, and special forms of acknowledgment.

There is a limited body of empirical data specifying appropriate performance measures to evaluate the effectiveness of research teams (Payne, 1990). They typically include indicators such as published written outputs; patents and prototypes; internal organizational reports and algorithms; contributions to science; recognition and reputation; social effectiveness of the team's work; training effectiveness of the team; administrative effectiveness (i.e., meeting budgets and deadlines); innovativeness; and effective applications. Considering these diverse measures of effectiveness, our teams are considered successful because of: (1) high levels of productivity in the completion of fairly large scale community surveys; (2) studies completed with fairly difficult to access drug using populations; (3) the established reputation of the research organization within and beyond target communities for accessing community members, understanding community dynamics, and providing useful data to the community; (4) innovative and culturally congruent sampling strategies; (5) timely completion of project deadlines; and (6) scores of reports written for, with, and on behalf of the community. Of particular relevance is the use of several of these reports to inform community initiatives with policy makers, businesses and local popular opinion. Beyond these objective measures of effectiveness, in other ways, we also recognize the strength of our approach to research team development. Team members demonstrated a personal commitment to the project through personal contributions of their time, effort, and expertise that far exceeded the call of duty. It was evidenced in their involvement in community projects that went far beyond their scope of work, about which we became familiar because of the project's involvement with the community. Finally, it was noted in the emotional bond which developed or was enhanced during the course of project implementation.

Supporting the Research Team

Supporting the research team requires attention to developing group cohesion and a sense of team spirit; establishing support mechanisms within the team to support individual and group needs; integrating the team into a broader context so that there is a feeling of membership in a larger community group; and maintaining group cognizance of the relationship between the project and community change processes.

Building team spirit requires attention to group process (Briggs, 1996) and establishing group cohesion. Strategies often involve creating the right interpersonal dynamics, a context, and a collective of people with a shared mission: a sincere and profound concern about the community. A functional, optimal team is encouraged to contribute by offering innovative ideas, procedures, policies, and interpretations to the project and its data (West & Farr, 1990).

Research can be a stressful and demanding process, particularly when the issues are directly related to serious social and emotional challenges that are recognized on a daily basis by members of the team. In such a context, attention must be given to the team's emotional needs and to social support mechanisms. This was accomplished through weekly "process" and sharing meetings with the teams; through team retreats; individual team member consultations; and connecting team members to support systems within the community. A number of factors have contributed to the maintenance of high commitment and performance within our research teams. Members were encouraged to be innovative and to routinely provide input on the project's operations. Wherever possible, opportunities were provided for the team to grow (i.e., in service training, conferences, training in different project roles). Emphasis was given to keeping the lines of communication open, providing opportunities for discussion as often as possible.

Highly effective research teams are characterized by innovation, cohesion and productivity, coupled with providing team members the opportunity to influence the conceptualization and scope of the research project (Briggs, 1997; West & Farr, 1990; Pinto & Prescott, 1987). These traits are positively influenced by leadership style and management within the team (King, 1990). Mohr (1969) found that leader motivation, conceptualized in terms of "ideology-activism," increases the frequency of innovation. Health officials who espoused more liberal ideologies and a more interactive role had higher levels of innovation. Pierce and Delbecq (1977) argued that "pro-change" values (values supportive of organizational/social/personal change rather than stagnancy) on the part of organization leadership facilitates innovation as well.

The teams for the Los Angeles based studies espoused pro-change values in which team leadership and team members were open to internal changes in procedures and policies. Moreover, they believed in the concept of community empowerment which often necessitated multi-level change (micro-, meso-, and macro-level systemic change) to adequately address community needs. In effect, the research team espoused ideology-activism in its value base and approach to research. This philosophical/ideological stance brought with it a level of commitment, motivation, innovation, and support within the team. The principle investigators of the L.A. based projects clearly demonstrated commitment to and belief in community and team empowerment. Subsequently, they were seen by the team in advocacy roles on behalf of various community causes. An organizational climate developed that was conducive to ideology-activism. This increased team members' sense of freedom to become involved in personal and community empowerment. While innovation was encouraged within the team the range of such creative expression in the completion of research responsibilities was made clear to all members of the team. Clear limits for organizational innovation which included and reflected a set of guidelines regarding project implementation and ongoing management were consequently emphasized.

Given that the majority of these projects were conducted among African American populations, Africentric values clearly influenced and guided the vision, management, and objectives of our projects. These values reflect basic cultural aspects of African American life such as spirituality, harmony, verve, affect, communalism, expressive individualism, orality, and social time perspective (Stevenson & Renard, 1993). Generally, these cultural values or principles thematically influenced the research enterprise. The driving African-centered value structure demanded from team members (1) excellence, (2) a sense of appropriateness, (3) an inclusivity which counters processes of alienation, (4) a sense of responsibility to the extended family known as the community, (5) a sense of competence and confidence, and (6) a recognition of the principle of consubstantiation (Nobles & Goddard, 1993) that, by definition, demands appropriate action and attitude toward others. Team members were encouraged to uphold these principles implicitly and explicitly in the pursuit of our research agendas. In several instances, our research teams and target populations were multi-ethnic (i.e., Hispanic and African American or multi-ethnic Asian/Pacific Island American). Under these circumstances, the cultural principles of the multiple groups were articulated and recognized. Oftentimes, the divergent cultural groups' principles were complimentary. Where there was divergence of thought, these differences were openly discussed and their implications for understanding, defining, or implementing research objectives closely examined.

Projects that operate within a clear structure, purpose, and base, add to the supportive processes of a team. Van de Ven (1986) suggests three principles for developing an "infrastructure that is conducive to innovation and organizational learning" (p. 605). The project must operate from a clear set of values and standards. Secondly, the organization needs to develop the capacity for "double loop learning." This means the project is able to discern and correct deviations from the standards it has set and discern and correct errors in the standards themselves. Double loop learning is also facilitated by an environment that does not cast human or procedural error within a negative light. Rather, errors and mistakes are expected and seen as a natural part of human endeavors, not a source of shame or embarrassment. Thirdly, the organization must indulge rather than shun uncertainty and diversity in its many forms.

In the L.A. studies, these conditions created a supportive environment that promoted a sense of cohesion, shared vision, and innovation. An organizational climate that is conducive to the process of innovation requires an atmosphere which at least supports freedom of expression and participation and simultaneously demands excellence in performance (Bower, 1965). The team must preserve rather than reduce uncertainty and diversity. Uncertainty about the soundness of a believed "truism" can provide fertile ground for creative thought and innovation particularly if a procedure appears to obscure critical examination of pertinent research issues. We found that creativity occurred best within an atmosphere which encouraged diversity. Therefore, diverse expressions of thought, style, and strategies were encouraged while dogma and rigidity of thought, theory, and practice were summarily de-emphasized. Even though guided by a set of cultural values, there was no need for a "party line" within our teams.

Finally, a most critical factor contributing to a successful research team is locating the team within the target community and establishing a bond/relationship with highly visible community based groups/agencies. Opportunities for team support emerge out of these relationships. As the members of the team and the project itself negotiate access, equal attention must be given to sustaining and nurturing emerging relationships. This often involves a fluid process of give and take with community institutions and leaders. The research must facilitate integration of project team members into the community organization/groups. It must see the interaction with these community groups/agencies as a continuous process of negotiation and mutual source of support. For example, in our projects, community connections have led to increased effectiveness and decreased stress in the completion of project tasks. Community collaborations have led to personally fulfilling experiences for members of the team as they grow in their perceptions of themselves as valuable contributors to community efforts. Personally meaningful relationships and sources of support were fostered and encouraged in the community relationships that emerged.

CONCLUSION

In a society where research directs the expansion of information, and information influences the development of public policy, evolving more efficacious strategies for gaining research access to historically oppressed communities-of-color is critical. It is only through appropriate access that the elaboration of more competent interventions within those communities can occur. Theory, methods, and action develop within a cultural context. The meaning of the world is not the same for all (O'Donnell, Tharp, & Wilson, 1993). The privilege accorded the "objective" voice of the intellectual or the scientist has now been substantially withdrawn, and the voice of "objective science" is seen as merely *one* in a multi-vocal social world. If there are multiple perspectives on a single event, and if one of them is not *ipso facto* privileged, then the issue of meaning becomes an area requiring radical and consistent confrontation. That is, if a single event can be reported and interpreted differently (with equal legitimacy) by multiple participants and observers, then we must develop ways to capture these multiple meanings, and we must develop a method for determining which meaning, if any, takes precedence in the construction of reality via the research enterprise.

How does research in substance abuse recognize and utilize the existence of multiple realities, particularly across ethno-cultural lines? It appears that the construction and management of a research team engaged in an action research partnership with the community must be continuously reassessed, reworked, and revalidated. Additional insights are needed into the critical elements that make these teams successful with diverse subjects and populations. This is a necessary condition if our goal is insight into the "truth" of reality for a particular population. Creating the effective research team is about creating the right process, a proper context, and a collective of people with a shared mission: a sincere and profound concern about *that* community.

REFERENCES

Andrews, F. M. (Ed.), (1979a). *Scientific productivity*. Cambridge: Cambridge University Press.

Andrews, F. M. (Ed.), (1979b). Motivation, diversity, and the performance of research units. In F. M. Andrews (Ed.), *Scientific productivity* (pp. 252-287). Cambridge: Cambridge University Press.

Benello, G. (1992). *From the ground up: Essays on grassroots and workplace democracy*. Boston: South End Press.

Betancourt, H., & Lopez, S. R. (1993). The study of culture, ethnicity, and race in American psychology. *American Psychologist, 48*, 629-637.

Bower, M. (1965). Nurturing innovation in an organization. In G. A. Steiner (Ed.), *The creative organization*. Chicago: Chicago University Press.

Boykin, A. W. (1991). Black psychology and experimental psychology: A functional confluence. In R. Jones (Ed.), *Black psychology*. Berkeley, CA: Cobb & Henry.

Briggs, M. (1997). *Building early intervention teams: Working together for children and Families*. Aspen: Aspen Publishers.

Hill, J. L. (1996). Psychological sense of community: Suggestions for future research. *Journal of Community Psychology, 24*, 431-438.

Hughes, D., & DuMont, K. (1993). Using focus groups to facilitate culturally anchored research. *American Journal of Community Psychology, 21*, 775-806.

Hughes, D., Seidman, E., & Williams, N. (1993). Cultural phenomena and the research enterprise: Toward a culturally anchored methodology. *American Journal of Community Psychology, 21,* 687-703.

Kelly, J. G. (1990). Changing contexts and the field of community psychology. *American Journal of Community Psychology, 18,* 769-792.

King, N. (1990). Innovation at work: The research literature. In: M. West & J. Farr (Eds.), *Innovation and creativity at work: Psychological and organizational strategies.* New York: John Wiley & Sons.

Lambert, W. H. and Teich, A. H. (1981). The organizational context of scientific research. In P. C. Nystrom and W.H. Starbuck (Eds.), *Handbook of organizational design* (vol. 2., pp. 305-319). Oxford, England: Oxford University Press.

Lorion, R. P. & Newbrough, J. R. (1996). Psychological sense of community: The pursuit of a field's spirit. *Journal of Community Psychology, 24,* 311-314.

Lykes, M. B. (1993). Community research crosses national boundaries: Multiple meanings of long-term residence in particular spaces. *American Journal of Community Psychology, 21,* 487-493.

Mohr, L. B. (1969). Determinants of innovation in organizations. *American Political Science Review, 63* 111-126.

Newbrough, J. R. (1995). Toward community: A third position. *American Journal of Community Psychology, 23,* 9-37.

Nobles, W. (1996). *Personal communication.*

Nobles, W., & Goddard, L. (1993). An African-centered model of prevention for African American youth at high risk. In L. Goddard (Ed.), *An African-centered model of prevention for African-American youth at high risk.* Washington, DC: U.S. Government Printing Office.

O'Donnell, C. R., Tharp, R. G., & Wilson, K. (1993). Activity settings as the unit of analysis theoretical basis for community intervention and development. *American Journal of Community Psychology, 21,* 500-520.

Payne, R. (1990). The effectiveness of research teams: a review. In: M. West & J. Farr (Eds.), *Innovation and creativity at work: Psychological and organizational strategies.* New York: John Wiley & Sons.

Pierce, J. L., & Delbecq, A. (1977). Organizational structure, individual attitude and innovation. *Academy of Management Review,* 27-33.

Powell, W., & Lovelock, R. (1991). Negotiating with agencies. In G. Allan (Ed.), *Handbook for research students in the social sciences.* London: The Falmer Press.

Price Waterhouse Change Integration Team. (1996). *The paradox principles.* Chicago, IL: Irwin.

Rappaport, J. (1977). *Community psychology: Values, research and action.* New York: Holt Rinehart & Winston.

Rowe, D., & Grills, C. (1993). African-centered drug treatment: An alternative conceptual paradigm for drug counseling with African-American clients. *Journal of Psychoactive Drugs, 25,* 21-33.

Sarason, S. (1974). *The psychological sense of community: Prospects for a community psychology.* San Francisco: Jossey-Bass.

Sasao, T., & Sue, S. (1993). Toward a culturally anchored ecological framework of research in ethnic-cultural communities. *American Journal of Community Psychology, 21*, 705-727.

Seidman, E. (1978). Justice, values and social science: Unexamined premises. In R. J. Simon (Ed.), *Research in law and sociology* (pp. 175-200). Greenwich, CT: JAI.

Stevenson, H., & Renard, G. (1993). Trusting ole' wise owls: Therapeutic use of cultural strengths in African-American families. *Professional Psychology, Research and Practice, 24*, 433-442.

Teper, S. (1977). *Ethnicity, race and human development: A report of our state of knowledge.*

Thomas, C. (1970). Psychologists, psychology and the black community. In I. Korten, S. Cook, & J. Lacey (Eds.), *Psychology and the problems of society.* Washington, DC: American Psychological Association.

Van de Ven, A. (1986). Central problems in the management of innovation. *Management Science, 32*, 590-607.

Vega, W. A. (1992). Theoretical and pragmatic implications of cultural diversity for community research. *American Journal of Community Psychology, 20*, 375-391.

Walsh-Bowers, R. (1993). The resident researcher in social ethical perspective. *American Journal of Community Psychology, 21*, 495-499.

Weinstein, R. S. (1994). Pushing the frontiers of multicultural training in community psychology. *American Journal of Community Psychology, 22*, 811-819.

Wicker, A. W., & Sommer, B. (1993). The resident researcher: An alternative career model centered on community. *American Journal of Community Psychology, 21*, 469-482.

CONCLUSIONS AND RECOMMENDATIONS

Conducting Drug Abuse Research with Minority Populations: Conclusions and Recommendations

Mario R. De La Rosa, PhD
Mitzi S. White, PhD, JD
Bernard Segal, PhD
Richard Lopez, PhD, JD

SUMMARY. Traditional theoretical and methodological approaches to the study of drug behaviors in minority populations need to be modified to address the special issues involved in studying these

Mario R. De La Rosa is Visiting Associate Research Professor, Boston University School of Social Work and Health Science Administrator, National Institute on Drug Abuse. Mitzi S. White is a Postdoctoral Fellow, Department of Psychology, Harvard University. Bernard Segal is Professor, Department of Psychology, and Director, Center for Alcohol and Addiction Studies, University of Alaska Anchorage. Richard Lopez is Director, Substance Abuse Program, Washington, DC General Hospital.

[Haworth co-indexing entry note]: "Conducting Drug Abuse Research with Minority Populations: Conclusions and Recommendations." De La Rosa, Mario R. et al. Co-published simultaneously in *Drugs & Society* (The Haworth Press, Inc.) Vol. 14, No. 1/2, 1999, pp. 269-283; and: *Conducting Drug Abuse Research with Minority Populations: Advances and Issues* (ed: Mario R. De La Rosa, Bernard Segal, and Richard Lopez) The Haworth Press, Inc., 1999, pp. 269-283. Single or multiple copies of this article are available for a fee from The Haworth Document Delivery Service [1-800-342-9678, 9:00 a.m. - 5:00 p.m. (EST). E-mail address: getinfo@haworthpressinc.com].

populations. Theoretical models need to be expanded to include the effects of cultural, community, and minority status factors. In addition, they need to be multi-disciplinary and dynamic, reflect differences both across and within minority populations, and identify assets as well as risk behaviors. Special methodologies for collecting data from minority populations must continue to be developed, and empirical data need to be collected to identify effective strategies. Training programs are needed which provide researchers and students with tools to create more comprehensive theoretical models, strategies for collecting data from minority populations, and knowledge of the cultures of various ethnic/racial groups. *[Article copies available for a fee from The Haworth Document Delivery Service: 1-800-342-9678. E-mail address: getinfo@haworthpressinc.com]*

INTRODUCTION

Researchers have been studying drug behaviors in minority populations for more than 25 years (see De La Rosa, Recio-Adrados, Kennedy, & Milburn, 1993; Trimble, Bolek, & Niemcry, 1992; Trimble, Padilla, & Bell, 1987). While valuable data have been collected, the theoretical models and methodologies employed primarily have been adapted from those used in the study of White populations. Only in recent years have researchers recognized that there are special issues attendant to the study of drug behaviors in minority populations, and as a consequence, traditional methodologies are often inappropriate. This realization has encouraged researchers to begin developing new theoretical models and methodologies which are more appropriate for the study and understanding of drug behaviors in minority populations.

The papers presented in this volume are at the forefront of the effort to develop theoretical models and methodologies which will increase our knowledge of drug behaviors in minority populations. As the papers illustrate, a number of researchers believe that models of drug behaviors in minority populations must include the contextual realities[1] embodied in community, societal, and cultural constructs (e.g., see Brunswick & Reir, 1995; Vega, Gil, Warheit, Zimmerman, & Aspori, 1993; Wallace, 1999), rather than simply focusing on constructs rooted in individual behavior. In accord with this focus on community, societal, and cultural factors, a number of papers stress the need for methodologies which involve the community in the research process and present methods for improving the researcher/community nexus.

Taken together, all the papers in this special publication stress that researchers, whether from or apart from the cultural group under study, have to recognize that cultural values and community involvement affect the conduct of the research involving minority communities. The editors of this volume believed that allowing overlaps in the discussion on the role of cultural values and community involvement across the sections of this collection would reflect the importance of these elements as essential for the successful conduct of drug abuse research with minority populations.

Despite this publication and progress in recent years in improving the quality of drug abuse research with minority populations, much work remains to be done in this burgeoning area. This paper will focus on identifying problems and issues surrounding the conduct of drug abuse research and make suggestions for improving future research. The first section of the paper will address issues related to the development of theoretical models which have increased explanatory power and utility for researchers and practitioners in the drug abuse field. The second section will focus on methodological issues which affect the conduct of research with minority populations. The third section will discuss the need for special training programs on conducting drug abuse research with minority populations and for more minority researchers and researchers with specializations in the culture of particular ethnic/racial groups.

THE DEVELOPMENT OF THEORETICAL MODELS
FOR MINORITY POPULATIONS

Theoretical models of drug behaviors serve to (1) identify key factors and constructs that should be measured in the course of research; and (2) delineate sets of relationships that have been experimentally established between variables affecting drug behaviors. In this latter capacity, as a delineation of the state of current knowledge about drug behaviors, models provide policy makers and health care providers with information that they can use in the prevention and treatment of drug abuse.

Theoretical models of drug behaviors in minority populations have often had limited utility in either identifying key factors and constructs which impact on drug behaviors in minority populations or in providing health care providers and policy makers with useful information. This is, in part, because models have tended to be far too narrow in their conceptualization of the factors which affect drug use behaviors. Most models of drug behaviors in minority populations confine themselves to psychological, sociological, and familial factors which have been found to affect drug behaviors. As a result, they have (1) focused primarily on risk behaviors, (2) neglected to take into account the vast array of cultural differences across minority populations, and (3) failed to capture the complexity of the mechanisms underlying drug behaviors.

In order to account for the myriad of factors which produce drug behaviors in minority populations, more comprehensive theoretical models need to be developed. It is recommended that theoretical models be (1) expanded to include cultural and community factors and variables based on the effects of occupying a minority status is the United States; (2) flexible in order that they can be easily modified to reflect the range of differences across minority populations and within ethnic/racial groups; (3) multi-disciplinary and dynamic; and (4) based on an asset as well as a risk behavior orientation. While these recommendations are not exhaustive, creating models which incorporate these recommendations should help to provide policy makers and health care providers with a better understanding of the factors underlying drug behaviors. Moreover, these models should also help policy makers and health care providers to be more responsive to the drug abuse problems affecting particular minority populations and to design more effective treatment and prevention programs for these populations.

Each of the above recommendations is discussed in detail below.

1. Theoretical models should be expanded to include cultural and community factors and variables based on the effects of occupying a minority status in the United States.

Traditionally, theoretical models of minority drug behaviors have failed to include cultural factors. Instead, they have tended to focus on factors which have been found to be important determinants of drug behaviors among nonminority populations in the United States. As a result, the models have inadvertently posited mechanisms and relationships which are based on cultural behaviors, values, and attitudes that are part of the European culture that until recently predominated in the United States. In order to understand drug behaviors among minority populations, it is essential that these models be modified to reflect the cultural behaviors, values, and attitudes of the population being studied. A model of children's susceptibility to drug use proposed by Brooks, Whiteman, Noruman, Gordon, and Cohen (1988) illustrates this point. Their model posits that the parent-child interactions are a key determinant of children's susceptibility to drugs. While this model may be valid for nonminority populations, it may not be applicable to many minority populations in which the extended family plays an important role in the child rearing process. For example, in Hispanic families, aunts, uncles, grandparents, and even more peripheral relatives are often involved in rearing a child. Therefore, in modeling Hispanic children's susceptibility to drugs, it is important to include constructs relating to the extended family. Failure to include such constructs in models will result in researchers omitting variables from their studies which may be important determinants of drug behaviors within particular ethnic/racial groups.

Traditional theoretical models also have not included the effect of community factors on drug behaviors. This too, in part, reflects a form of cultural bias. Minority groups which are the focus of drug abuse studies often live in dense impoverished urban areas in which the community has a much greater impact on individuals' lives than in more affluent nonminority communities in which individuals are insulated from each other. Thus, community factors such as poverty, poor schools, inadequate housing, rampant unemployment, and a lack of law enforcement have a greater effect on drug behaviors in these communities.

As part of the inclusion of community factors in models, researchers also need to include the drug behaviors of residents of the community. These behaviors affect the behaviors of other residents who may or may not engage in drug behaviors. For example, open air drug markets provide youth in the community with easy avenues to drug abuse behaviors and may affect youth drug use. Similarly, open drug markets may lead community residents to organize to eliminate drug dealing resulting in youth being exposed to strong community sanctions against drug use. Therefore, it is important that models include factors which focus on prevailing drug behaviors in communities.

Traditional theoretical models have also failed to include factors related to minority status. Minorities often have experiences which differ markedly from those of members of the dominant culture. Discrimination, in the form of racism, is a common experience of all African-Americans in the United States, and also of many Hispanics, but it is rarely experienced by Whites. While the full extent of the effects of discrimination is not clearly understood, it is generally agreed that it has a negative impact on the lives of minorities and creates a sense of hopelessness or, alternatively, anger which can contribute to drug behaviors. Similarly, recent immigrants often experience acculturation stress in their attempt to adapt to the American culture (Vega et al., 1993). Models which exclude minority status factors, such as racism and acculturation stress, may provide an incomplete picture of the causative mechanisms underlying drug use among minorities. For example, Kaplan, Johnson, and Bailey (1987) have proposed a self-derogation model which stresses the importance of low self-esteem as a determinant of drug using behavior. This model, however, may be inappropriate for use with minority populations in which experiences of racism and acculturation stress may underlie low self-esteem. (See Goodstein and Ponterotto [1997] who have found that ethnic/racial identity affects Blacks' levels of self-esteem, and Vega et al. [1993] who have found that the stress which foreign born Hispanic youth experience in learning and adapting to a new culture undermines their perceptions of self-worth.)

As part of including cultural, community, and minority status factors in theoretical models, researchers should also hypothesize and test the interactional relationships between these factors. Social science variables rarely act independently. Given the close substantive relationships that exist between culture, community, and minority status factors, it is likely that there will be strong interactions between these factors which should be accounted for in models.

2. Theoretical models should be flexible so that they can be easily modified to reflect the range of differences across minority populations and within ethnic/racial groups.

Researchers are becoming aware of the wide range of differences both across and within minority groups living in the United States. Racial classifications, such as African-American, Hispanic, and Asian are far too broad. Numerous behavioral and cultural differences exist between ethnic groups within these classifications. Cuban Americans have different values and attitudes than immigrants from South American countries like Peru and Argentina. In addition, there is a growing population of youth of mixed race or ethnicity (e.g., youth of mixed African and Asian, African and Hispanic, or Asian and Hispanic ancestry) in the United States who share cultural values from several ethnic/racial groups.

Researchers also are finding that there are strong differences within ethnic groups which limit the generalizations that can be made about individuals within the same ethnic group. For example, Vega et al. (1993) have found differences between Cuban adolescents who recently have immigrated to the United States and those who either have been born in the United States or have resided in the United States for longer than three years. Cuban adolescents who are recent immigrants have values toward drug use which correlate more highly with those of their parents than adolescents who are born in the United States or long-term residents.

To develop theoretical models which reflect this myriad of differences would be impossible, potentially an exercise in futility. Flexible theoretical models need to be developed which can be modified to incorporate the ethnic/racial differences of the particular group being studied. Such models might contain meta-components which do not identify particular clusters of variables, but rather point to processes which can be used to identify the key cultural variables which act on behavior in a particular minority group.

3. Theoretical models should be multi-disciplinary and dynamic.

Current theoretical models of minority drug behavior are primarily grounded in the sociological and psychological sciences and to a lesser degree the biological sciences. Researchers are beginning to be aware that limiting the study of drug abuse behaviors to these disciplines results in an incomplete picture of the multiplicity of factors that produce drug behaviors. As a consequence, researchers are developing models which include constructs from other disciplines. For non-minority populations, Huba, Wingard, and Bentler (1980) and Glantz (1992) have developed models of drug behaviors which integrate constructs from the domains of biology, economics, organizational behavior, sociology, and psychology. This work needs to be extended to minority populations. Moreover, researchers should also consider incorporating constructs from additional disciplines into their models. Disciplines, such as government and education, have constructs which can also add to our understanding of the etiology of drug behaviors in minority populations.

In developing models, researchers also need to recognize that drug behaviors and the factors acting on them are not frozen in time but are dynamic. For example, Kandel, Kessler, and Marguiles (1978) have found that adolescents, regardless of their ethnic/racial backgrounds, usually progress through different stages of drug use initiation with each stage facilitating escalation to greater use and increasing the severity of illegal drug types. Social and economic conditions are also dynamic factors which change over time and may facilitate or impede drug behaviors at different points in time. For example, a lack of public and private resources paired with high unemployment rates can create conditions which are conducive to the development of drug distribution businesses and networks (Johnson, Williams, Dei, & Sanabria, 1990).

4. Theoretical models should be based on an asset as well as a risk behavior orientation.

Most theoretical models developed to explain drug use behavior in minority populations follow a risk behavior orientation (De La Rosa et al., 1993). These models have focused on identifying the deficits in a minority individual's personality, family, or environment which are responsible for their drug behaviors rather than protective factors which prevent the individual from using drugs. While some drug abuse researchers have begun to examine the role of protective factors (De La Rosa et al., 1993), the risk behavior orientation continues to drive most drug abuse research conducted on minority populations (Glantz, 1992). The development of models which have an asset behavior orientation and examine protective factors is particularly important because of the contribution that these models can make to the design of effective prevention strategies for minority populations.

This readjustment of focus to identify protective factors is also important because there has historically been lower prevalence of drug use for African-Americans and Hispanics than for Whites. Moreover, a recent review of drug use by African-American youth by Wallace, Bachman, O'Malley, and Johnston (1995) suggests that African-American youth continue to be less likely to use drugs than White youth. The protective factors responsible for these lower rates may be quite different than those in White communities because drugs are often readily available in minority communities in which there is extensive poverty.

METHODOLOGICAL ISSUES

Studying drug behaviors in minority populations has proven to be a difficult endeavor. Drug behavior is often illicit, populations hidden, and minority individuals frequently view researchers from outside the community with distrust. In an attempt to reach these populations, researchers have used a wide range of quantitative and qualitative research methodologies but despite these efforts, they have had only limited success (Collins, 1992; Tucker, 1985). In recent years, researchers have begun to rely more heavily on ethnographic methods (see Adler, 1990; Dunlap & Johnson, 1999). These methods have been found to be particularly well suited for gaining access to hard-to-reach minority subgroups, such as female crack dealers, intravenous drug users, and gang members (Carlson & Siegal, 1991; Dunlap & Johnson, 1996; Ramos, 1990; Yin, Valdez, Mata, & Kaplan, 1996). The success of these researchers appears to lie in their gaining the trust of subjects by establishing a rapport with them and creating a presence in their communities through use of indigenous workers and involvement of the community in the research process.

Despite the wide range of methods that have been used to reach minority populations, statistical evidence of the effectiveness of either traditional methods or more recent ethnographic methods is sparse. While a few studies have tackled this critical question (see Krohn & Thornberry, 1999; Thornberry, Bjerregaard, & Miles, 1993; Rogler, Barreras, Santana-Conney, 1981), most data that exist are anecdotal. In order to determine which methods are effective, researchers need to systematically collect empirical data on the effectiveness of strategies that they use to meet, recruit, and retain minority persons. Researchers need to describe these strategies in detail in publications and reports to funding agencies and provide statistical data on the recruitment and retention rates associated with each strategy. Metanalyses should also be performed across studies to identify strategies that consistently have proved to be effective. For example, the recruitment and retention rates for studies that use community advisory boards need to be compared with studies that do not use advisory boards. Similarly, the effect of different types of incentives and the use of indigenous workers on recruitment and retention both need analysis. To encourage drug abuse researchers to collect these data, funding organizations should require researchers to report these data, and journals should require that it be included in the methodology sections of manuscripts.

Researchers should also be encouraged to use flexible research designs in which they replace ineffectual strategies with more promising strategies in the course of the research process. As part of this process, however, they need to collect data which statistically substantiate their decisions to introduce new strategies. To encourage such experimentation, funding organizations should not place rigid restrictions on research designs. Rather they should allow researchers to change strategies if they discover that the present one does not work. For example, if a drug abuse researcher is funded to use a monetary incentive and finds it to be ineffective, he or she should be able to try alternative incentives.

As the body of data on the effectiveness of various strategies for gaining access, recruiting, and retaining minority populations grows, handbooks need to be written which delineate these strategies. These handbooks should not only provide information on what strategies are most effective with various populations but provide information on the types of minority populations and communities in which they are effective. Another approach is to develop discovery models of processes that can be used to analyze target communities. An excellent example of this approach is Tashima, Crain, O'Reilly, and Sterk's (1996) community identification (CID) process. This process was developed to direct the collection of public health risk-related behaviors and values in communities targeted for education and intervention programs. It provides a systematic and flexible process to identify and describe the target community and identify individuals both within and outside of the community who are knowledgeable about the community. In addition, the CID process includes methods of analyzing and interpreting the data collected in order to use them to design effective strategies for access to the communities. Models like this need to be expanded to address the special issues involved in studying drug behaviors and gaining access, recruiting, and retaining minority populations.

TRAINING ISSUES

Expanding Academic Training

Academic programs to train students in conducting drug abuse research primarily provide substantive knowledge of psychological, sociological, and public health constructs related to drug behaviors and a traditional repertoire of statistical and methodological tools. As a result, many drug abuse researchers in the field limit their study of drug behaviors to these substantive domains and use methodologies that are often inappropriate for use with minority populations. In order to better prepare students for the special problems attendant to studying minority populations, programs need to be expanded to provide substantive information on cultural, community, and minority status factors. As part of this expansion, programs need to teach students how to measure these factors in minority populations. In addition, programs need to encourage students to expand their knowledge of constructs from other disciplines which are relevant to drug behaviors. Finally, programs need to teach students ethnographic and other methods which have been found to be effective in collecting data from minority populations. In order to fully appreciate the difficulties inherent in collecting data from minority populations, students should be required to spend time in the field working with researchers who are experienced in studying minority populations.

Training Programs for Researchers

In addition to expanding academic programs to train students in conducting drug abuse research with minority populations, training programs need to be developed for extant researchers in the field. These programs should not only teach researchers new methods to gain access to minority populations and increase their substantive knowledge base but also provide a forum for the development of new methodologies and theoretical models. Foundations and the federal government should be encouraged to fund and promote such programs.

The Development of Minority Researchers and Cultural Experts

While the issue of whether minority researchers are better able to gain access to, recruit and retain subjects from minority populations than White researchers is complex and controversial, more minority researchers are needed in the field. Anecdotal evidence suggests that the presence of minority researchers encourages studies to incorporate cultural and community factors into their design (Marin, Burhansstipanov, Connell, & Gielen, 1995). Similarly, the use of minority researchers and outreach workers appears to facilitate access to minority populations (see Anderson, 1992; Becerra & Zambrana, 1985). Moreover, few would challenge the contention that researchers who are members of a particular ethnic/racial group are an invaluable resource in the study of those groups and can help improve our understanding of drug behaviors in those groups. Therefore, a clear goal of the field should be to develop programs and provide funding for the training of minority researchers who are committed to studying drug behaviors in minority populations.

While in an ideal world, every research project would include a minority researcher who is familiar with the culture of the ethnic/racial population that is being studied, this may not be possible. This problem is further compounded by the wide range of cultural differences that exist within broad racial categorizations. For example, the classification "Hispanic" encompasses a wide range of cultures. Mexicans have behaviors and values that are different from El Salvadorians. Even within a racial/ethnic group, such as Cubans, foreign born members have different values than American born members. Therefore, while it is important to train more minority researchers, this may not be sufficient because of the logistical difficulties in finding researchers from each ethnic/racial group who are willing to study drug behaviors in their particular ethnic/racial group. Moreover, minority researchers may not want to be limited to studying their own ethnic/racial group. Thus, training programs should provide specializations in particular ethnic/racial populations. Researchers, regardless of ethnicity, will then be provided with the opportunity to become specialists in a range of ethnic/racial populations and will be able to make a contribution to our understanding of drug behaviors in more than one ethnic/racial group.

CONCLUSION

Traditional theoretical models and research methodologies need to be refined to address the special issues attendant to studying drug behaviors in minority populations. Researchers are becoming aware that the etiological mechanisms underlying drug behaviors in minority populations are complex and a product of a wide range of societal, cultural, and individual forces. In order to advance the knowledge and understanding of drug behaviors in these populations, theoretical models need to be expanded to incorporate cultural, community, societal, and minority status factors into their explanatory matrix. Models also need to be multi-disciplinary in their approach and recognize that variables are often dynamic over time. In addition, because of the wide range of ethnic differences within racial groupings, models need to be constructed with flexible components which depict processes for selecting cultural variables which are relevant for the particular ethnic/racial group being studied. Finally, in order to provide information which can be used by policy makers and health care practitioners for prevention programs, models need to include asset-based variables rather than simply risk-based variables.

Efforts to develop theoretical models which provide comprehensive explanations of drug behaviors in minority populations have been hampered by the special problems attendant to the collection of data on drug behaviors from minority populations in impoverished communities. In response to these problems, researchers have begun to develop new and potentially more effective methods to gain access to these communities, but little empirical data exist as to the effectiveness of either these or more traditional methods. Data need to be collected on the effectiveness of these new strategies and more traditional strategies. In addition, metanalyses need to be performed across studies to identify strategies that are effective across a range of contexts. These data can then be used to develop handbooks and discovery models for conducting research with minority populations.

The special problems that exist with regard to developing theoretical models of drug behaviors in minority populations, and collecting data from minority populations, make it essential that academic and professional training programs be developed which focus on these issues. These programs should concentrate on expanding students' and researchers' knowledge bases and providing them with a proven repertoire of strategies to use in collecting data from minority populations. In addition, more minority researchers need to be trained and programs should be offered which specialize in the cultures of various ethnic/racial populations. The goal of these specializations should be to develop a cadre of specialists to assist researchers in collecting data from various ethnic/racial populations.

NOTE

1. The term "contextual reality" refers to the community factors and societal forces which may affect the drug behaviors of minority persons. Community factors include such variables as high neighborhood crime rate including the availability of drug markets, poor public schools, poor public transportation, dilapidated housing conditions, and lack of appropriate police protection against crimes. "Societal forces" includes such variables as racism, the flight of private industries from minority communities, and the lack of federal, state, and local government investment in improving the school systems in minority communities which may affect minority persons' opportunities for obtaining a quality education or gaining gainful employment (Simcha-Fagan & Scwartz, 1986).

REFERENCES

Adler, P. (1990). Ethnographic research on hidden populations: Penetrating the drug world. In E. Lambert (Ed.), *The collection and interpretation of data from hidden populations* (NIDA Research Monograph 98, Pub. No. (ADM) 90-1678, pp. 96-112). Rockville, MD: U.S. Government Printing Office.

Anderson, M. (1992). Studying across difference: Race, class, and gender in qualitative research. In J. Stanfield, II & R. Dennis (Eds.), *Race and ethnicity in research methods* (pp. 39-52). Newbury, Park, CA: Sage Publications.

Becerra, R., & Zambrana, R. (1985). Methodological approaches to research on Hispanics. *Social Work Research & Abstracts, 4,* 42-49.

Brook, J., Whiteman, M., Noruman, C., Gordon, A., & Cohen, P. (1988). Personality, family, and ecological influences on adolescent drug use: A developmental analysis. *Journal of Chemical Dependency Treatment, 1,* 123-161.

Brunswick, A. & Rier, D. (1995). Structural strain: Drug abuse among African-American youth. In R. L. Taylor (Ed.), *African-American youth: Their social and economic status in the United States* (pp. 225-246). Westport, CT: Praeger Press.

Carlson, R., & Siegal, H. (1991). The crack life: An ethnographic overview of crack use and sexual behavior among African-Americans in a Midwest metropolitan city. *Journal of Psychoactive Drugs, 243,* 11-20.

Collins, L. (1992). Methodological issues in conducting substance abuse research on ethnic minority populations. In J. Trimble, C. Bolek, & S. Niemcry (Eds.), *Ethnic and multi-cultural drug abuse: Perspectives on current research* (pp. 59-78). Binghamton, NY: The Haworth Press, Inc.

De La Rosa, M. R. Recio-Adrados, J., Kennedy, N., & Milburn, N. (1993). Current gaps and new directions for studying drug use and abuse behavior in minority youth. In M. R. De La Rosa & J. Recio-Adrados (Eds.), *Drug abuse among minority youth: Advances in research and methodology* (NIDA Research Monograph 130, Pub. No. 93-3479, pp. 321-340). Rockville, MD: U.S. Government Printing Office.

Dunlap, E. & Johnson, B. (1996). Family and human resources in the development of a female crack-seller career: Case study of a hidden population. *Journal of Drug Issues, 26*(1), 175-198.

Dunlap, E., & Johnson, B. (1999). Gaining access to hidden populations: Strategies for gaining cooperation of drug sellers/dealers and their families in ethnographic research. In M. R. De La Rosa, B. Segal, & R. Lopez (Eds.), *Conducting Drug Abuse Research with Minority Populations: Advances and Issues* (pp. 127-149). Binghamton, NY: The Haworth Press, Inc.

Glantz, M. (1992). A developmental psychopathological model of drug abuse vulnerability. In M. D. Glantz & R. Pickens (Eds.), *Vulnerability to drug abuse.* Washington, DC: American Psychological Association Press.

Goodstein, R. & Ponterotto, J. G. (1997). Racial and ethnic identity: their relationship and their contribution to self-esteem. *Journal of Black Psychology, 23*(3), 275-292.

Huba, G. J., Wingard, J. A., & Bentler, P. M. (1980). Framework for interactive theory of drug abuse. In D. J. Letterie, M. Sayers, & H. W. Pearson (Eds.), *Theories on drug abuse: Selected contemporary perspective* (NIDA Research Monograph 130, Pub. No. (ADM) 84-967, pp. 95-101). Rockville, MD: U.S. Government. Printing Office.

Johnson, B., Williams, T., Dei, K., & Sanabria, H. (1990). Drug abuse and inner city: Impact on drug users and the community. In M. Tonry & J. Q. Wilson (Eds.), *Drugs and crime* (Crime and Justice Series, 13, pp. 9-67). Chicago, IL: University of Chicago Press.

Kandel, D. B., Kessler, R., & Marguilies, R. (1978). Antecedents of adolescence initiation into stages of drug use: A developmental analysis. *Journal of Youth and Adolescence, 7,* 13-40.

Kaplan, H. B., Johnson, R. J., & Bailey, C. A. (1987). Deviant peers and deviant behavior: Further elaboration of a model. *Social Psychology Quarterly, 50,* 277-284.

Krohn, M., & Thornberry, T. (1999). Retention of minority populations in panel studies of drug use. In M. R. De La Rosa, B. Segal, & R. Lopez (Eds.), *Conducting Drug Abuse Research with Minority Populations: Advances and Issues* (pp. 185-207). Binghamton, NY: The Haworth Press, Inc.

Marin, G., Burhansstipanov, L., Connell, C. M., & Gielen, A. C. (1995). A research agenda for health education among underserved population. *Health Education Quarterly, 22,* 346-363.

Milburn, M., Gary, L., Booth, J., & Brown, D. (1990). Conducting epidemiologic research in a minority community: Methodological considerations. *Journal of Community Psychology, 19*(1), 3-12.

Ramos, R. (1990). Chicano intravenous drug users. In E. Lambert (Ed.), *The collection and interpretation of data from hidden populations* (NIDA Research Monograph 98, Pub. No. (ADM) 90-1678, pp. 128-145). Rockville, MD: U.S. Government Printing Office.

Rogler, L., Barreras, O., & Santana-Conney, R. (1981). Coping with distrust in a study of intergenerational Puerto Rican families. *Hispanic Journal of Behavioral Sciences, 3,* 1-17.

Simcha-Fagan, O., & Schwartz, J. (1986). Neighborhood and delinquency: An assessment of contextual effects. *Criminology, 24,* 667-703.

Tashima, N., Crain, C., O'Reilly, K., & Sterk, C. (1996). The community identification (CID) process: A discovery model. *Qualitative Health Research, 25*(1), 23-48.

Trimble, J., Bolek, C., & Niemcry, S. (1992). *Ethnic and multicultural drug abuse: Perspectives on current research.* Binghamton, NY: The Haworth Press, Inc., 57-74.

Trimble, J. E., Padilla, A., & Bell, C. (1987). *Drug abuse among ethnic minorities* (NIDA Research Monograph Series, DHHS Pub. No. (ADM) 87-1474). Rockville, MD: U.S. Government Printing Office.

Thornberry, T., Bjerregaard, B., & Miles, W. (1993). The consequences of respondent attrition in panel studies: A simulation based on the Rochester Youth Development Study. *Journal of Quantitative Criminology, 9,* 127-158.

Tucker, M. (1985). U.S. minorities and drug abuse: An assessment of the science and practice. *The International Journal of the Addictions, 20*(6&7), 1021-1047.

Vega, W., Gil, A., Warheit, G., Zimmerman, R., & Apospori, E. (1993). Acculturation and Delinquent behavior among Cuban adolescents: Toward an empirical model. *Journal of Community Psychology, 21,* 113-125.

Vega, W., & Gil, A. (1999). A model for explaining drug use behavior among Hispanic adolescents. In M. R. De La Rosa, B. Segal, & R. Lopez (Eds.), *Conducting Drug Abuse Research with Minority Populations: Advances and Issues* (pp. 57-74). Binghamton, NY: The Haworth Press, Inc.

Wallace, J. (1999). Explaining race differences in adolescent and young adult drug use: The role of racialized social systems. In M. R. De La Rosa, B. Segal, & R. Lopez (Eds.), *Conducting Drug Abuse Research with Minority Populations: Advances and Issues* (pp. 21-36). Binghamton, NY: The Haworth Press, Inc.

Wallace, J., Bachman, J., O'Malley, P., & Johnston, L. (1995). Racial/ethnic differences in adolescent drug use. In G. Botvin., S. Schinke, & M. Orlandi (Eds.), *Drug abuse prevention with multiethnic youth.* Thousand Oaks, CA: Sage Publications.

Yin, Z., Valdez, A., Mata, A., & Kaplan, C. (1996). Developing a field-intensive methodology for generating a randomized sample for gang research. *Free Inquiry in Creative Sociology, 24*(2), 195-204.

Index

Page numbers followed by "t" designate tables; See also refers to related topics or more detailed topic breakdowns.

For Product Safety Concerns and Information please contact our EU
representative GPSR@taylorandfrancis.com
Taylor & Francis Verlag GmbH, Kaufingerstraße 24, 80331 München, Germany